Warren,
Glad to learn that you are
doing so well. I hope you
enjoy this read.
Douglon 07-29-13

FOOTLOOSE IN TIME:
Tall Ships, Dreamwork, and an Appointment with the 16th Karmapa

Don O. Dyer

Dedicated to H.H. the 16th Gyalwa Karmapa, Rangjung Rigpe Dorje, who died in November 1981 in Zion, Illinois (USA), and to H.H. the 17th Gyalwa Karmapa, Orgyen Trinley Dorje.

Contents

Chapter 1 – Open to the Public

Tibetan Buddhism was not part of my upbringing. Born in Los Angeles in 1947 and raised poor in Southern California and Oklahoma, I was one of those curious kids who grew up wanting to know how things work: the weather, technology, literature, osmosis, the human condition. By the time I reached age twenty-seven, when this story begins, I had survived a childhood in foster homes; starting anew every year in a different school; military service in the Vietnam War; the passions and perils of social change in the '60s; an ill-prepared attempt at higher education; and cofounding and abandoning a wholesale art company. I also had a hard-earned and sensitive understanding of how the world works and a desire to discover how I fit into it.

That discovery came about in a way I would never have imagined, through a series of five dreams that proved to be prophetic and that made me realize that I could not stop dreams from coming true, although I nearly went crazy trying. Along with this discovery came the realization that our minds are more expansive and cosmic in scope than we realize, that the human mind can and always will aspire to reach beyond immediate experience, beyond the prevailing concepts that proscribe our condition.

My journey began on New Year's Day, 1973, when I packed my belongings in a Volkswagen and relocated from Norman, Oklahoma, to San Francisco. My ambitions centered on opening a coffeehouse for artists and hanging out with Richard Brautigan and other Bay Area writers and poets. With a frustrated attempt as an art student behind me and a shoebox of poems to prove it, I regarded myself as a misunderstood poet and artist whose talents would blossom in a more sophisticated art scene. In San Francisco, that portfolio qualified me for a burger-flipping job at a fast food joint overlooking the bay on Van Ness Avenue.

Midway through Day 1 of my new job at the burger joint I glanced through the open back door to see a freighter making its way across the bay, not a surprising occurrence in San Francisco—and yet it sent a jolt down my spine. I had pictured this scene exactly—me, wearing a white chef's hat, working over a sizzling grill as a small freighter, visible through an open back door, slowly coursed across the blue rectangle of bay framed by the doorway—but the image had come to me months earlier, in a dream I experienced half a continent away in landlocked Oklahoma, where there are no blue-water ports or freighters.

For a moment I lost my place in time: was I at work at a fast-food joint in San Francisco or half-awake in a bed in Oklahoma? How was it possible to experience something that I had dreamed two months earlier? For the next few days, the question of "how could I have foreseen all of it?" rumbled in my consciousness. A week later it lingered as a conversation piece. And a month later this dream-come-true was old news and I had a great new job and a great new place to live.

What I didn't know is that I would experience four more prophetic dreams within the year and that they would soon propel me along a pilgrim's path where I would be catapulted across an ocean and turned inside-out, to land bedazzled at the feet of the 16th Karmapa, one of Tibet's most powerful incarnate lamas. And ultimately I came to realize that he had a hand in all of it.

*   *   *   *

On paper my new job was night watchman at the San Francisco Maritime Museum. But at the end of the first night, as I witnessed dawn arrive from the "crow's nest" on the *Balclutha*—a 300-foot, three-masted, square-rigged sailing ship that had been christened in 1886—it didn't feel like a watchman's job. In truth, with the whole Bay Area bathed in the lambent glow of dawn and the ship's ancient joints creaking beneath me, I felt on top of the world. Farther up the mast, a luffing sound beckoned as a breeze moved across the ship's only sail. On it, in bold script, was a message to attract tourists: Open to the Public.

Starting that summer, I began restoring the *Balclutha's* woodwork during the day and working at night, when needed, as a watchman. In the fall I moved onboard the *Eppleton Hall*. The *"Eppie"* was a turn-of-the-century, steam-powered, paddlewheel tugboat that had been donated to the San Francisco Maritime Museum. A floating antique, she had been built from stem to stern of teak and brass with old-world craftsmanship, then tricked out in black and white paint with red trim. She lay moored alongside the *Balclutha* and was slated for restoration and eventual relocation to the museum's primary venue at the Hyde Street Pier. Meantime, I lived onboard with Zak, who had been working on the *Balclutha* for more than two years.

Having moved onto the *Eppie* months earlier, Zak lived in the captain's quarters, located below-decks and aft of the pilothouse, and I was allowed to set up in a tiny stateroom next to the galley and just forward of the pilothouse. Our arrangement with the museum required that we put in five full days each week working on the two ships. The work, the living arrangements, and the modest paychecks all seemed a fair price for living on what we regarded as the Bay Area's largest and coolest waterbed. The price went up steeply in the winter months, since the *Eppie* and most working ships from that era did not include heaters.

The spring of 1974 in San Francisco was a delirious time that encompassed the beginning-of-the-end for the Nixon presidency; the peak of the streaking fad; cars in lines for hours wrapped around city blocks due to the OPEC oil embargo; and the early mystery days of Patty Hearst's ordeal. However, working the night shift taught me to appreciate the uncluttered potential of mornings, and whenever possible I headed high into the ship's rigging at sunrise to watch the city awaken.

While perched near the top of the rigging on just such a morning in March, I watched as horizontal shafts of early morning sunlight illuminated Alcatraz Island and lit up like a lampshade a perfectly rounded cloud bank just beyond the Golden Gate Bridge. The damp morning air held sound low to the ground. I watched as a white-tipped wake from a passing freighter arrived. Below, the *Eppie* teetered over the arriving wake, fell, then wallowed in the backwash. Predictably, a few minutes later the stern hatch cover slid open and Zak emerged.

As I watched from aloft, Zak paused on deck, struck a regal pose with feet apart, and cocked his head to regard the new day. I had seen this morning ritual dozens of times and had decided that months of living next door to a tourist attraction had instilled in Zak an appreciation for the theatrical art of grand entrances and exits. I hastened down to join him for a cup of coffee in the galley.

Zak had moved to San Francisco from Milwaukee, where two generations of his family had been union workers for the city. He was Polish with dark hair and, oddly enough, a

Mediterranean complexion. He seemed to prefer the art of conversation over any other activity, espoused a mild brand of socialism, assumed a macho attitude around his slender Italian girlfriend who cooked for us, and had a rabid aversion to ethnic jokes.

Halfway through our second cup of coffee, the sound of Troy's keyring jingled by overhead. Troy was our boss. He had arrived early. I headed up the double-wide rope ladder that served as stairs between the *Eppie* and *Balclutha*. The jingling sound had moved from left to right, which meant Troy probably had gone to the ship's office in the stern section.

The main deck was vacant when I topped the railing, properly called a gunwale, and stood there weighing my options. I could hear Troy shuffling through the mess on his desk with a heavy hand. I had started in that direction when a tall, barrel-chested man strode around the corner of the deckhouse. A tremendously imposing figure, easily over six feet tall with shoulder-length, fiery red hair, the man stopped at the main hatch cover and stroked his beard. The beard fanned across his chest when he released it. Topped with his burning bush of red hair and wearing a black leather jacket and black denims, he stood out like a match struck in the dark. The man scanned the mainmast rigging above from left to right and top to bottom, then stroked his beard again. He looked like a Viking prince gone to seed but packaged in tight-fitting Hugo Boss attire. When he saw me, he shared a gold-toothed smile that flashed in the morning light. I returned the gesture, hoping not to disclose my discomfort.

"Morning gents," he said, his eyes fixed on something behind me. It was Zak, holding a steaming mug of coffee in his left hand and clenching a bagel in his teeth while clumsily tucking his shirt in with his right hand. With the bagel "beak" added to his angular facial features and disheveled black hair, he looked like a wounded hawk trying to straighten his feathers. So much for grand entrances.

A jingle of keys and a slammed door informed me that Troy had exited his office in the ship's stern section. Zak and I took a step in that direction only to have Troy breeze by with a yellowed sheaf of blueprints in his hands.

He spread the blueprints on the main hatch cover and pointed to the upper topsail yard on the main mast. "I'm guessing it weighs twenty-two hundred pounds," said Troy to the red-headed stranger. They looked in the rigging at the yard, a horizontal spar, approximately sixty feet long, that supports a large square sail directly above the ship's mainsail.

"What's cooking, gentlemen?" asked Zak. He and I looked upward into the rigging. Usually Troy kept us up-to-speed on all shipboard activities.

"Have you met Dalton Ames?" asked Troy absently, leafing through the blueprints. "Dalton, this is Don and Zak." He looked up, finally. "They'll be at your disposal," he told Dalton.

Dalton nodded toward us. "Gents," he said. He took a step forward with an outstretched hand and a disarmingly open smile. We shook hands. He took the same step back and stroked his beard.

"So, what's up?" Zak asked Dalton.

Dalton didn't answer. Instead, he produced a blue tobacco pouch from his jacket pocket and rolled a cigarette while looking over Troy's shoulder at the blueprints. Zak had a flair for drama and liked to be the center of attention, and Dalton seemed to have similar traits, so I had a feeling the two of them were going to bump heads. Dalton sucked his teeth with a squeak, then raised the cigarette in a haughty manner to his lips. He looked to Zak. "Got a match?"

"Not until somebody tells me what's going on," said Zak.

Dalton took a side step toward Zak, raised his arm in a slow arc, placed it on Zak's shoulder, then pulled the much smaller Zak closer in an avuncular way, and cast his gaze into the rigging. Using a thick-tongued Shakespearian brogue, he said, "We're going to strike yon upper tops'l yard, my good man." He whacked Zak on the back and exploded into laughter. It was a booming laugh that was held momentarily in the waist of the ship, then spilled overboard and fanned across Embarcadero Street. We all joined in nervously. Zak was the first to catch his breath and stop.

"Now," continued Dalton in his brogue, "wherefore art my match?"

There was a second round of laughter. Zak and I joined the merriment again. Dalton's eyes held a lawless glint as he scanned our faces. When he finally stopped laughing, the glint had taken on a hard edge that signaled "Don't mess with me, laddie."

Zak swung fire up to Dalton's cigarette. He had deferred, but only temporarily.

Troy closed the folder of blueprints and turned his attention to Zak and me. "Dalton's a master rigger. He's en route to Denmark from Japan but has agreed to help us strike the upper tops'l yard so we can refurbish it." Dalton smiled with satisfaction as he puffed his cigarette.

The explanation opened a new avenue for Zak. "Don and I might be going to Denmark in a few weeks," he told Dalton. "To sail a 127-foot schooner back with Captain Hofman."

Dalton arched an eyebrow. He was a handsome man in spite of the massive red mane. Unexpectedly, like light playing off quicksilver, his dark, discerning eyes and brows disclosed a change in sentiment. Beneath all the hair there was the face of a sensitive and self-conscious man. Without a discernible reason, his every expression changed to one of approval, his every motion of gregarious ease.

"You guys can talk about that later," Troy declared. He was in his get-things-done mood. "We've only got Dalton for one day." He tossed the sheaf of blueprints onto the hatch cover. "Let's get moving."

"Okay gents," said Dalton with a show of gold, "we're going to need a big snatch block fixed to a deck cleat over there." He pointed his long finger with the thumb up like a gun as he described the configuration of blocks and tackle needed to deploy the capstan—a human-powered turnstile winch on the foredeck—to lift then lower the 2,200-pound yard. He examined it for a long moment. "We're going to need at least a dozen men," he told Troy.

"No problem with the manpower," answered Troy. "I'll muster the rest of our guys and a few of the Hyde Street crew."

"No problem," mimicked Dalton. He tucked his hands into the pockets of his black leather jacket and swaggered off, head high, walking a straight line as the ship's deck see-sawed beneath his feet. He stopped at the foot of the main mast, spun on his heels, and looked into the rigging. "We're going to have to go topside and have a look." He cocked an eyebrow. "I'd like to get this done by nightfall." He looked to see who was listening, then added, "I'll be flying to Denmark as soon as we drop that cookie." He leaped with ease onto the port gunwale, shared a grin, then climbed the shrouds into the topside rigging. I followed.

Dalton looked worried when I caught up with him on the yard. He sucked a squeak through his teeth, stroked his beard, and studied the huge clamp-like iron hardware called a parrel that held the yard. "This thing's locked up tighter than Queen Victoria's snatch," he proclaimed. "Bet we end up cutting it off." He hauled out his tobacco pouch again and sprinkled tobacco onto a paper, undaunted by the altitude, swaying ship, or breeze.

"I hope we do get this done today," I told Dalton. "I'm scheduled for a tonsillectomy tomorrow."

"No shit?" he replied with mock sincerity and no effort to disguise it. He licked his cigarette paper. "Want a smoke?" He held the tobacco pouch my way. I was struck by how quickly this man of charm and charisma had turned first into an aggressive brute and now into a bored supervisor. "It's the best tobacco in the world. Drum tobacco. From Holland."

I nodded. He tossed the pouch. I rolled a cigarette and tossed it back. "I have to get the tonsils removed before I can crew-up with Captain Hofman." I couldn't tell if Dalton was listening. He seemed preoccupied with Zak on deck below. "The 127-foot schooner that Zak mentioned," I finished.

"Look at that fool down there," said Dalton, gesturing with his head at Zak, who had carried block and tackle gear to the main deck and had turned to fitting spars into the capstan. "What's his name?" he asked.

"It's a long Polish name. We call him Zak."

"Zeke," he bellowed, "we ready to weigh anchor yet?" He tossed his head back and laughed derisively.

Zak waited until Dalton had fallen silent and then replied, "Aye-aye, your royal behindness," in his own Shakespearian brogue. The rejoinder was quintessential Zak. We all laughed. I hoped that it would help relieve the tension between them, but knew better.

After several hours of running lines, fixing blocks, slackening braces, and adjusting gear, the work crew arrived and were assigned jobs. Everything was ready for a final inspection. Zak, holding a line from the port end of the yard, was on deck explaining the task at hand to a group of tourists. The plan was simple. Once the yard was winched up a few inches by the crew turning the capstan, the hardware that joined the yard to the mast would be detached. Using the lines attached to each end, the free-hanging, sixty-foot, 2,200 pound-yard would be turned slowly until it pointed fore and aft, and then lowered to the main deck.

The main deck was crowded with tourists. They scattered as Troy ran frantically from the office phone to the main deck and the different workstations, advising, clarifying, and consulting with Dalton, who stood arms crossed, feet apart, on the main hatch cover. I was thirty feet up on the yard, sitting comfortably and holding a short-handled, eight-pound sledgehammer. Famished and exhausted after working nonstop for thirty hours, I watched as a portly tourist on the deck below stuffed himself on a shrimp cocktail and fries. I was fading fast.

Finally, Troy returned to the command post on top of the deckhouse and nodded his approval. "Here we go, boys," called Dalton. He turned to the foredeck and gave the capstan crew a signal. After half a turn the manila line cut the air with a tuning-fork strum as it tightened. The shackle over the upper tops'l yard snapped upright on the taut line. I shifted into position under the parrel and banged the big hammer on the bottom of the flashlight-sized pin that kept the parrel jaws locked in place. The pin did not budge. I banged the pin repeatedly until exhausted. No movement. Dalton took my spot. "Cranky, is she?" he asked with sarcasm. I gladly handed him the hammer, as my lungs were heaving.

"Okay, sweetheart," he cooed, "daddy's home." He struck the pin with a crushing blow. Paint chips flew. He struck it again and again, but still no results.

Troy tried. "It's no use," he said, gasping. "We'll have to cut it off."

Darkness had arrived by the time Zak and I gathered the welding gear from two sources and returned. A new crowd of tourists lingered on deck, cameras at the ready. My mind and body seemed detached by exhaustion. I had worked double shifts for weeks, sleeping during the day. On this day, however, I'd had no sleep and nothing to eat since breakfast. My eyes felt rusted in their sockets. Troy caught us from behind as we hauled the cutting torch and equipment up the gangway. "We can get it done tonight," he said. I could tell by his hurried speech and aggressive tone that he had been drinking.

Troy was something of an enigma to me. He was well-educated, articulate, a good boss, and knowledgeable in a broad range of academic and everyday subjects, yet he purposefully cultivated a rough-hewn, macho image that surfaced as a reckless streak when he drank. Hence, Zak and I exchanged nervous glances as Troy explained that the welding gear would have to be hauled into the rigging.

At the precise moment that all the gear was assembled aloft, Troy ignited the torch and focused the flame to a point. Rocking with the tide, the cylinders of welding gas rolled noisily back and forth between the mast and a ditty bag of tools on the small crosstree platform. The cap from one of the welding bottles rolled off and fell thirty feet to the crowded deck with a dull clang. Sensing Troy's condition, Monty, a *Balclutha* coworker handling a line on deck, forced the crowd against the rails. Dalton climbed onto the yard beside Troy.

The actual cutting lasted minutes only, but my weary nervous system colored the operation with a timelessness. Working feverishly from the footropes just below me, Troy nearly fell due to an unexpected swell from the bay, but he had hooked his leg around the footrope as a precaution. Still, the cutting torch fell and swooshed in slow-motion arcs as it swung untended at the end of the supply hose. With a hand from Dalton, Troy scrambled back into position and retrieved the hissing blue flame as if he were Zeus toying with a comet. "You all right?" a voice called from the crowd. But it was one of those moments when words and people and things seemed to occupy different realms, and no reply was expected.

Troy resumed. The hissing blue flame of the torch splintered on contact with the hardware and sprayed into sheets of white light in the cool moist air. Blinding pulses of light flashed as if a furnace door was opened and closed in turns. The smell of bubbling paint and scorched iron baked in my nasal passage. Below, the upturned circle of faces on deck was blanched under the pulsing light. They raised flat arms from the chasms of darkness between them and, like pilgrims witnessing a miracle, shadowed their eyes from the mystery above.

Dalton gave me a thumbs up, his face flushed red from drink and masculine delight. The shock of red hair around his face pulsed to fluorescence in the spasms of torch light and streaming sparks. The gold in his broad smile glinted. Looking down from the rocking platform amid the rumble of rolling welding bottles, garish light, and the spellbound gaze of the crowd, I felt suspended in a fanciful prop for some Wagnerian drama unfolding below me. It all seemed unreal and other-worldly. With the cutting complete, Troy extinguished the torch, worked his way to the crosstrees, and handed the torch and goggles to me. Dalton followed. Once again the single floodlight on the "Open to the Public" sign softly illuminated all that had moments before been bathed in a brash, pulsating light. Troy's face was cinder-specked and sweat-streaked except for two clean circles around his eyes that had been protected by the goggles. He looked like a Hollywood pirate in a close-up, but he was instructing me to get some sleep. A moment later, he and Dalton swashbuckled down the capstay to the main deck where they were embraced by the open arms of the crowd.

Later in the evening when Dalton invited me to come to Denmark to work with him "on a real sailing ship," I didn't think about how much I detested his behavior or the misery he heaped upon those around him. Rather, I only heard his flattery and only envisioned a square rigged sailing ship gliding over a boundless sea of blue with me onboard and gulls hovering to stern. It was a fantasy, I knew, as we shook to seal the agreement later in the evening, and I knew that working for him would be much worse than working with him. I had no way of knowing then that I would learn this lesson the hard way well before winter arrived.

Three hours later, Taylor, another *Balclutha* coworker, awakened me. "Shit, man, I thought you left for the hospital already," he said, then laughed. "Sorry, man." In my exhausted state, it took a while to understand that Taylor had forgotten to wake me. I knew from the liquor on his breath that the work on the yard had been finished and duly celebrated. I was too tired to care.

The Polk Street bus was empty and parked at curbside when I got onboard for the trip to the hospital. The driver arrived moments later with a cup of coffee from the Eagle Cafe and opened a newspaper on the steering wheel. I glanced across Embarcadero Street to the *Balclutha's* floodlit rigging. The extra lines in her rigging gave her a cluttered look. Where the upper tops'l yard had been there now was an emptiness as if her tonsils had been removed. I half-heartedly thought about the hidden meanings, but was too tired for symbolism too. "You need a transfer?" the driver asked into the mirror. The doors slapped shut and the bus heaved forward toward the hospital, a stop-and-go journey that would change me from subject to object.

Chapter 2 – A Dream Comes True

The *Balclutha* lay motionless on a low tide as I made my way up the gangway with a quart of post-tonsillectomy ice cream for my throat. The upper topsail yard that we had struck lay on blocks along the port side of the main deck and a family of four stood on it, admiring the *Eppie*. I joined them for a moment and then, with a tip of the head, continued over the gunwale and down the rope ladder toward my bunk. Zak's face shined in the soft light emanating from the galley as I descended the forward ladder. "Hey, man, how you feeling?"

I shrugged an OK. It hurt to speak. "Hear from Captain Hofman?" I whispered.

"Not a word," said Zak sympathetically.

I resumed working double shifts the next evening. I needed the extra money to pay for the tonsillectomy and air fare to Scandinavia. I felt renewed and eager when Monty awakened me for the night watch. A day of additional bedrest and ice cream had helped my throat as well. When I reached dockside, Monty was chatting with a pair of happy young lovers beside the ticket booth at the end of the gangway.

Monty was an American Indian of some sort with long black hair, almost always in a ponytail, dark eyes with long lashes over cheekbones that could cut glass, and a cheerful face bracketed by premature crow's feet from laughing too much. His naturally dark complexion, confident presence, and lean athletic frame made him irresistible to women. Monty and I had arrived in San Francisco the same week and met in a Sutter Street residence hotel that catered to new arrivals. We became immediate friends at the front desk when I overheard the clerk read the name on his driver's license—Montgomery Hart. He made me swear an oath on the spot to never repeat it. That had been a year earlier.

The happy lovers left. Monty and I headed aft then up a ladder to the poop deck, where the helm is located. It offered a panoramic view of the north and west Bay Area. The night was remarkably cool and clear. A horizontal strand of twinkling lights ringing the Bay Area shoreline stretched out before us, interrupted only by the imposing bulk of Alcatraz directly to stern. "Too bad you missed the actual striking of the yard," said Monty. "It was damn hectic." He offered a cigarette. It was the first tobacco I'd had since the tonsillectomy. It irritated my throat a little but tasted good.

"I had to get those tonsils out. Captain's orders."

"Dalton really knows his stuff," he said, returning to the subject. "But he and Troy got into it a couple of times."

"Zak told me."

He nodded. "It didn't surprise me. A classic case of an immovable object against a . . ." He searched his thoughts for a moment and then said, "I've forgotten the rest."

"Take a look at that baby," said Monty after a moment's silence. A gigantic freighter slowly emerged from the darkness into the lights along the waterfront to the west. "I'll bet those tugboat pilots are making a mint right now." A tugboat at the freighter's bow diligently pressed the freighter toward the pier. As the ship slowly turned, another tug appeared to her stern. From a quarter of a mile away, it all had the bright-edged look of a Hollywood production.

"Let's go aloft for a better view," I suggested. Monty took the starboard shrouds, I took the port, and we met in the rigging thirty feet up. "It looks like they're going to put her in over there." I pointed beyond the harbor cruise ferries to a long pier that serviced freighters. As if confirming the observation, the overhead lights at the pier came on.

Monty spoke as he slowly swept his arm along the horizon in a 180-degree gesture before us. "I really dig this whole waterfront scene. It's always looked like some kind of an exaggerated G.I. Joe harbor toy to me. Just look at it."

He was right. Within a two-block stretch of waterfront, starting on the east, there were a dozen harbor tugs and water taxis, a floating helicopter pad, the moored Alcatraz tour boats, the island itself halfway across the bay, and a three story arch for transferring railroad cars from ferries to the tracks that ran up and down Embarcadero Street. To the west were harbor cruise ships, a postcard-perfect fishing-boat marina, an observation platform with coin-operated telescopes, and then the huge freighter that was now closer to its mooring space along the pier. "You're right, it looks contrived," I said.

Although a quarter of a mile away, the pier lights illuminated the waterfront for a hundred yards or more. The tugs working the huge freighter provided the only movement in a serene bayside still life. Darting expertly from one side of the freighter to the other, they powerfully, yet gently, nudged her toward the pier like so many worker ants attending a queen. The freighter's movement was nearly imperceptible.

"Wow," exclaimed Monty, "it'd be wild if they rammed that thing into the pier." He grinned like a teenager. "How much do you figure that thing weighs?"

I considered it for a moment. "Thousands of tons, for sure."

Suddenly, the sound of crunching timbers ripped through the silence. The freighter had rammed the pier in slow motion. It was a slow, high-pitched, wrenching sound intermixed with the squealing sound of twisting, splintering planks, and deep snapping noises. Monty's eyes bulged in disbelief.

"Goddam, Don," said Monty. "They've run that thing into the pier!" The slow crunching rumble continued for several agonizing minutes as the tugs labored furiously to stop the motion of the ship. A second ear-splitting noise cracked over the bay as the stern of the freighter crunched into the pier. For all the noise, crunching, and frantic tugboat activity, the huge ship appeared dead in the water.

Monty and I braced ourselves against the mast and watched the slow-motion collision. As the clamor and drama unfolded before us, a similar scenario unfolded in my mind. However, the image in my mind's eye was the *Balclutha* sinking with the same gut-wrenching crunch of timber. My eyes locked on the horizon beyond the Golden Gate Bridge and lost focus. The image had come from a dream I'd had in the hospital. What a coincidence. Eerie, really.

"I'll bet that ship's not moving at one mile per hour," said Monty as the slow crunch produced a disturbing soundtrack of snapping and buckling planks. Men's voices commingled frantically as the noise diminished. Soon the timbers had fully absorbed the ship's momentum, and with a shrill, twisting squeak they decompressed until the ship no longer pressed against them, leaving the feeble sound of men shouting.

"I can't believe it," said Monty, shaking his head. "I'll bet those guys on the pier need to change skivvies."

I was still transfixed by the dream. Sensing something unusual, Monty fell silent.

"Monty, I had a dream in the hospital. I just remembered it." Monty turned away, toward the bay, as if needing to contemplate the gravity that had entered my voice before proceeding. I recounted the *Balclutha* Dream:

Monty, Taylor, Chris, and myself—plus one unidentifiable person—are motoring down a highway in a convertible. I am driving. The convertible top is down and the wind is blowing through our hair. We are talking excitedly. The weather is perfect. Monty is turning the radio tuner in search of something upbeat. The only thing on the broad landscape is an inland channel running parallel to the highway on the right and clouds in the distance.

The mood and pace of the dream changes as a mammoth wall of storm clouds forms on the horizon and the *Balclutha* appears under full sail in the channel just ahead. As the ship approaches, we notice that she has too much sail up for the building gale. Soon, she begins to heel over. Everybody in the car concentrates on the scene of impending disaster. I slow the car as the wind blows harder and harder and the ship lists farther to starboard. The seas continue to build until the mainsail hangs in a swell, instantly fills with seawater, and, with a terrifying splintering sound as the yard buckles, the weight of the water in the huge sail tugs the ship downward.

Held at a stark list to starboard for that brief moment, another wave snags a sail. More timbers snap. Another swell swamps the entire starboard side of the ship, causing it to wheel abruptly to a stop. Amid the crunching timbers and toppling sail, the crew scrambles over the side into the sea and swims for shore. Behind them, the ship is buoyed for a long moment in a bank of froth, and then plunges bow first below the surface with an elongated slurp, and a moment later, it drags down a trailing tangle of lines, timbers, and sail through a roiling patch of foam.

I yank the car to the side of the road and we rush to the shoreline. There, eerily, each of us—Monty, Chris, Taylor, myself, and the unknown fifth person— stand among huge stones along the shoreline with outstretched hands, and each of us pulls a clone of ourself up onto the bank. The unknown passenger pulls out a man with a featureless face. In the background, debris from the ship drifts away as we stand helplessly on the rocky shore with puzzled expressions.

A moment passed before Monty spoke. "Shit, that's one freaky dream."

"What's just as freaky is that I never remember dreams, not since I was a kid anyway." Monty shot me his skeptical look, wondering, I supposed, if I was setting him up for a practical joke. "It's true," I told him. "As a kid I used to have a recurring dream. But that stopped and I never remembered dreams again until once last year, just before I moved to San Francisco."

"So what do you think it means, this dream?" He offered another cigarette. I accepted.

"I don't know. Some people say that dreams are just a way of tidying up unfinished business. You know, to keep too many loose ends from tangling up things in real life . . . I guess." We lit the cigarettes.

"You don't sound too convinced," said Monty. He paused to study his cigarette. "I don't know either. I mean, it probably does work that way in some cases. But look at your dream. It creates unfinished business instead of clearing it up." We both looked over to the newly arrived freighter as some of the pier lights were shut off. "Guess they got her tied down," said Monty. "But you can bet your bippy somebody's gonna get their ass kicked over that."

We watched and smoked as one of the tugboats pulled up alongside the freighter and a man descended on a rope ladder from the freighter to the tugboat. "I agree with the unfinished business stuff," I said, testing to see if Monty was still interested. "In the sense that dreams come from your imagination and that the imagination spans all of your lifetimes. Not just the present one."

"You mean reincarnation?" asked Monty. He was suddenly struck with a thought. "So you're saying that we have been sailors before? That we've gone down with a ship in a previous life?"

That one took some thought. I didn't want the conversation to deteriorate into a gab session on parlor mysticism. Monty was thinking it over too. He didn't say anything for a while, so I broke the silence. "When I moved to San Francisco, I used to come down here a couple times a week to absorb the ambience and just sit on the pier and watch the *Balclutha* move with the sea. I loved it. I'd sit there on the pier and just watch it sway and listen to the creaking and smell the tar, salt air, and wet canvas. And though I never thought about it this way before, it all seemed to communicate to me like a voice from the past. A familiar voice from the past."

"I used to do the same thing," said Monty excitedly. "Isn't that wild?" He took a last puff on his cigarette and flicked it toward the bay. It fell short and lay smoldering on the poop deck below. It would have to be retrieved quickly before it burned into the wood. We hurried down. Monty tossed the cigarette over the side. "Do you think it means the deal fell through with Captain Hofman—the dream, I mean?" "Who knows?" I shrugged. "It'd be nice if the skipper would get back with some news one way or the other."

"Or send a postcard," suggested Monty. After considering it for a moment, we laughed at the thought.

Again there was silence. Monty, I suspected, was thinking about his girlfriend at home in bed. Instead, he asked, "Do you think we'll get to go . . .?" His voice trailed off.

I knew the rest of the question: ". . . if the skipper puts together a crew for the ship?" We worked our way toward the gangway. I needed to let Monty off the ship before I could lock the gangway gate. "It's hard to say. Troy seems to think so. That's why he's letting us work all these extra shifts."

"Zak's not saving for the trip. He said that if the ship deal turns real, word will get out and sailors will spring out of the woodwork. Sailors with tons of experience that you and I could never compete with." He paused, then added the obvious. "You know, like Dalton."

There was another pause as we both acknowledged Zak's assessment. Zak usually was right. "Our chances are probably one in a million." He lit up another cigarette then looked at his watch. "Shit, Don, I need to get outta here." He headed for home and a warm bed. I locked the gangway gate behind him and returned to the rigging where we had witnessed the freighter disaster. It had been an eerie incident, a second eerie dream.

Chapter 3 –Traveling Man

April arrived before we heard from Captain Hofman. Zak and I had just sat down to lunch in the galley on the *Eppie* when Troy shouted. "Don . . . Zak." It was Troy's familiar call from the deck of the *Balclutha*. "Your boss is here." A few seconds passed before the meaning registered.

The skipper was back!

Captain Hofman pinned me with his pale blue eyes the moment I vaulted over the gunwale. His face radiated confidence. The familiar pipe in his mouth and worn seaman's cap were never before so welcome a sight. And his eyes were full of good news.

He propped a foot on the main hatch cover amidships and rested a clipboard on his knee. As always, he was perfectly groomed—dapper, really—in pressed khakis, polished boots, and a classic black and white seaman's cap over close-cropped, silver-gray hair. The firm facial muscles crinkled around his eyes when he smiled. His perfectly shaped goatee looked as if it had been plucked from a Rubens canvas. "And how are you, Don?" he asked firmly, but with a touch of mirth. He stood in a circle of familiar faces—Troy, Benny, Monty, Chris, and Zak. He was every bit a man in his element. The Skipper.

He turned back a couple of pages on the clipboard until he uncovered a sketch of the rigging plan for the *Marite*. "She's as sound as the Rock of Gibraltar," he said. "From stem to stern we found one deck leak. One." He smiled triumphantly. "Otherwise, her hull is pickled hard as a barnacle." He turned to me. "But there's a lot to be done."

A rush of pride and anxious joy swelled in me. He had singled me out! It meant that I had been chosen to be on his crew! Monty placed a hand on my shoulder and whispered "Congratulations."

"For one thing," continued the skipper, "the foremast has been moved forward eight feet." He let the pages on the clipboard fall back. "We'll just have to move it back," he said steadfastly. "And she'll have to be flush-decked." He removed the pipe from his mouth, casually glancing into the bowl. "Do you know what that means?" I assured him with a nod that I did. "She's been a dory fishing boat in Greenland waters for the last forty years." He made direct eye contact with Troy and said, "Not a trace of wormrot, never took on a drop of water. I went through all the logs." He paused to rework the tobacco in his pipe.

Troy took the opportunity to express his congratulations to the skipper, then made excuses and departed for his office. "She's quite a lady . . ." The skipper resumed his description of the *Marite*, but his words fell into that chasm that opens between men when emotional departures arise.

For me, it was both a joyful and painful moment of realization. It meant I would be leaving the *Balclutha* soon. Perhaps others would be leaving too. Suddenly, the distance that Troy had maintained all those months made a little more sense. A flourish of emotions swirled in me as I watched his sturdy frame disappear into the shelter deck. He had always been like a fun-loving, appreciative father to me, and yet detached. When the probability that I might be shipping out with Captain Hofman arose, he had immediately insisted that I work all the hours I could handle in order to save money for the airfare and a tonsillectomy. The tonsilectomy was mandatory, as the skipper had seen a young man's tonsils removed while at sea and did not want to experience it again.

I recalled a simple and delightful evening when Troy invited me to his home for supper with his family. The evening was etched in my memory by two things: Troy and I discovered that we had both just read James Michener's *The Source*, which prompted a long, animated discussion. Second, it was during that conversation and the spaghetti dinner that Troy told me I had started working on the *Balclutha* at just the right time, that I had better timing than Gordius.

When I cocked my head quizzically, he poured us another glass of wine, said "Greek mythology" in a dramatic tone, then moved from the head of the table to the chair directly across from me. He enjoyed sharing with his crew what he had learned at the university. He explained that the myth of Gordius and the legend of the Gordian Knot came to us from the ancient Greeks. Gordius was a commoner who became king when an oracle instructed the local elders to anoint as their next king the first person to arrive in a wagon in the public square. Gordius happened to be in a wagon at the right place at the right time, and recognized it. In gratitude for his good fortune, he dedicated the wagon to the gods and bound it to a temple with an elaborate knot. The knot itself soon became famous as people from all over tried to unravel it, but failed even to find the ends of the rope. A saying arose that whoever succeeded in untying the knot would become ruler of the world. According to legend, a steady succession of would-be rulers tried and failed to untie the knot. However, when Alexander the Great tried and failed, he promptly drew his sword and sliced through the knot, and that's what inspired the expression "to use the Gordian Knot approach." With that, Troy held up his glass for a toast.

"I moved to San Francisco in a wagon," I told him, "a Volkswagen. And drove straight to Ghirardelli Square. When I saw the 'Open to the Public' sign on the ship, I got back in the car and drove to the *Balclutha,*" I added. "Maybe that's why I was lucky."

"Well, here's to looking up your old address," he said, more than a little tipsy. We clinked glasses. "It's better to be lucky than good."

The memory of the supper at Troy's faded as the skipper's words reclaimed my attention: ". . . of course you'll have to dress for it," he said with authority. "The Faroes are only a few hundred miles from the Arctic Circle."

Zak slapped me on the back. "You lucky dog."

"You'll need to be outbound by the end of the month," said the skipper, sharing the blue of the North Atlantic in his eyes. "I'll make a map with instructions to get you there. Tvoryori is not an easy port to find."

"The Faroe Islands," I whispered reverently. "Square tops'l schooner. Scandinavia. Arctic Circle. The *Marite.*" There was an irrepressible mystique and romance in the character of the words. My feet padded softly behind the skipper as we headed for his pickup truck, parked along the pier.

The skipper poured two fingers of gin into plastic cups that he kept in the glove box. Following his lead, I downed my glass in one gulp. He poured another. "The foremast has been moved forward eight feet." He raised his cup and held my eyes in his gaze. "We'll have to put it back where it belongs." It was the third time in half an hour he had mentioned the relocated mast. I took it as a pact of some sort between us. We drank. He quietly took the cups, wiped them clean with a paper towel, and stowed everything neatly back inside the glove box.

"Did Mr. Heflin say anything about air fare?" I asked. Mr. Heflin was the main sponsor for the *Marite* enterprise, had recruited the investors, and had sent the skipper to the Faroes to inspect the ship. According to Zak, Heflin had already secured most of the needed funds from the distributors of an unnamed Scottish whiskey. In exchange for restoration funds, the *Marite* would deliver a cargo of specially labeled scotch from Britain to San Francisco, which would be widely promoted along the west coast. "I'm guessing Cutty Sark," Zak confided. It seemed like a brilliant scheme to me.

"You'll be reimbursed for your traveling expenses after I return to the ship in about one month," the skipper said absently as he leafed through the material on the clipboard. A wry smile spread over his face when he removed a letter and clipped it on top. He pointed to the letterhead. It featured a square-rigged sailing ship, top-center, with *Adventures In Time, Inc.* imprinted on a slender, streaming pennant to the left and *San Francisco, California* on a matching pennant to the right. "Starting on April 27th, you will be employed by Adventures in Time, Incorporated," he proclaimed.

His words hung in the air like a fluttering banner. It was a dream come true. I would leave in three weeks to refit and sail a 127-foot square topsail schooner from an island in the North Atlantic to San Francisco. I was benumbed by my good fortune.

Monty awakened me a few hours early on departure day. He wagged a bottle of tequila in front of my eyes. "Come on, Dee," he beckoned, "it's time to get up." Behind him were the voices of three other *Balclutha* crew members—Chris, Benny, and Taylor—echoing the message. Getting up was difficult. I had worked sixteen- and twenty-hour days for months to raise the one-way airfare to the Faroe Islands and pay for the tonsillectomy, and I was tired down to the bones. I joined the party on the main deck of the *Balclutha*, but didn't feel like partying. The crew was so intoxicated that even tourists had been allowed to join the carousing.

"On this slalom occasion," joked Zak with one foot raised precariously, "the party of the first part do hereby propose a toast to the party of the second part . . ."

"Knock off all that legal talk and let's party!" said Chris. He raised a silent toast to me and added a tip of his head to the perpetual smile on his face.

"Bon voyage," said Monty in his own private toast. Whatever he had planned to add was interrupted when Benny strode up.

"You feeling all right?" he asked after looking me over. Benny worked part-time onboard the *Balclutha*. However, he was a bit of an outsider because his interests centered on zoological studies at the university instead of ships, booze, and women. I admired him for sticking with his studies.

The going-away party turned into a going-crazy party after Zak returned with the fourth bottle of tequila and received a hero's welcome. My body was crying out for a square meal, coffee, and a hot shower. Instead, I got tobacco, tequila, and a dousing. "I hereby anoint you King of the Weather Deck," announced Zak as he poured seawater from a bucket onto my head from the poop deck above.

"He's jealous," Chris told me. "You've bumped him off his self-appointed throne."

Troy made his way over with a tourist shadowing him. "They make the best hammocks in the world," said the tourist as they stopped.

"Don, I've got to go," said Troy. "I promised the little lady that I'd get home at a respectable hour." He shook my hand solidly. "Good luck, and don't forget that you promised me a letter."

The tourist beside him started to shake my hand, but his arm suddenly shot upward. "My God!" he cried, pointing.

"Zak!" shouted Troy with gravity, but then he broke into laughter. "Get your ass down." Everybody looked into the rigging as a volley of laughter exploded simultaneously. Zak was *streaking* in the rigging! He was naked in the rigging!

"Yeah," cried Benny exuberantly, "get your ASS down!" The laughter rolled across the deck like a wave over-topping a sideboard as everybody, including giddy tourists, contributed to the fun.

"It's a full rectal eclipse of the moon," said Troy to Chris and me, as Zak carefully slid down a stay to the crosstrees.

"No, it's a three-toed sloth!" shouted Monty.

"Zak, you're an animal," cried Chris.

Zak glided down the final capstay in his genitalia-sans-regalia, flaps-gone-white descent to the port gunwale and disappeared over the side on the rope ladder to the *Eppie*.

Two hours later, I staggered past a broken tequila bottle on the pier to somebody's car, stuffed my bags into the trunk, climbed into the backseat, and headed for the airport in a drunken stupor. As the car lurched into the traffic along the Embarcadero, Monty, Chris, and Taylor flapped their arms good-bye from the foredeck overhead. The three of them had been in the *Balclutha* Dream. I had a feeling I would see them again, soon.

The transatlantic flight, with stops in Dallas and New York, transported me to a near-freezing dawn in Reykjavik, Iceland. What I could see of the city as I descended the ramp to the runway was a scattering of buildings crowded among rocky outcroppings and stacked on slate-colored knolls. With the first sign of light the eastern horizon emerged as a sawtooth ridge of peaks tearing at the underside of a bank of dark clouds. Reykjavik, I recalled, had been selected as neutral ground for the Cold War chess summit between American wunderkind Bobby Fischer and Boris Spatsky, a Russian. To me, the atmosphere seemed more Cold War than neutral as I headed for the terminal.

After a wait at the customs gate, a pair of sleep-starved men in olive-green uniforms wheeled in luggage carts, stamped passports, and said "Velcome to Reykjavik." One of them pointed across the hangar-like interior to double doors and added, "Terminal nine." I gathered my bags and exited.

While inside, however, the Icelandic landscape I had discounted earlier had magically been transformed by the full light of morning. Indeed, Iceland was green! And white! And blue! Iceland was beautiful! What a difference a sunrise can make. The colorful landscape leaped into my eyes from all directions. Overhead, balmy clouds elbowed for space, and fluted pillars of light streamed between them. Light splashed across buildings and sparkled on edges. The eastern horizon had been transformed into a snow-covered range of pristine mountains. I dropped my bags in disbelief.

Beyond the airport fence, a milk truck turned from a thoroughfare down a slope past the terminal building and headed up an opposite slope toward a stand of sherbet-colored houses nestled at the foot of a ridge. Everything seemed at arm's length in the perfectly clear air. The environment was delightfully invigorating.

Across from the terminal building, a fireman hosed down the driveway to the airport fire station. His whistling fit in perfectly with the alpine setting. "Godt morning," he said. "It's nice day." He stooped to spray under the fire truck in the driveway but watched me search the surrounding buildings. When I neared enough to make eye contact, he said "You are Amerikan?" He shut down the nozzle and pointed at the U.S. Mail bag that held part of my gear. I nodded.

"You need taxi to Reykjavik?" he asked unevenly.

"Terminal nine," I answered, then surveyed the outlying buildings a second time.

"You go to Faroes?" he asked with urgency, then glanced at his watch. "A moment, please."

I could see through the glass in the firehouse door as he spoke animatedly into the phone, listened, spoke again, his face lighting up each time a voice returned from a pause. He disappeared behind a door and then returned to the driveway after a moment. "Your plane vil vait," he explained hurriedly, then snatched up my duffel bag on the run. "Come . . . please." He heaved the duffel bag onto the back of the small fire truck. I grabbed the other bags and followed, tossing them on the layers of folded hose that filled the rear section as he started the engine. It was a vintage fire truck, the kind with an open cab, a freestanding windshield, and a shiny bell perched over the driver's shoulder on an arching bar. Like the bell, every valve, gauge, and handle was polished metal. All else was red, shiny red. The fire truck was moving when I hopped on the chrome running board at the rear, realizing the fire truck would be my taxi.

The fireman gave the bell a couple of clangs and steered a circular path around the firehouse. He unexpectedly turned straight up a grassy embankment behind the station, reached a tarmac surface, turned abruptly, and made a beeline toward a group of small hangars at the other side of the airport. I could just see his head beyond the hoses, his short hair whipped by the wind. He shot me a tight-lipped smile and rang the bell again. It was a wonderfully scintillating ride—the over-sprung truck; the enthusiastic fireman; the panorama of light, shadow, and color; and the stiffening cold wind. It stripped away my fatigue. I tightened my grip as the truck sped onward. Soon it was clear that we were headed for a small plane with both props spinning. He steered a wide circle around it, pulled up forty yards short of the cockpit, smiled again as he stood to oversee my off-loading, said something against the roar of the plane's engines, and snapped off a crisp salute as I headed for the plane. I don't know precisely what he said but I like to think it was, "Velcome to Skandinavia!"

The boarding hatch just behind the cockpit of the twin-engine Fokker was hinged down and a section of steps folded down from it to the tarmac. The copilot, standing between me and the spinning propeller, helped heave my bags inside. I climbed onboard and followed a willowy blonde flight attendant in a navy blue uniform to a seat amidships with a view under the port wing. The attendant buckled my bags into an empty seat. "You must fasten your seat belt and leave it so," she said with an authoritative German accent. Four other passengers were onboard, all smiling as if they had arrived by fire truck too.

The flight between Reykjavik and the Faroes was a visual feast of lava- and ice-sculpted terrain. Icy rivers fingered through a moss- and tundra-covered landscape of white-capped mountains, faulted knolls, jagged cliffs, glazed crater pools, and sapphire-blue lakes, with only the occasional signature of man—a square dot.

The flight to the south coast lasted eight or ten minutes only. We were lucky, the attendant told us, she had never before seen it so clear. Along the coast, most of the passengers and the attendant shifted to the port side of the plane for a few minutes to gaze out the windows at the spectacle of a glacier calving icebergs a thousand feet below. As the plane climbed, the newly born icebergs joined a procession of hundreds of icebergs sweeping across a serene sea of blue, caught in a long curving current and looking like bridesmaids in streaming white gowns en route to some distant nuptial event.

The approach and landing at Vagur was equally memorable—but for white-knuckled terror. The skipper had aptly described the experience as comparable to landing in the Grand Canyon. Still, I wasn't prepared for the terrifying touchdown between gnarled rock faces, the smudged images just yards beyond the wingtip outside my window, and the sound of screeching brakes trapped between stone walls. As the plane stopped abruptly at runway's end, my jittery eyes looked over a cliff at a rolling blue wave as it crashed onto a rocky shore 500 feet below. When the engines revved again, my instincts screamed *escape* until I realized the pilot was merely turning the craft around to taxi back to the Quonset-hut terminal. A biting wind raked the terrain as I descended the ladder. It was a welcome confirmation of my survival. A pair of short, bow-legged men in heavy, hand-knit sweaters checked our passports and directed us to the taxis outside. I had made it safely to the Faroe Islands.

In Thorshavn, the capital, I caught the *Smyril* to Suderoy, the southern-most island of the eighteen-island chain. To the

Faroese, a nation of boat builders and fishermen, the sea-going ferry *Smyril* is a thing of national pride. "She's a sturdy vessel," a traveling teacher informed me. She was a little wide in the beam but undaunted in an expanse of the North Atlantic that turns boats into driftwood for a hobby. After sharing a short history of the islands with me, the teacher went his way and I collapsed onto a padded bench. Despite a rough sea that night, I slept until awakened by slamming hatches and heavy footfalls on the deck overhead. I had a dream while sleeping that night. A strange dream. However, another six weeks would pass before I recalled it, and, as with the *Balclutha* Dream, impart it to Monty.

I was on deck topside in a cold wind, eyes sorting through unlit objects along the waterfront when the *Smyril* made port in Tvoroyri (pronounced T-where-row-ree) on the island of Suderoy. After traveling some 6,000 miles in fewer than forty hours with only nominal sleep, little to eat, and only four dollars left in my pocket, even Wally Beardon's face was a welcome sight as he caught the mooring line and secured it to a bollard. At three in the morning, in fact, it seemed an overt act of warmth and generosity.

"It's about time you got here," he shouted while helping the deckhands set the gangway. Wally Beardon was engineering officer onboard the *Marite*.

"It feels good to be here." I replied.

"How'd you like that flight in from Reykjavik?" He added his familiar chuckle, more of a muted rattle, actually, that I had not heard in months. Wally and Captain Hofman had arrived together weeks before to inspect the *Marite*. I had known Wally in connection with repairs he had done on the *Eppie*. He was a first-class engineer, nobody questioned that, perhaps even brilliant, considering his ability to improvise, but he had another full-time occupation wherever he went or whatever he did: Wally was a spinner of tall tales. Some would say he lived in a delusional world of fiction. Others called him a liar. However you looked at it—raconteur, liar, delusional storyteller—he was a unique and complicated American character.

"The copilot passed out on us," he said. I had yet to put a foot on the dock and he was already spinning a tall tale. "For a while I thought the skipper or me was gonna have to help set her down." He took a bag and grinned. He was a big man, just over six feet or so, and had an honest and intelligent face that was made pink by miniature bacilli-like squiggles in his cheeks, all of which gave him a certain caloric glow. Up close, his soft blue eyes shifted as if uneasy with proximity, but they steadied and became engaging at other distances. He was a heavyset man, overweight actually, who looked like a cupid all grown up, wingless, of course, and he smoked a pipe incessantly. Invariably he wore khaki trousers, one of several plaid hunting shirts, an unzipped, camouflage hunting jacket, and an orange hunter's cap with the earflaps turned up. I cannot recall ever seeing enough hair on Wally to ascertain the color; he kept it cut short. Probably pushing fifty years old, Wally still had perfect vision, or at least some reason to claim that he did.

"Where's the *Marite?*" I asked after studying the orchard of masts in the miniature harbor.

"You'll have to wait 'til daylight to see her," said Wally. "But she's right over there." He pointed, strangely enough, to where I had concentrated my gaze. I re-examined the masts in the dimly lit area but saw nothing that resembled a 127-foot sailing ship.

"Why don't you get some sleep? The *Marite* will be there in the morning." I agreed and Wally escorted me up a short hill in the darkness and into a small but handsome hotel where I quickly gave in to the sleep of the travel-weary.

Chapter 4 – Adventures in Time, Inc.

The Tvoroyri Hotel was built into the steep bank of the fjord overlooking the man-made harbor. From the lobby the dining room opened to the right and held perhaps twenty rectangular tables joined end-to-end in sets of two or three, running in parallel lines and all covered with red and white checkerboard tablecloths. The walls were surfaced with beaded pine paneling and crowded with framed photographs. Boston ferns hung at regular intervals from the ceiling. Plate glass windows on the wall facing the harbor permitted a nearly seamless view of the fjord and harbor below. Wally and another man were hunkered over the midday meal at a table in the far left corner.

I stopped beside their table and introduced myself to Hutch, who was the navigator for the *Marite.* My hair was wet from a shower. He acknowledged me with a nod, but lifted a forkful of potatoes to his mouth anyway, then chewed and swallowed before speaking. "Bet that shower felt good," he said between bites, looking, measuring. He exchanged a disapproving glance with Wally. Wally didn't like the length of my hair, which nearly touched my collar. By appearances, Hutch didn't like it either.

I took a step to the window and swept my gaze over the dozen or so ships in the harbor. Most of them were small fishing boats. I saw no sailing ship. My pulse quickened.

"We got a telegram from the skipper telling us you were on the way," said Wally, food in his mouth.

"It just barely beat you here," added Hutch with a short laugh.

"Where's the *Marite*?" I asked. There was silence until their forks clinked on their plates They joined me at the window.

"She's right there," pointed Wally. "Can't you see?"

"Those were my exact words when I first got here," said Hutch with irony. He laughed again, a slow laugh that was really a series of verbalized HA-HA-HAs, as if he had learned to laugh from an instruction manual.

I examined the three largest ships again. There was no sailing ship among them.

"It's right there . . . in the middle," said Wally. "You'll be more impressed once you look her over."

"I can vouch for the hull," said Hutch. "It's as hard as a rock."

"You better dive in," said Wally as he returned to the table.

I sat down to mutton, potatoes, and Brussels sprouts, plus the unshakable image of three haggard freighters moored side by side. There was nothing about the ship in the middle that had insinuated a sailing ship to me. She looked more like a dismal little freighter.

"This is Hutch's favorite dish," said Wally sarcastically. "Mutton." He handed me the serving spoon with an uneasy smile.

"Yeah . . . sure," answered Hutch. He looked over sympathetically.

"How about you, Don?" interrupted Wally.

"What?"

"You like mutton?"

"I like everything except buttermilk," I told him.

Hutch's eyes brightened. I thought the remark had won his approval until the real object of his admiration arrived from the kitchen. "Wait until you see this Faroese gal," he whispered.

"Hay-lo," said the waitress in a thick accent. With her pink cheeks and big smile she looked like Heidi in blue jeans, tight blue jeans. "Just von more too-day?" She was the picture of rosy-cheeked health and innocence. "I come back," she said after surveying the table.

"Now just hold on," said Hutch to the girl in his slow, undulating delivery. "Wait a minute. We want you to meet our new man." Hutch's eyes revealed infatuation.

"I come back," she said, and left.

"Hutch, I think that gal's sweet on you," I toyed.

"Oh-h . . . now, I'm old enough to be her father," he declared, almost embarrassed.

"If they're old enough to bleed, they're old enough to breed," said Wally breezily. Hutch shot him a scowl. I had forgotten how crude Wally could be. The Faroese girl returned with a platter of cookies and that glowing good health. Wally reached for the cookies before the tray was on the table. "Only decent food in the place," he said of the cookies. The waitress imparted a fleeting sneer, then returned to the kitchen.

From the hotel it was two short blocks downhill to the quay. A cold, wet wind nipped at our ears. Hutch extended a formal handshake, which he had withheld in the hotel, before narrating en route what he knew about the village of Tvoroyri. He was a big man, mostly muscle, with a slow and measured manner in speech, in thought, and in his gait. Perhaps forty years old, his blond hair, blue eyes, pink complexion, and high cheekbones looked Scandinavian. The impression was enhanced by the Faroese sweater and knit cap he wore. An unbecoming combination of bowed legs and droopy pants gave him the appearance of a man with no butt. He had sailed a number of ships in the past, he told me, including a two-year trip around the world.

The concrete quay, shaped like a sideways L, extended perpendicular into the fjord about seventy yards then turned ninety degrees right and continued for another 150 yards. The seaward side of the dock provided temporary mooring berths; the sheltered side was for longer term moorings and repairs. A dozen or so craft were moored inside the quay. Most of the local fishermen anchored their boats in the fjord to avoid port fees.

The *Marite* was moored between two small freighters. To get to her, we crossed the steel deck of the freighter *Skeinvagur*. I paused at the gunwale where the two ship hulls ran parallel and recalled the grand vision of the *Marite* I had imagined. Slowly the skipper's words fell into context with what I now saw. Previously they had only confirmed and colored my own romantic image. But now I was looking reality in the face: the *Marite* had been refitted into a dingy little freighter, and the mast that needed relocating was being used to support a cargo boom.

"Not much to look at, is she?" said Wally truthfully. "But she's a dandy. The skipper and I went through all the logs. She's never taken on water and she's spent the last forty years as the mothership for small dory fishing boats working the waters near the Arctic Circle."

I followed Hutch and Wally over the gunwale. "Anytime you buy a ship you're only buying a hull," said Hutch consolingly. "She's a little dirty, I'll grant you that, but she's pickled as hard as a rock." He threw back the canvas hatch covering on the main hatch and removed two of the twelve-foot planks that spanned the opening. Daylight spilled into the hold.

A noxious odor came out. The interior walls of her rounded belly were discolored by a grey-green glaze. "This hull is pickled from the rock salt they spread over fish in the hold."

"It's as sound as a Yankee dollar," said Wally. "The skipper and I went over her with a fine-toothed comb."

I surveyed the ship once more. The prow stood high in the water, well above the prows of the freighters on each side, and from stem to stern she had the contour of a sailing ship. I let my imagination remove the clutter of add-ons to the weather deck—the deckhouse with a pilothouse on top, the sheltering bulkheads that enclosed the stern deck, and the stubby masts fore and aft. She was a sailing ship. The skipper had a keen eye. He had said it would be flush-decked, stripped to the main deck.

"Let's show him his new bachelor pad," said Wally, grinning, pipe clenched in his teeth.

"I don't think we're gonna have time," said Hutch looking skyward. Wally dashed for the ladder to the pilothouse. The rain caught Hutch and me replacing the planks and refitting the hatch cover. In less than a minute, we were soaked.

Hutch and I scurried up the ladder to the pilothouse. Wally had taken a seat on an oak barstool beside the ship's wheel and placed his tobacco kit on the window sill. "Who's turn for the stool?" he asked.

"Who cares?" said Hutch, suddenly angry. He turned to me, his jaw clenched. "It's the same every frigging day. Rain, rain, rain." Conversation ceased. The rain drumming on the roof made me feel trapped inside the five-by-eight-foot pilothouse. Soup-bowls of pipe ashes cluttered the window sills. A hotel towel was draped over the ship's wheel. The ship's compass, suspended in a large brass binnacle to the right of the ship's wheel, bore the smudged look of neglected brass. Their silence

and the competition for the barstool told me that Wally and
Hutch had spent a lot of time in the pilothouse staring at the rain
and unchanging landscape.

Recognizing a captive audience, Wally seized the moment
to educate us about bouncing raindrops that he had witnessed in
the Colorado high plains. "Damnedest thing, to stand out in the
rain without getting wet." He attributed the anomaly to the high
iron content of Colorado dust.

His tall tales had probably been their primary pastime.
Clearly they had needed one, for they had been in Tvoroyri for
weeks without having raised a finger. "So what needs to be
done before we can move onboard?" I asked. "The skipper
mentioned moving the foremast. Obviously, that will require a
shipyard. But what can we do now? Today?"

Hutch stared blankly out the window.

"We don't own it yet," said Wally. A silence followed.
After a short while, Hutch wiped the condensation from the
window with the towel. The rain was coming down in sheets.

"Why don't we move onboard?" I pressed.

"That's not for us to decide," said Hutch.

A real pair of adventurers, I concluded. I looked again at the
Marite as she endured the rain. "She's a sturdy one," the
skipper had said. "Built in Fécamp, France in 1913. A square
tops'l schooner." Vainly I indulged in that sleek vision of a
sailing ship that had occupied my imagination. How different it
was from the real ship before me.

The rain let up enough to see again. I toweled a window
then studied the village of Tvoroyri and environs. Although
colorful and perfectly clean, it seemed an uninspiring little berg
perched on the south bank of a fjord. I turned my eyes westward
to the clock on the steeple of the little white church with a red

roof near the hotel. It had stopped at 6:15. "Welcome to Adventures in Time," I told myself, acknowledging the ready-made irony.

Almost a week passed before Hutch agreed that we should move onboard. Wally signed on reluctantly. Hutch and I approached Mr. Hansen, the ship's owner, and pitched it as a plan to clean up the ship before Captain Hofman returned.

Mr. Hansen was a practical man. Besides owning the *Marite*, he had a thriving business that traded in everything from lumber and hardware to clothing and dynamite. A handsome, formal man with a gentrified manner, he spoke impeccable English, was perfectly groomed, and always dressed, Hutch told me, in a grey wool suit, his shirt buttoned at the collar and a black beret over silvering black hair. He gave a green light to our proposition.

Hutch and I remained at his dining room table to plot priorities. First we would clean the officers' quarters so we could move onboard, then we would work our way on deck. Next stop was the ship chandler, who had extended a line of credit for the ship's needs to Mr. Heflin and Adventures in Time, Inc. The current needs were brooms, scrub brushes, detergent, a pair of buckets, and two sets of raingear.

Hutch and I spent the next few weeks cleaning. The officers' quarters were the easiest of the clean-up projects, requiring a full day only. Hutch and I moved onboard.

Located belowdecks, the officers' quarters were a small, triangular compartment that was fashioned from the rounded interior section of the ship's hull all the way to stern. The space had a beehive feel owing to the built-in honey-hued oak furnishings, low ceiling, and stacked bunk units with identical drawers beneath each bunk. A narrow table with built-in benches occupied the space between the port and starboard bunk units. An antique brass lamp hung over the table. The captain's cabin, a mere eight-by-ten-foot cubicle, was accessible by a door on the starboard side of the officers' quarters toward amidships. The ladders to the engine room below and the deckhouse above were accessible in the opposite space on the port side.

Hutch turned out to be a good companion and a hard worker as we labored through rain and wind and cold, slowly, steadily, making our way through the squalid compartments. After three weeks of toil, we had cleaned most of the ship. Wally began to show up for an hour or so every day. He would start the engines, let them run for a short while, then return to the hotel to read. Sometimes he would stay long enough to spin a tall tale.

The day after we had scoured the captain's cabin, however, Wally moved into it while Hutch and I were out. Although Hutch and I felt as if an outsider had invaded our space, we neither spoke of it nor acknowledged our disgust. For his part, Wally seemed oblivious to the enormity of squatting in the captain's cabin. He only seemed interested in his own comfort and convenience. Hutch attributed it to the length of his stay, as if it represented some sort of sensory deprivation.

One day Hutch and I returned to the *Marite* to find the ship's electrical generator running and Wally reading in the mess, the ship's small dining area. Despite its location in the engine room below decks, the generator was loud and drowned out normal speech. Wally grinned as we made our way through the hatchway and sat. "I got a little present for you, Dee," he yelled, pointing into the galley. "I just couldn't hack those pygmy sandwiches and the mutton anymore." Wally had arranged to buy food and diesel on credit. It was a coup for our better well-being. The *Marite* no longer seemed merely a cold wooden object and the focus of our labors. She was our home.

By request, the first meal was sausage, eggs, fried potatoes, and gravy. "We have fire," was the message that passed from eye to eye over that meal. Cafe Prometheus.

Toward the end of May, the island was blessed with its first clear and windless day of the year. Small flowers miraculously appeared, transforming the landscape into a carpet of green flecked with colors. We proclaimed it a day of rest. I spent the morning at the Konditari, a bakery, sipping coffee and updating my journal, and soon found myself chatting with three insatiably curious teenage girls—Frieda, Birthe, and Larla. Larla's father owned the *Marite*. They wanted to know about California. I wanted to learn Danish. They taught me to read the menu. I loaned them *Planet Waves*, a Bob Dylan album on cassette tape. Thus began a lovely friendship and my first Danish language lesson.

With the advent of spring, a steady stream of freighters began arriving with goods for Mr. Hansen. One day he asked Hutch and me to help unload his cargo. Having been penniless for weeks, an opportunity to earn money sounded good, even if it involved hours of lifting 110-pound bags of cement.

For Hutch and me, the money improved things. But it created a problem since Wally, who avoided physical labor, was broke. As a courtesy, Hutch and I replenished Wally's tobacco supply. And though he took the tobacco without hesitation, he was too proud to regard our goodwill as anything but charity.

We saw less and less of him. When he did join us for meals or in chance encounters, they usually ended in senseless spats.

Increasingly, his anger and frustration also showed in not-so-subtle ways. Like running the generator all night so he could read. The more we earned, or so it seemed, the later he ran the generator and the less he responded to our complaints. Finally, Hutch exploded, called Wally "a worthless slob," and tossed his belongings from the captain's cabin.

Things changed. Wally holed up in the hotel. Hutch turned angry and moody. I packed my stuff and moved from the officers' quarters, which were all the way aft, to the forecastle all the way forward (and commonly known as the fo'c'sle). A few days later Hutch called for a meeting in the mess.

At first we just sat there, Wally puffing on his pipe, Hutch on the opposite bench peering into a cup of coffee. His voice barely broke the silence. "Things weren't supposed to be this way," he complained. "The crew was supposed to be here a month ago, the skipper included." He shook his head as he spoke; his voice had taken on a hushed tone. "I mean, we should be in Copenhagen right now." He paused to draw a breath, then looked up. He looked tired, distraught. "Hell, I'm a navigator, not slave labor. I'm not some kind of hippie-dippy dreamer. You think I hired on to unload freighters and be a human conveyor belt for slimy bags of fertilizer? Hell no! I am a navigator." His fist rose between us. "I have guided ships around the world, finer ships than the *Marite*, and that's no tall tale." He wanted to pound his fist on the table, but lowered it instead.

"Give it a few more days, Hutch," I reasoned. "The skipper'll show up any day now." I looked to Wally but got no help. He seemed in another world.

Hutch didn't answer immediately. "I'm giving it one more week, then I'm throwing in the towel," he said finally. "I've seen this sort of thing before. You are free to do what you want." He slid to the end of the bench and exited in a wearied swagger.

Hutch and I were unloading bags of chemical fertilizer on a rainy day when Chris strode through the narrow doorway of the storage shed. "Chris!" I dropped my bag of fertilizer and ran to greet him. He was smiling so hard he couldn't speak. I wanted to hug or tackle him but settled for a double handshake because of the fertilizer slime on my clothes.

We were still backslapping excitedly when Hutch body-slammed a bag of fertilizer on the stack, like a late night TV wrestler. He propped his hands on his hips. "If you're going to be one of my men, you're going to need a haircut," he declared. His wide frame stiffened into a menacing posture.

Chris' eyes narrowed, then turned to me with an expression that said "What's his trip?"

A stony silence ensued. Then, just as suddenly, Hutch apologized for his behavior and returned his attention to the fertilizer bag. I threw up my hands for Chris' sake. "Have you seen the *Marite* yet?" I asked neutrally. "Hutch and I have got it looking pretty good."

"Oh, yeah. And I saw Wally." He shrugged and looked anxiously at Hutch.

"You talk with the skipper before leaving?" asked Hutch without friendliness.

"About two weeks ago." He turned to me with a bright grin. "I hitch-hiked to New York and then flew over. It was fun and saved a lot of money"

"I wish I would have done that."

"And dig this," he said privately, "I caught a fishing boat in from Iceland to here." His broad smile returned. "Now that was a trip!"

There was an elemental beauty to Chris' way of doing things. Some would say he had a passive personality type. To me, his behavior was less about following the path of least resistance, as it appeared, but more like avoiding stationary objects. Instead of stopping to challenge red tape or confront obstacles, Chris moved through the world without making judgments. A judgment, after all, is simply a stationary thought. Chris just flowed, that is how he described his lifestyle, and he was happy to be alive and part of the structure and flow he experienced around him.

Hutch moved another bag from the forklift outside the door to the stack we were building in the shed. As he headed back to the forklift he grumbled "We ain't getting paid to sit around and gab."

Chris bristled. "Hey, I've been here two minutes now and have got nothing but flack. What's the beef?"

"Beef?" growled Hutch. "I guess they don't teach proper English in school anymore. What's the beef? You think I'm some kinda butcher or something?" He tossed another bag down onto the pallet. "Things are going to have to change around here, I can tell you that."

"So, what's the problem?" Chris asked.

"You guys got a lot to learn if you think life onboard the *Marite* is going to be one big bed of roses," he grumbled.

"I thought sailors were supposed to drink and bitch about food and live on an hour's sleep," I said. "All work and . . ."

Hutch interrupted again. "You two aren't sailors." His eyes riveted on Chris. "You're just a couple of aimless hippies with long hair."

"Is that what all of this is about, Hutch? Are you pissed off about our hair?" I held out a lock. "Christ, Hutch, it's only hair. You needn't make it out to be something diabolical." I shook my head in disbelief. "Correct me if I am wrong, Hutch, but didn't the term Jack Tar come from sailors using a dollop of tar to bind their hair into ponytails?"

"Well, that might be," he said, simmering, "but it doesn't make sailors out of you two."

"What difference does it make anyway? You just told me a few days ago that you were throwing in the towel, giving up, and that I was free to do what I want."

"Well, for your information, and this goes for the two of you," he scowled, "I am still your superior onboard this vessel and what I say goes." He stiffened.

"So which of you am I to believe?" I shot back. "The one who threw in the towel or the one who wants to be in charge?" There was silence as Hutch tried to stare me down. I lifted a lock of hair. "It's just hair, Hutch. To us, it's a freedom flag, that's all."

Chris waited with a smile, then spoke to Hutch. "The skipper is my boss and he doesn't care about my hair . . . or yours," he said to Hutch. "I'll just wait and see what he says." His voice was controlled and confident, and he didn't wait for a reply. "This is your hang-up, man. The skipper doesn't care."

The next morning I conjured a decent breakfast despite the circumstances. "Ya know, with four of us onboard now, maybe we should start eating supper onboard too," said Wally.

"Who's going to cook it and clean up," I asked Wally. "Have you forgotten we don't have a cook onboard yet?"

"You're not doing too bad," he grunted. Hutch sat stone-faced beside him. Secretly, I was delighted that they appreciated my cooking, though I'd never admit that to them.

Over the weeks Sunday had become host to a couple of traditions. We laundered our clothes and met at the hotel for the big mid-afternoon meal. On this particular day we learned that Wally had kept a room at the hotel even though he had lived for all but a few days in the captain's cabin. The revelation surfaced as the innkeeper scolded Wally in a wretched scene for snatching cookies from another table after the guest had gone. The blood drained from Hutch's face as the innkeeper, wagging a finger like a castigating schoolmaster in suspenders, unloaded on Wally for every grievance attributable to the Americans over the months. The kicker had been the owner's final words as he stomped off in his wooden clogs: "There vil be no more showers on credit." It meant added hardship—not for Wally, he had not put in a single hour of work since I had arrived—but for those of us who got dirty working every day. The owner had also asked for payment in full for all charges to date, which we did not have. It had been an embarrassing incident in a roomful of hotel guests.

Wally was unmoved throughout the scolding. Apart from waiting until the owner left to finish off the cookies in his hand, he seemed totally in another world. The incident revealed to us that Wally was little more than a shell of a man. No conscience, no principles, no scruples, no shame, nothing.

Chris and I refrained from commenting on the ordeal until outside. The confrontation had not been amusing, but we laughed uproariously about it. We laughed about the cookies, mimicked the waggling finger and the innkeeper's pot-bellied tirade. We laughed about Hutch, who had sat white-faced in his chair through the torrent of abuse. We laughed about the presence of the other diners, the lost access to the showers, the embarrassment, the indifference, the ensuing silence. Like adding machines, we laughed and laughed until the list was the sum of our misfortune, and then we laughed about that. We finally were honest enough to laugh about our disgrace and our pain.

To get away, Chris and I climbed the mountain behind Tvoroyri. It was a mere 800 or 900 feet, not really a mountain, but the last few hundred feet was a vertical wall of dark grey stone jutting out from the mossy green slope. "And if it rains, who knows, it might do us good," declared Chris. I agreed. The incident at the hotel had left me feeling like a flimflam artist. The idea of climbing a mountain had a spiritual allure, a quality that appealed to my need to reaffirm my purpose and being. A little rain could only help.

The climb to the top took less than an hour. We prudently avoided the sheer rock surfaces in favor of the crevices that rockslides and rainwater had chiseled into the stone over eons. Having reached the crest, we followed a ridge running parallel to the fjord toward the open sea until we reached a sheer drop overlooking the clear blue north Atlantic. Here was a truly awesome vista that I would see many times in the Faroe Islands with undiminished awe: a sheer cliff falling hundreds of feet to the deep blue sea below, a grey ceiling of clouds just overhead, and hundreds of birds describing arcs in the timeless space between. As the image of the church steeple with the broken clock increasingly became the logo for Adventures in Time, Inc. in my mind, this ubiquitous cliff-side vista surely was the address. And the soundtrack, should I score it for a movie, would include the distant hungry cry of birds on wing. I succumbed to the beauty, the awe, and felt my body being towed ever so gently as the earth beneath me spun through the cosmos. I loafed and invited my soul, as Walt Whitman expressed the feeling a century earlier on the same planet and during the same eternity.

And after a long time of just absorbing the experience, quietly, every now and then throwing a stone toward the sea, the rain came, slowly at first. The wind picked up, the sky took on a menacing cast, and we fled for the ship.

It seemed an angry world that pelted us with cold rain and wind as we hastened along the ridge, running when we could. The swift change in conditions bore all the markings of a brawny storm. We found our point of descent behind Tvoroyri and began the dangerous vertical descent over cold and wet stone. The wet, spongy moss, a comfort when damp on the way up, became a lubricant underfoot on the way down. At one point I stopped to reset my feet on a stone when Chris came sliding by uncontrollably. He skidded over the wet moss for forty yards or so before plowing into enough loose gravel to slow his descent.

"Hey . . . Dee," he shouted gleefully in the cold rain. "You ought to give that a try. It's fun . . . and fast!" Rainwater ran down his face and dripped from his spindly goatee. He launched himself on another skidding descent and came to a halt in loose gravel again. "Come on," he called from eighty yards downhill and beckoned with a large wave of his arm.

I sat on the back of my heels as he had, leaned back, and with a slight push skidded downhill on my butt. It worked wonderfully. Following Chris' path, I soon joined him at the base of the rock. Tvoroyri lay a mere 200 yards beyond, the *Marite* the same distance again.

The storm continued unabated all night and into the next day with gale-force winds, thrashing waves, and unremitting rain. Chris and I donned raingear for the short dash from the fo'c'sle to the galley. The ship rocked so much that coffee cups were half-filled. Hatches were dogged. Wally, we learned, selfishly had run the generator most of the night so he could read. Hutch should have been in an awful mood, but somehow seemed unaffected. Like old buddies, the three of us chatted naturally over coffee about the storm and other things. Without saying it, the reconciliation was a recognition that, like it or not, we were the captain's choice of crew. We all had to get along in order to accomplish the higher goals of getting the *Marite* seaworthy and sailing her to San Francisco.

Later that morning Hutch hauled out his charts and instruments and showed us how to plot a course on a navigational chart. Chris, who owned and lived on a thirty-six-foot Navy surplus whaleboat that he planned to refit as a ketch and sail, was especially appreciative. Hutch had given him part of the wherewithal to do just that. In the spirit of things, Chris announced that he was getting a haircut. I agreed to get one too. When we returned from the barber, Hutch invited us to move into the officers' quarters.

Another swing of the pendulum.

Wally remained impassive through it all. Although unstated, we worried about his mental health. But none of us knew him well enough to judge whether he had gone over the edge or was naturally this detached and insensitive. Another issue left unstated was the matter of the ship's finances. We all had paid our own way to the Faroes with the understanding that we would be reimbursed once the skipper returned. But the skipper had not returned as scheduled, and we all knew now that the bills were not being paid. No doubt every adult in Tvoroyri knew it too. Securing capital for the project had been Mr. Heflin's domain from the beginning. Our roles occupied a different column in the Adventures in Time ledger.

Hutch's mood swing continued up the scale to euphoria. At supper time he pitched in to help Chris and me prepare a meal of flounder, potatoes, and carrots. Bouncing around the galley with plates in hand and fetching condiments, his face showed a color and vitality that had been in short supply for weeks. He even whistled "Camptown Races" for a short while until Chris threatened to put *Goats Head Soup,* the Rolling Stones album, on the tape player. The title was enough to command silence.

As if by notice, Wally showed his face at mealtime. We had not seen him since the incident at the hotel. "Fish and potatoes again?" he asked wearily. "We might as well be eating at the hotel." He lit his pipe and then checked the coffee pot. He was smirking about something. "I got a surprise," he told us. After two trips to the captain's cabin, he assembled on the table a cache of new books that he probably had just swapped with a trawler crew that had holed up in Tvoroyri during the storm. The cache of trade goods included a portable Smith-Corona typewriter in a carrying case. Wally rubbed his palms excitedly, his pipe going strong.

"I pulled this one out of storage just for you," he said of the typewriter. His eyes shifted from mine to the typewriter and back.

It looked like a tall tale in the making, but I took the bait. "That's your typewriter?"

"Sure is," answered Wally. "I've turned out many a good short story on that little jewel." He went to fetch a cup of coffee from the galley but continued talking, yelling almost. "I had planned to write my first novel during this little expedition, but the weather and the hotel food has got my creative energies all screwed up." I held my thoughts in check. "So I'm looking to trade her away." He returned to the galley with his eyes trained on mine.

"What if the mood strikes you later on?" I asked.

"Once the skipper gets here there'll be no time for anything but sailing," he replied. He raised a paperback copy of *Puppet on a Chain* from among the books on the table. "Ever read this one?"

I shook my head. "How much for the typewriter?"

"Whatever I can get. I figured it might help you learn Danish, since most of the letters are the same." We settled on 150 kroner. In the local English-language typewriter market, $25 was more than fair. And he was right, the Danish and English alphabets were close cousins and the girls enjoyed typing vocabulary lists and writing me playfully seductive notes in Danish. With no radio or TV, we all had time on our hands.

Chapter 5 – The Pecking Order

Cold, stormy weather seemed to be the norm in the Faroe Islands, but by mid-June the rain was warmish and arrived on a spring-like wind. Hutch returned from Mr. Hansen's warehouse with a broad smile. "Good news, fellas," he said. He filled his coffee cup and took it and the smile into the mess. "Two crewmen are in Thorshavn," he said at last. He shifted his weight onto an elbow on the table. "Apparently they have run out of money, so Mr. Hansen arranged to have them put up in the hotel and to get them onboard the *Smyril* this afternoon."

"Ya-hoo," cried Chris. "I'll bet it's Zak and Monty."

"We don't know who they are," said Hutch, "just that there are two and that they are worn out."

Monty and Taylor arrived that night. The exhilaration of having made it to journey's end kept them up for a while, but they soon surrendered to total exhaustion. They emerged from their sleeping bags the next afternoon talking about how good a shower and shave would feel. Therein lay their first big disappointment.

Chris recounted the saga of the lost shower privileges as the three of them set places for dinner. I was cooking, but noticed that Hutch and Wally overheard part of it. The arrival of Monty and Taylor, I hoped, would inaugurate a new phase in the social dynamics onboard the ship. But when all hands gathered for the evening meal, Chris, Taylor, and Monty benched themselves on one side of the mess room table and Hutch and Wally sat on the other. Not an auspicious arrangement.

"We're going to start calling you Chef-boy-are-Dee," quipped Monty as I placed grilled cod and boiled potatoes on the table.

"Chef, boy-are-this-boring, would be more like it," said Wally with his mouth full.

"Maybe you comedians will yield the floor for a minute," said Hutch. "This is my first time to talk with our new guys and I've got some questions."

"Commodians is more like it," said Wally with a grin to Hutch.

"First of all, let me introduce myself. I'm Harold Crutchfield. Most people end up calling me Hutch, and that's just fine." He set his fork down and wet his lips with a sweep of his tongue. "I'm navigational officer onboard the *Marite*. Second mate." He paused for the formal exchange.

"I'm Monty Hart, deckhand or rigger, I guess."

"I'm Randy Taylor," he said with food in his mouth. "Sorry about the food, I'm famished." He swallowed. "You can call me Randy or Taylor. These guys call me Taylor." He returned to his plate.

"Chris and Dee are going to have to show you the way to the barber shop," said Wally. "And you too," he nodded toward Monty.

"I don't have to get a haircut unless I want," declared Taylor. He had a long, black, curly head of hair that would have made a Bourbon monarch proud.

"Now, now, hold it," said Hutch. "Who's got the floor here?"

"I don't care who's got the floor," snapped Taylor. "My personal habits and hygiene are not items on a ballot that Silent Majority boneheads vote up or down." He poked a forkful of potatoes into his mouth without looking up.

"Dee and Chris got haircuts," said Wally.

Hutch restrained Wally with a hand on his forearm. "Okay now, just hold on, everybody." Hutch glared at Taylor until, in the silence, Taylor casually looked up from his plate. "There is a chain of command on board this ship," said Hutch sharply, "and right now I am at the top of that chain of command." He was ready for dissent, but got silence instead. "And until Captain Hofman returns each of you is under my command. You will do what I say or you're out of the picture." He spoke very slowly but in a wavering, emotional voice. We all nodded in agreement.

"Does that include Wally?" asked Taylor.

"Shut up," snapped Hutch. "Right now I want silence. S-I-L-E-N-C-E. Understand?"

Everybody nodded.

"We'll get to that later, and we'll get to the matter of personal hygiene later," said Hutch. "Right now I just want the floor, okay?" A long silence turned into an uneasy exchange of glances. Hutch seemed to be reorganizing his thoughts. Taylor calmly returned to his food.

"Go ahead and eat," said Hutch. He stared straight ahead for a long moment, thinking before speaking again. "I don't want you new guys to get the wrong impression of me or anything. I'm not a slave driver or the bossy type. I'm sure you've talked with Dee and Chris about it."

Hutch was looking my way, expecting support. "We've been getting along just fine," I said.

On cue everybody looked to Chris. "You don't see me complaining," said Chris.

"And I'm sure we'll all get along," continued Hutch. He looked to Monty. "Did the skipper give you guys any instructions to pass along to me?"

Monty cleared his throat. "Not me," he said. He looked over to Taylor.

"Me neither," said Taylor. He drank some coffee.

"Did he give any indication when he would be returning?" asked Hutch. He, too, now took a bite of food.

"Real soon is what he told me," answered Monty, holding his fork but not eating. "He said Heflin had signed up twenty-two students and that . . ."

"Twenty-two students," blurted Wally. Hutch's face registered the same shock. "That's all we need, a bunch of dingbat students," said Wally to Hutch.

"Where are we going to put twenty-two students?" asked Hutch to Wally.

"In the hold," said Wally flippantly, "and then we could take'm out to sea and dump'm." He took a puff on his pipe to keep it going and then leaned it against his plate.

"Do you think we could modify the hold to accommodate twenty-two students?" asked Hutch rhetorically. "That's a lot of people." He turned to Monty again. "Are you sure he said twenty-two?"

"Yeah. Fairly sure." He looked to the other faces.

"Did you have a sense of how soon 'real soon' was?"

"A week or two, I'd guess," said Monty. Taylor stood and began spooning more food on his plate. He didn't look at Hutch or he would have seen clenched jaw muscles and an icy glare.

"What about you, Taylor? Did he give you any idea as to how soon he would return?"

"Not really." Taylor looked at Hutch briefly then turned to me. "Any dessert?" My expression must have conveyed the absurdity of the question, as he responded with a short burst of laughter.

Hutch let the levity pass before speaking again. "But do you agree with Monty that a week or two was what he had in mind?" Hutch was seething beneath the surface over Taylor's casual attitude.

"I guess," said Taylor, not really listening. He nudged me and scooted my way with his cup. He wanted more coffee.

"Now just a minute," reacted Hutch. He had almost stuttered. "We're still having a meeting here." He stirred in his seat.

"I was just going to get some coffee," said Taylor. He clunked his cup down. "Christ," he murmured in frustration. He sat with a plop.

"I'm not one to single out people, Taylor, but you and I are going to be going to Fist City if you can't learn to show some basic human respect." His quavering voice conveyed the depth of his anger, and his restraint.

Taylor expelled a breath in surprise. "Are you threatening me?" asked Taylor. He looked around the faces at the table. "In front of witnesses? Is that what that means? A ship's officer is physically threatening a deckhand on his first day?" He looked for verbal support but got none. "This is 1974, Hutch, not the nineteenth century. There are international laws protecting . . ."

"It's just an expression," said Hutch. "You know that and you also know what I mean." He had made his right hand into a fist but slowly uncoiled it. "I have enough problems around here without having to take guff off you."

"Threatening a crew member is not the way to—"

Monty interrupted. "I think we're both still frazzled from our trip. I know I'm edgy, jet lag and all." A silence intervened. When Taylor moved to respond, Chris gave him a "What's the point?" shrug.

"I've said all I need to say," said Taylor. "I'm sorry if it has rocked the boat around here."

The unintentional pun loosened Hutch's stern expression a little. Even Taylor smiled nervously.

"Oh, I get it," said Monty, quick to see a face-saving opportunity.

There was a small sigh of relief around the table, and nervous smiles followed. "There are plenty of potatoes left," I announced. I looked to Hutch. Mealtime held a certain reverence with Hutch. It was sort of like Family Time with Dad to him. Taylor had picked a poor time to confront him. But then Taylor had never let timing get in the way of expressing his opinions.

My food was cold once I got to it. We ate in a strained silence until the gathering showed signs of breaking up. There was a tacit acknowledgement, however, that Hutch needed to make the first move.

"You guys don't go too far away from the galley after supper," said Hutch in a soft but official voice. "Wally and I need to do some brainstorming so we can figure out a schedule and whatnot." It was an invitation to leave. We were more than happy to get away.

"I've got five bucks that says we're going to the brig," quipped Chris as we headed forward on the main deck.

"I just hope he doesn't retaliate with a night watch or something," said Taylor.

"You ya-hoos stay onboard," interjected Wally, his plump face centered in the open porthole as we passed. He had heard our remarks.

Monty offered us a Marlboro once we were a safe distance from the galley. We hadn't seen an American cigarette in weeks. "Troy told me to remind you about the letter you owe him," Monty told me. We all lit up. "And guess who took over your killer hours after you left?" He blew out a puff of smoke as if it was the question mark to his sentence. "Da killer did," he said slowly, both thumbs pointing at his chest.

"Hutch like this all the time?" asked Taylor. He had gone over to the port gunwale and was looking at the collection of boats in the harbor. Technically it was nighttime, but there was still enough light to read a newspaper. In these latitudes the advent of spring also meant the arrival of the Midnight Sun.

"It's jet lag," countered Monty with a wink.

"Hey, look who's coming." Chris pointed to the road that led down to the quay. In the spring light there moved three familiar female figures: Larla, Birthe, and Frieda.

"Women?" said Monty. He licked a fingertip and smoothed his eyebrows in a comical display of preening. Taylor had yet to take his eyes off the girls.

"They're too young," said Chris with profound disappointment.

"There's a set of jugs on one that would do wonders for my girl back in Baghdad-by-the Bay," said Taylor.

"That's Birthe. She's the youngest of the three. Probably fourteen," I said.

"How old are the other two?" asked Monty. We all turned slowly as we watched their progress along the dock amid the masts and harbor obstructions in the foreground.

"Sixteen," said Chris. I nodded. "Larla's dad owns the *Marite*," he added.

"The skipper told us all about good public relations and our ambassadorial role." Monty stopped and pointed to Chris and me. "Did he tell you guys too?" When we smiled, Monty slapped his hip. "I knew it." He howled in delight. "With little plastic cups of gin from his glove box?" He and Chris exchanged a friendly push. "I can't believe it."

The three girls reached the dock beside the *Skeinvagur* and waved excitedly. "New mens on board?" called Birthe, her voice carrying over the deck of the freighter to the *Marite*. They crossed the freighter's deck and we met and talked, separated by the pair of gunwales.

"Vee came to say hay-lo to new mens," said Birthe. She was all smiles as her eyes swarmed over Monty and Taylor without inhibition. Frieda and Larla were equally excited but more reserved.

"I'm Larla. This is Frieda. She is Birthe." Monty and Taylor extended greetings.

"Taylor and Monty are friends from San Francisco," I said.

"They are friends you wait for?" asked Larla.

"You like Tvoroyri so far?" asked Frieda, her eyes bright as usual. She had an extroverted personality and a round smiling face that almost glowed with enthusiasm.

"So far," said Monty. "Except for the meals." He poked me in the ribs.

"Hotel food is wery bad," said Birthe with a shake of her head.

"I think he's talking about our first meal onboard the *Marite*," said Taylor. "It was unpleasant in more ways than one."

Frieda and Larla looked to Chris and me for an explanation. "Wally and Hutch didn't like their hair," said Chris.

"I think it's bootiful," said Birthe, eyeing Taylor's long curly dark hair. There was envy in her eyes and voice.

"It's more than just the hair," declared Taylor philosophically. "They are just a couple of has-beens and they're worried because they're outnumbered and they don't have the balls or the brains to dominate us."

Chris clapped loudly and cheered him on. "Right on!"

"Goddam radicals," said Monty, his fist thrust overhead.

"Goddam radicals," mimicked Birthe. Hearing it, Monty apologized for the profanity.

"That okay," said Larla. "You should hear Birthe's papa." They all laughed.

"Yeah. You should hear him when he drinks schnapps," said Birthe. "He says many bad words."

"Uh-oh," said Frieda. She shot a glance to me. "Here come Hutch." Her expression turned pleasant as she turned to face him.

Hutch was smiling his sugary PR smile for Mr. Hansen's daughter. "Ho-ho," he said cheerily. "What have we got here? Faroese sirens?" The girls looked to Chris then to me for a translation.

"Yeah. We got a three-alarm fire here," said Monty under his breath.

Hutch hadn't paused. "Sorry to break up this little gathering, but we've got business to discuss in the mess." He looked to all of us and then to the girls. "How about a rain check?" He chuckled.

The girls understood the meaning, if not the humor, nodded, and waved good-bye as they exited. We headed for our meeting in the mess.

Hutch and Wally had decided that until the skipper returned we would all put in an eight-to-five workday, five days a week, and that the crew would be responsible on a rotating schedule for cleaning up the mess and galley after meals, the cook exempted. As a show of courtesy and leadership, although they did not mention these motives specifically, Hutch and Wally would do the clean-up on this night only. All in all it seemed more than reasonable and even-handed.

Chris and I had been berthing in the officers' quarters since the reconciliation. However, since there was not room there for the entire crew, we were assigned to the fo'c'sle with the other crew members.

The fo'c'sle housed twelve bunks in identical three-high tiers port and starboard with a large drawer under each. The floor plan was a reverse of the officers' quarters. Also, the fo'c'sle was smaller and less elegant in terms of design, materials, and workmanship than the officer's quarters.

A lot was accomplished in the days before the skipper's arrival. Morale improved and everybody got along. We holystoned the officers' quarters and mess, a back-breaking job that involved scrubbing off a thin layer of wood from the hardwood deck with a special, porous brick. Whenever the rain stopped we stripped the old paint from the hull and applied a fresh coat of glossy black. The ship's metalwork was burnished and then rustproofed with red lead oxide paint. The brightwork—portholes, instruments, the ship's bell, anything made of brass—was made to gleam, even in the rain. With the exception of the engine room and areas within Wally's domain, the *Marite* had been scrubbed and polished—and showed it.

Chapter 6 – Footloose in Time

The skipper arrived unexpectedly on a freighter at midday instead of onboard the *Symril* in the evening. When word got out, the crew swarmed on deck to greet him. Hardly noticed was the young sailor behind him, a teenager with pimples and shoulder-length, stringy blonde hair. The skipper directed the bunch of us into the mess where he promptly pulled a bottle of vodka from his jacket pocket. Chris bounced into the galley for cups.

"Glad to have you back," declared Hutch, his round face aglow. "We were beginning to wonder."

"Where's Wally?" asked the skipper. "I want *all* of my crew here so I don't have to repeat myself."

Monty, who stood nearest the hatchway, darted below to the officers' quarters and returned moments later with Wally thirty seconds behind and a smile just for me. Monty had caught Wally hurriedly moving out of the captain's cabin, I knew. I smiled back as the skipper passed out cups of vodka to all and raised a toast. "To the crew of the *Marite*."

"And her skipper," added Hutch.

The skipper nodded graciously, his polished smile and raised cup moving from face to face as he toasted. We all downed the vodka. The cups were refilled. "By all accounts you gentlemen deserve a couple of stiff ones." He raised another toast. "I've received nothing but excellent reports from Mr. Hansen on your behavior and," here he paused to admire the freshly refurbished deck in the mess, ". . . your work habits." He made another visual round of all hands and proclaimed, "Congratulations and well done!" He placed a paternal hand on Wally's shoulder to his left. "And for some of us that goes double." Like the rest of the crew, I silently disagreed with the skipper's remark, but I found the vodka agreeable.

Having the skipper onboard produced a positive change in attitude. The mood shift showed in everybody's eyes. Despite our submission to Hutch and begrudging willingness to do his bidding, as a man Hutch was neither respected nor appreciated. We recognized him to be generally fair, knowledgeable, and a hard worker, but undercutting all of that was a visible and pervasive insecurity. He clearly was no leader. But with the skipper now in charge we could afford to extend full confidence and respect to Harold Crutchfield, navigation officer.

"Now, let me introduce you all to our new crew member." The skipper reached over to the young man and pulled him firmly to his side. "This is my son Billy, or William as his mother admonishes me to call him." The skipper tried unsuccessfully to suppress his pride. Billy was two inches taller than his dapper father, but they shared the same wiry frame. He had the pale complexion and soft muscle tone of a bookworm. He shifted his weight sheepishly as his father made the round of names, but he looked up and shared a diffident smile once his father was finished.

"His mother only reluctantly let him come," said the skipper. He turned to his son. "We can untie her when we get back." The crew erupted into a hearty laugh.

"What's this about twenty-two students?" asked Hutch. There was admiration in his eyes but doubt in his voice. "Where are we going to put them?" He gestured to illustrate that the mess was essentially full with just the eight of us packed in.

"Just one question at a time," answered the skipper cheerily. "There is time to answer all of your questions and to solve all of the problems. We have time." He smiled reassuringly to Hutch and the rest of us. He then pulled some papers from a folder while Wally poured us all another cup of vodka. The top drawing was a freehand sketch of how the ship's hold would be sectioned into berthing compartments. He passed it around as he explained that ballast would have to be taken onboard to put the *Marite* into sailing trim. This could be done, he told us, with built-in cribs along the sides of the hold that could be filled with Faroese stone.

The more we drank, the fewer the questions. The proceedings quickly degenerated into a welcome-home party as a second bottle appeared and idle talk turned into backslapping banter. The skipper's son sat on the bench beside Chris and Taylor, and the three immediately struck up a conversation. The skipper looked so travel-weary that the knife-edge creases in his starched khakis seemed the only thing holding him upright.

Monty and I slipped out of the mess. Monty was one step ahead and waiting on the weather deck. "Here's one to keep in your back pocket . . ." he said, but paused until we had walked past the porthole. "When I went down below to get Wally, you know, when we were all waiting in the mess?" I nodded. "Well, Wally was in the middle of getting all of his stuff from the captain's cabin and I caught him hiding porno books in the engine room!" He let his jaw drop for emphasis. "I mean, can you believe it?"

"Does he know? Did he see you?"

Monty shook his head. "No way. His back was to me. I waited until he returned toward the officers' quarters to tell him to come up."

"It really doesn't surprise me. As far as I'm concerned he's just half a rung above Charles Manson," I said.

Monty agreed. "I think I'm gonna hang his ass with'm," said Monty. "The next time he comes after me with one of his stupid sermons I'm gonna zap his ass." The thought made for amusing possibilities.

The skipper came out on deck. He glanced around pleasantly. "If we could bottle and sell this air in New York," he remarked, "we'd have our own sailing ship, eh?" He removed his cap, massaged the bridge of his nose, then replaced the cap loosely on the back of his head. He tried unsuccessfully to stop a yawn. Jet lag took no prisoners, I thought, not even on such an eventful day.

The party moved back into the mess where the skipper had supplied another pint before turning in. Everybody was pleasantly drunk. It was a special day. The skipper had returned. The crew of the *Marite* was whole now. Monty inched over. "Billy's got some pot," he whispered. He elbowed me, a big smile spread mischievously across his face. "Can you believe it? The skipper's son!"

Like a father granting permission to well-behaved sons, Hutch magnanimously gave us the remainder of the day off. Monty, Chris, Taylor, Billy, and I headed for the mountains. An alternative route that the girls had shared got us to the top faster and easier. We stopped at a rock ledge a safe distance from town and smoked a joint. Afterwards, we meandered along the ridge to a spot overlooking the *Marite*. Everybody was laughing and joking. The weather was excellent for the Faroes—chilly with a breeze.

As we walked, Monty placed a hand on my shoulder to hold me back from the rest of the group. I was expecting more about Wally's porno books or a gag. "I guess you noticed that your dream came true."

I nodded vaguely but hadn't really thought about it.

"The arrival of the unknown crew member was the clincher." He nodded toward the skipper's son. "I've been keeping track."

The observation stunned me. I looked to Monty. His swarthy face seemed suddenly ashen. My thoughts shot back to the *Balclutha* Dream. It seemed a lifetime ago. We walked a few steps, him expecting me to respond, I suppose. Finally he spoke. "Goddam, Dee, what does it mean?" There was an uncharacteristic gravity in his voice.

"I don't know, Monty."

Monty recounted the content of the dream out loud. "We were cruising in a car along a channel . . ." He pointed to the fjord below and to our right. "And we were passing a joint. You and I were in the front seat talking."

"Were we passing a joint?" I asked in earnest. "I don't recall that."

"Come on Dee, it doesn't have to be exact. You sound like one of those Bible-belt preachers who . . ." When he saw me nod he didn't complete the thought but went back to the dream. "Anyway, so the crew of the *Balclutha* swim to the shore and we stand along the edge and pull clones of ourselves out." He was emphasizing every word. "Don't forget Billy. He's the sailor with the blank face. And remember, Zak wasn't in the car."

"So what do you think it means?" I asked, not really wanting to discuss it stoned and half-drunk. "Is the *Balclutha* gonna sink?" I added, "Or does it represent the *Marite*?"

"I can't believe I'm hearing this from you, Dee," said Monty, irritated. He picked up a rock and threw it down the side of the mountain. We continued along the rock edge. "I mean, you're the one with the philosophical inclinations. Usually it's you who sees the metaphysical side of everything. And for once I'm seeing it too and you're acting like you don't understand." He kicked a rock over the edge.

"You're right," I apologized. "I'm sorry. But this dream thing has got me confused."

"Yeah, well you mentioned the *Balclutha* sinking," said Monty in a hurried voice, "Try this one. When Chris, Taylor, and I left, only Zak remained to work onboard, and he decided to move in with Lisa. Now, that's not exactly the picture of a sinking ship, but it is a ship without a crew."

We had stopped. There wasn't any point in disputing it. He was right. The interpretation fit. I surveyed the landscape that rose to the left. It was spangled with tiny colorful flowers set in a deep lush blanket of green that rose steeply amid scattered outcroppings of rock. It was ideal for the thousands of sheep that thrived on the islands. We must have stood there for some time, for when I looked up the rest of the group had put a hundred yards between us and them. Chris was trotting back our way. "What are you guys doing?" he shouted. Monty threw his arms up and shrugged. Chris stopped within shouting distance. "Dee, let's show them our monster slide."

"What's he talking about?" asked Monty.

"Yeah," I called back to Chris. We hurried to catch up with the others. I was happy to have a diversion from the dream discussion. It was a short-lived diversion.

Chris led the way through the crevice in the rock ledge. I stood at the top, feet planted firmly, and gave a hand to lower Taylor and then Monty. A shock wave jolted my body: before me was an exact image of the rescue scene from the dream, but in reverse motion. The realization pulsed in my head at the speed of light while the images—the rocky ledge, the blue water, hands extended to a crewman among huge rocks—remained motionless on my retina. My grip went slack as I helped lower Billy. He looked up with a puzzled expression. I wanted to explain but a paralysis gripped my vocal chords. One thought swirled in my head: the dream had come true. Then a wrenching wave of emotions crashed over me like breakers over rocks. I staggered away from the ledge. More waves rumbled over me. I breathed slowly to regain control. I could hear Chris explaining the slide technique to the others below, but it seemed far away, otherworldly really, like the interred eavesdropping on the living through a wall of earth.

Monty had joined them. I was alone. My hands trembled. I needed to regain my inner balance. This isn't happening, I told myself. It's the vodka and the pot. An hallucination. But the dream had not been a hallucination. And neither was this.

A strong urge to rejoin the group seized me. I needed to get off this rock ledge, I was being bombarded with more than I could comprehend. Something akin to a voice was telling me to run. I felt top-heavy, off balance, as if suddenly burdened by the physical weight of a world of unknowable dimensions. I wanted to ignore it but knew that I could not turn back the hands of time. It would take more than facts and evidence to explain another dream-come-true.

The human mind, I have learned in hindsight, is a resilient entity that is so well conditioned in the art of self-preservation that it allows us to live and act with deliberation in a world that is essentially inexplicable. In this environment of limited understanding, we build cities, send colleagues to the moon, transplant organs, split atoms, and gainfully tap the earth's wealth for our comfort and utility, all without ever knowing who or even what we are. Few things divert us from these activities, stop us in our tracks, and compel us to look imploringly at the insecurity and uncertainty that is life. Having a dream come true is one such phenomenon. Like an earthquake, it upends the most basic assumptions about the world in which we live, dismisses the assumption that we live on terra firma. Having a dream come true months after the fact amounts to knowing about something before it happens. It violates what philosophers and physicists describe as the arrow of time, the realization that events in time unfold in one direction only. When faced with such a dilemma, one must either deny it happened or acknowledge that your explanation of the world is flawed.

I inched forward to the ledge and looked down at the group clutching the ragged side of the rock face, the wind blowing their hair, none of them really comfortable with Chris' idea. My eyes locked on the face of the steeple clock below. It was still fixed at 6:15. Adventures in Time, Incorporated. The dream. The sum of facts was overwhelming. And yet no meaning appeared beyond the fact that it had happened under those circumstances. Sure, there was symbolic meaning, but life cannot be lived symbolically. Or can it? Was all of this a product of having read too many novels? Of willingly suspended disbelief one time too many?

Chris' words were louder, as if repeating himself for my benefit. "It's easy, just ask Dee," he said. The moment had an unadorned existential quality to it. The cold, windswept landscape, the desperate band of anxious beings clinging to a cliff with stiff hands on a stony path, eyes darting. And there was the confident leader, Prometheus 1974, steadfastly showing the way, smiling, the steeple clock over his right shoulder like the clock in Frost's *Acquainted with the Night.*

"Come on, Monty," urged Chris, "follow me." Monty eased past the others until poised beside Chris. At that moment Chris nudged himself forward. "Geronimo," he cried. After a few yards of skidding on his boot soles, he switched to a squat and then just slid down the gravel on his butt at breakneck speed. Monty followed, then Billy. Taylor and I followed.

Moments later we all stood on the moss-coated gravel at the base of the ledge. The outlying houses of Tvoroyri were just below. The slide down the slope had worn a large hole in the backside of my jeans. I only had two pairs of jeans, and now my underwear showed beneath one of them.

I didn't know then that other dreams would follow and that they would be connected by similarly inexplicable events. And, looking back, as crazy as it seems, that hole in the back of my jeans would figure prominently in the resolution of the fifth dream and play an instrumental role in one of the most uncanny and important events in my life.

The skipper called a meeting of all hands after breakfast. He reiterated what he had covered the previous day, gave out work-party assignments, and invited an airing of any grievances. Taylor immediately broached the topic of reimbursement for our air fare. According to the last telegram the skipper had sent before returning, we were all to be paid in full when he arrived. He did not yet have the money, he told us. Beyond laying the blame on Heflin, he offered no explanation for the lack of funds and unfulfilled promises.

Sensing that the grumbling around the table would soon get out of hand, Hutch asserted control with a raised hand. "Okay,

okay. The skipper's still got the floor here," he declared slowly and firmly. With that he stepped back and nodded for the skipper to resume. But the skipper had nothing else to say. A few murmurs arose.

"What about testing the pumps?" interjected Hutch clumsily.

The skipper's face brightened. "Yes, thank you, Hutch," said the skipper. He looked back at us with his pale blue eyes. "As you know, the North Atlantic is *the* stormiest body of water on earth. It is essential to have all survival gear in topnotch condition before we depart for Copenhagen." He turned briskly to Wally. "I trust that you and your crew can clean, test, and have all of our gear running properly within a week." It was a question.

Wally nodded. "Hope you don't mind getting your nails dirty," he told Taylor, grinning from one side of his mouth. Taylor had been assigned to work with Wally.

"If that's it," said the skipper, "then I'll leave the work parties in your good care, Mr. Crutchfield, and go iron out a few details with Mr. Hansen and the hotel."

"One more thing," inserted Taylor. The skipper pulled up short, an attentive expression on his face. "We need to talk about hair. Some of us are getting flack and I don't . . ." The skipper held up both hands briefly then resumed collecting his notes and said with patience, "We'll just have to get to that at some future date." The meeting was adjourned.

Hutch, I learned, had petitioned the skipper to better equip the galley. The needs were self-evident. The galley was small, approximately ten by ten feet, and equipped with a battered assortment of outdated pots and pans that were designed to prepare ten-gallon vats of gruel. The skipper returned an hour later with an extended line of credit and had Hutch and me make up a shopping list for cookware.

Our timing was perfect. A young nurse appeared from the side of the road as the two of us hurried to the supply house with the list. She was twenty-five yards ahead on the same road, going the same direction. Even from that distance I could tell she was a winner: tall, slender, with glossy black hair that turned up at her shoulders. She wore a pale blue, knee-length hospital smock that whipped in the wind. The skipper joined us with good news as we walked past the library. He had settled the dispute with the innkeeper and arranged for us to eat lunch and dinner there and to shower as well. The news effervesced into an exultant cry of "Ya-hoo!" from Hutch as we strode along.

Hutch's cry caused the young nurse to stop and turn. We gained distance on her as she studied us, fussed with her hair, and then darted into SuperMarked, Tvoroyri's grocery store.

"I need to stop in here for some tobacco," I said as we approached.

"Hey, you're not fooling anybody with that routine," proclaimed Hutch, his face big and round and full of fun. "Right, skipper?"

"I've learned over the years to never come between a man and his habits," he answered deftly. He placed a gracious hand on both our shoulders and steered us to the entrance.

The SuperMarked was small, about the size of an American convenience store, and had extra-wide aisles and shoulder-high shelves. She was reading a label in the far corner. The distance between her and the tobacco at the check-out counter meant I needed to stall.

"Hallo," I said to the lady behind the cashier's counter. It was the local greeting. "Hvordan har de det?" I asked nervously. I had spent many hours studying Danish with the girls but had never attempted to speak it in public. The skipper nodded in a demure expression of pride.

"What do you want?" the woman behind the counter asked in Danish. She was all business.

"*Drum tobac, behage.*" I said clumsily. I looked over my shoulder nonchalantly. The nurse had moved closer and even glanced my way.

"*Tolv kroner,*" the counter lady replied curtly. Nervously I produced the twelve crowns, and it was over, the stalling. Carrying on that much of a conversation in Danish without help and under duress had emptied me of strategy. I stood there dumbfounded.

After a brief moment of silence the skipper stepped back over. "Let me see that package," he said. He looked it over. "Are you sure this is fresh?" he asked me. Immediately he turned and addressed the cashier in Danish. And just as suddenly the woman was gushing with warmth and courtesy. She smiled with red painted lips and rose onto her tiptoes to look beyond us at the nurse, who seemed to be browsing. She and the skipper chatted again, Hutch nudged me in the ribs and broke out in sporadic laughs.

As I reached over to get the package of tobacco that the skipper handed me, an all-but-buried memory burst into my consciousness. This had all happened before: the reflected light playing off the shiny blue plastic wrapper, was indelibly imprinted in my mind, and the image of the shiny container floated away from our hands and slowly tumbled in my imagination through walls, space, and time over a blue ocean to a dream that I had onboard the *Smyril* while en route to Tvoroyri.

The actual dream had been little more than the single image of the two of us in the store, but in the dream the blue object the skipper handed me had been a flat, shiny-blue gun. After that, the whole image wavered as if reflected off the surface of an undulating sheet of glass.

The dream imagery invoked an unmistakable connotation: we had robbed the store with a plastic gun.

I stood there immobile, my mouth open and dry. Then I turned and *she* was standing beside me with a coquettish smile tensing on her lips, warm vapors shimmering on the rounded surface of her big, brown eyes. She blinked once, slowly.

"Hallo," I said with a hasty smile and a slight nod of the head. She wore a white nurse's uniform under the blue hospital smock. I geared up for a command performance in Danish.

"Hallo?" she said quizzically. "I thought you were American?" She spoke English! Perfect English. I nearly exploded with relief.

"I am," I said, exhaling heavily though still tensed.

"If I may," said the skipper. He had turned to face us. "I am Captain Clive Hofman of the *Marite* and," indicating Hutch, "this is Mr. Crutchfield, the ship's navigational officer" His words were sincere, almost solemn. Then he said, tipping his head toward me, "This is Mr. Dyer, an able seaman . . . and I would be careful around this guy if I were you."

Hutch exploded into laughter. He spun on his heels and slapped his knees. I was caught off guard too, but held my laughter to a broad smile.

"I've heard," said the nurse with an unflappable, almost world-weary smile.

I extended a hand, wanting to touch the nurse's hand.

"And I'm Hutch," clarified Mr. Crutchfield.

"Glad to make the acquaintance," she said dryly. "My name is Gretchen." With that she stepped through us to the counter and set down a small bottle. "I must be going." She opened the front of her smock to reveal the nurse's uniform. "I'm on duty and we have a problem brewing." Again, the mischievous smile, and she turned away.

"We can take a hint," said Hutch. I wanted to boot him for the remark.

She paid up, spun quickly on her heel, and said, "I hope to see you again." There was no smile, no hint of innuendo, nothing. She left and a draft of cold air took her place as she hastened out the door.

"She's Danish," said the skipper, "let that serve as a warning." He turned and spoke politely with the woman behind the counter.

"Wow! Dee, I'd say that's one helluva woman!" said Hutch. "You might want to try to latch onto that one."

The remainder of the walk to and from the chandler's warehouse was a confusing commingling of sexual imaginings and that haunting image from the Robbery Dream. I reviewed the dream in my mind. The meaning seemed unmistakable: we had robbed the store with a blue plastic gun. That is, we had purchased thousands of dollars worth of food and fuel and gear on credit and had yet to pay for them. And if the dream was an indicator, we would not be paying those bills. I hadn't yet come to grips with the implications of the Burger Joint Dream and the *Balclutha* Dream, and now there was a third one. The weight of the situation was starting to press in on me from all sides.

I had remembered three dreams in my adult life and all three had now come true. And if the prescient nature of the earlier dreams was an indicator, this latest one offered a glimpse into the future. If so, it meant that the *Marite* enterprise would soon default on its debts or run off without paying them. Either way, the Robbery Dream seemed to preview some future humiliation.

The possibility that the debts might not be paid was bothersome. The fact that I had dreamed it and somehow had suppressed it for weeks until the re-enactment in the store cast a shadow over my every thought and perception. Again, I felt singled out. The world seemed to be sending me messages. Was I some sort of medium? Or was this the onset of some life-altering psychosis? And what about that soul-jarring moment on the rock ledge with a hand extended to my crewmates? The growing list of questions seemed trapped in my head.

Monty was below decks working in the chain locker, the compartment that holds the ship's anchor chain when it's not in use. The chain would not budge. I volunteered to help Monty find out why. In truth, I desperately needed to talk. At first we talked about Gretchen. He was excited and asked the same questions about her that I was asking myself. "What about other nurses?" he probed. When that topic waned, I steered the discussion toward the dreams.

"Monty," I said as we removed a bulkhead plank so we could see inside the chain locker. "I had another weird dream." He looked my way with a slow turn of his head. "I'll tell you about it if you'll keep it under your hat."

The chain locker was a sturdy six-by-six enclosure located just forward of the ship's hold. After removing a second bulkhead plank, we climbed inside and confirmed Wally's guess that the chain was rusted to itself.

"You're turning into some kind of weirdo, Dee. I don't think I want to hear about it. Besides, when I wanted to talk about it the other day, you basically told me to go to hell."

I told him about the dream.

It was too dark to work in the compartment, so we sat on the pile of chain while Wally cranked up the generator and ran an extension cord for our work light. Two slender shafts of sunlight squeezed through the hawsepipe, the opening in the deck overhead through which the anchor chain fed into the compartment. The light passed into the dark folds of chain between us without illuminating the space. Monty extended his hands into the light to roll a cigarette. "So does it mean we're gonna run up bills and leave without paying, or what?" he asked. His voice had an eerie, distant quality in the darkness as his hands, seemingly disembodied in the shafts of light, expertly worked the tobacco and paper into a perfect cigarette. His hands withdrew from the light as he licked the gum. "Dee, what are we going to do if this whole thing falls through?"

"Go to Denmark. Dalton will have work," I replied. He handed me the cigarette through the light and started one for himself.

"Yeah, and how long do you think that would last? I mean, how long could you put up with Dalton's Dr. Jekyll–Mr. Hyde bullshit?"

He was right. Working for Dalton would be an awful experience.

We lit up. The light from the match illuminated Monty's face in the crowded space, and then it was dark again. The slender shafts of light reappeared like slices in a swirling body of smoke. Monty's cigarette arced up to his mouth, his Native American features sharpened in the sudden glow of the cigarette tip as he inhaled. He nodded grimly. We smoked in silence, keying our ears to the clumpity-clump of footfalls overhead. The sound indicated that Hutch was running the extension cord to us since he was the only crew member who had purchased clogs.

"You guys still down there?" called Hutch through the hawsepipe. He turned his head to someone nearby and said, "This is like one of those mineshaft rescue movies." Wally laughed in the distance.

The cold rain returned during Sunday supper at the hotel. It had never been that far away. The *Rosstindur*, her weather deck laden with tons of wet lumber, arrived as I studied the rain through the dining hall window. So I wasn't surprised when Eric, Mr. Hansen's oldest son, intercepted us on the way back to the *Marite* to ask if four of us could unload the lumber. With the skipper's blessing we agreed, weather and all, and headed for our raingear. Taylor had already departed somewhere and Billy was going to the discotheque with Larla, Frieda, and Birthe, so that left Monty, Chris, and me to unload the ship.

Afterward, we poked our wet and weary heads in the doorway of the discotheque to see what we had missed. The "discotheque" was really a small community center two doors up the hill from the hotel. Billy was the center of attraction, unpretentiously surrounded by teenagers, somebody's sailor's cap plopped on his head, and dancing feverishly with an unruly crowd of high-schoolers. When he saw us he bounced over to the DJ's microphone and said, "Come on in and celebrate, you orthos It's National Potato Week!" The three girls were doing their best to imitate the old flapper routine, hands on knees, switching them back and forth in time with the music. They never even saw us. We trudged back to the ship to remove splinters.

One morning during breakfast, the *Marite* and the small freighter alongside to port began drifting from the *Skarveinur,* the freighter alongside the *Marite* that moored the three ships directly to the quay. The harbormaster, we learned later, needed to pull the *Skarveinur* out for repairs and had done so without informing the skipper. In the end the *Marite* was returned to the middle position among a threesome of ships moored again in parallel, but with the *Azelda T,* a freighter no bigger than the *Marite*, now moored directly against the quay. The *Skarveinur* was relocated to the bitter end of the quay where, days later, a crane removed her pilothouse in order to replace the engine below it.

With only a week to get the *Marite* in trim for the voyage to Copenhagen, the crew worked nonstop. That also meant there was only a week to get to know Gretchen. A full day had passed since I had met her, so, after the evening meal and a shower, I put on my good jeans and headed for the hospital, located uphill behind the bakery. Rain looked eminent as I entered the long, dormitory-like building. A chubby nurse with a pale mole beside her nose gave me simple directions and the door number. She spoke English quite well and said that if Gretchen wasn't there I should try Hans' apartment. In the end neither was at home. I left a note in Danish on Gretchen's door.

Halfway back to the ship, I was surprised to see that a luxury liner had tied up at the quay. The *Kronprins,* a small ocean liner, was making the first of its weekly spring and summer runs between the Danish coast, Thorshavn, and Tvoroyri. Approximately 300 feet in length, with a white hull, red piping, and two red stacks, the ship towered over the entire port. From dockside, the ship's hull loomed three stories above the quay that was crowded with a hundred or more Faroese. The ship's retractable gangway, which served as a stairway between the ship and the quay, rolled back and forth among the crowd as the ship gently moved with the sea.

The hubbub created by the *Kronprins* didn't interest me. I stretched out on my bunk and tried to still the question marks that ricocheted inside my head. Did I have a chance with Gretchen? Who was Hans? How could I know in advance about the things revealed in the dreams? Who am I? Uncertainty had taken root in my mind, and I didn't know how to stop it, to stop the mushrooming sense of dread that the dreams would come true.

In practical terms, the deepening mystery of the dreams was like having an appointment with an identity crisis. I noticed it first in my journal entries. Over the last several weeks my writing style had evolved from a personalized shorthand that I had developed over the years to a stream of consciousness outpouring, to passages that resembled word salads. The entries had felt perfectly sane when I wrote them, but weeks later seemed the work of a stranger. Without thinking, I had ripped out the offensive pages. But as I discarded them I realized that the documentation was gone but the problem had not changed: I no longer knew who I was. I had seen unknowable future events weeks in advance. That was not possible in the world in which I lived.

Chapter 7 - The Hospital Connection

The skipper broke the bad news over lunch. Mr. Heflin had not sent the money as promised. The departure for Copenhagen was postponed. Hutch dropped his fork onto his plate with a clink. His face, normally round and pink, slumped into a funk. Surprisingly, that was the only immediate response from those at the table. Everybody internalized the shock. The unthinkable had occurred. In our rush to ready the *Marite* for her voyage, there had been no time to imagine any other scenario.

"I'll bet Heflin spent the money chasing tail at the Playboy Club," said Wally.

Taylor sighed heavily from the end of the table. "Did he say when the money would get here?" he asked.

"There was no mention of it in the cable," said the skipper.

"So what are we going to do?" asked Chris. His jaw muscles pulsed as he waited for a reply.

The skipper looked down the table at us. "It can be nothing more than a temporary delay," he confided. "Mr. Heflin has all the funding in line. I saw it in black and white before I left San Francisco."

"I've been keeping up with all of this Watergate stuff on the BBC," said Taylor. "You don't suppose *it* could have an effect on the funding or anything, do you? You know, a lack of investor confidence or whatever?"

"That's all on the east coast," said Hutch. "The skipper is talking about west coast money. It's all separate."

Taylor regarded Hutch with a single shake of his head and a sniff. "A thing like Watergate affects the whole nation, Hutch."

"It ain't nothing Nixon can't handle," said Wally.

"We've gotten off track," said Hutch. "Can we get back to the question of what to do?" He spoke authoritatively, yet stared blankly out the window. He turned to the skipper.

"We've still got a lot to do," said the skipper. "For one thing, we need to check the lifeboat and davits to make sure they are working properly."

His response did more to sow doubt than to answer the question, since everybody knew that the lifeboat and davits had been checked, were shipshape, and the skipper had been informed.

"Is it safe to say that this postponement is only for a few days or a week?" continued Hutch. "I mean, can we proceed with loading ballast?"

Everybody leaned forward for the answer. It was slow in coming. "That is something I will need to take up with Mr. Hansen. Until we have actually purchased the ship it is not considered good form to move her, insurance and all." Seeing doubt in more than one face, he continued. "There is nothing to worry about. It means a few more days in Tvoroyri . . . Hutch's favorite place, eh?" That brought a few mirthless smiles. The humor restored Hutch's facial color to normal. The waitress arrived moments later with cookies and coffee. But things weren't really the same.

"So what have you been hearing about Watergate?" I asked Taylor as we walked back to the ship in the rain.

He was holding the hood of his rain slicker away from his hair as if contact might flatten his curls or something. "Nixon's refused to turn over the tape recordings that Congress subpoenaed. He's claiming executive privilege. There's finally some serious talk about impeachment."

"The way you talked there was another stock-market crash in the wings."

"Hutch is full of shit," he sneered. "I don't have to tell you that. A scandal of this size affects everything. When there's no confidence in government lots of stuff grinds to a halt, the economy sours. Everybody is afraid to commit their money." We climbed over the dockside gunwale of the *Azelda T.* "On the BBC last night they talked about the economic impact it has already had on Europe. It's pretty intense. They can calculate stuff like that in terms of diminished economic activity," he explained.

"How about Patty Hearst?" I asked. "Whatever happened to her?"

We climbed over the gunwales of the two ships and stood in the rain on the main deck of the *Marite*. "God, Dee, you really have been under a rock, haven't you?" He paused, recollecting. "I guess you heard that she robbed a bank a few weeks ago, eh?"

"Robbed a bank," I repeated incredulously. The shock must have shown on my face as well.

Like a couple of loons, we stood there talking in the rain until Wally came along, removed the toothpick from his mouth, and said, "What you idjits doing out here in the rain?" He strode right past us, shaking his head in disbelief.

By Sunday afternoon the rain had ceased. I had washed my clothes, bathed, updated my journal, and was set to join Monty in a climb when a young man with a droopy moustache and a knit cap put his face up to the porthole and said, "I look for Don."

"That's me," I said. The man moved toward the hatchway.

"William Beresford Tipton the Third," whispered Monty. He was referring to the TV show in which a philanthropist gave a million dollars to random people just to see how it would change their lives. The visitor proved to be the mysterious Hans. Hans Valsberg, the cook at the hospital. He had come with an invitation from Gretchen. My heart did a cartwheel.

Hans explained the situation as we walked. "Gretchen worked last night for Margit, so Margit works dis afternoon for Gretchen so we can have drive in my car too-day."

"Sounds great."

"It is a wery small car, petrol is so dear, but it is good for four people." Like Gretchen and others on the staff at the hospital, Hans was in the Faroes on an exchange program with Danish hospitals. They worked here for three months in the summer while Faroese counterparts worked their job slots on the mainland. Hans had shipped his car over onboard the *Kronprins*. "Gretchen just now is awake," he continued. "She tole me to find you so we have more time for picnic."

We hopped in Hans' red Saab and sped the five blocks up the slope to the hospital. Gretchen and another young woman were sitting on the steps of the hospital dormitory when we pulled up. At their feet was a huge stainless steel bowl covered with a red and white checkered tablecloth. "That is Olivia, my wife," said Hans. He knew it would be welcome news and grinned to show it.

Poised casually on the steps in blue jeans, turtleneck sweaters, and hiking boots, they looked like a pair of models from an Eddie Bauer catalog. Gretchen was taller than Olivia. The casual clothes permitted a better viewing of her slender, inviting body than the nurse uniform had permitted. She had not got enough sleep; it showed in her face.

I was offered the front passenger seat because of my long legs. Gretchen, who also had long legs, squeezed into the backseat with Olivia. The bowl of picnic goodies fit into the trunk.

The road paralleled the shoreline to the landward end of the fjord and a fork in the road. We headed north to Sandvik, a fishing village with a clear-weather view of other islands. The weather seemed cooperative. The road continued inland for several miles then took a sharp turn uphill.

"Vee come to tunnel soon," said Hans. He downshifted to second gear as the grade and the load strained the small engine. The road hugged the rocky face of the mountain around a miles-long curve. "Der's de tunnel," said Olivia. She pulled herself forward to study it. Gretchen did the same. The blacktop widened at the approach but narrowed to one lane at the entrance.

"It's long," said Hans. He stopped briefly to switch on the headlights, then proceeded slowly, the four of us craning our heads to study the interior of the tunnel.

The tunnel was dark and wet and seemingly hacked out of the mountain with stone axes. Unlike tunnels in the U.S., there were no lights, no smooth surfaces, no finishing touches; just a rough-hewn passage carved and blasted through the mountain. Halfway through, the one-lane blacktop roadway widened into two lanes for forty yards or so to enable vehicles from both directions to pass. Water fell on the other side of the turnout, splattering loudly on the pavement as we drove by. Hans engaged the windshield wipers for half a minute. "I like it here," he said. "It's like tunnel of love." I detected his hand probing between the seats and suddenly Olivia jolted, giggled noisily, and slapped his hand. She said something in Danish which brought a hearty laugh. Joining in the fun, Gretchen reached up and over Hans' shoulder and blew the horn. The sound exploded inside the craggy chamber and splintered into a hundred thousand reports. In rapid succession, she blew the horn again and again. The noise jarred loose a few pebbles that fell on the hood. Hans intercepted Gretchen's hand on the next thrust. "You are going to break de paint," he said in English.

"He means damage the paint," corrected Gretchen in the darkness. "Hans learned to speak English by watching football on TV."

"It is called soccer in America," Hans corrected.

"Dat's true," agreed Olivia. The dash lights provided enough light to see her nodding.

"Look!" cried Hans, pointing. "End of tunnel. Light." He sped up as we approached the exit but stamped on the brakes when we emerged. The abrupt change in light was blinding. We all laughed. Hans resumed driving after his eyes adjusted.

Sandvik was unimpressive at first glance. A kiosk not much bigger than a telephone booth stood at the fork in the road where its main street began. The town consisted of a few dozen homes and commercial buildings along the waterfront and a mix of fishing boats and smaller craft crowded around a dock. The spectacular view changed our opinion. From the slope on the north side of the fjord where the little town perched you could see to the blue edge of the earth. And there, close though miles away, two green islands were majestically framed between the steep sidewalls of the wide fjord in the foreground. Hans stopped the car in the middle of the road and all four faces formed a line facing forward as the engine murmured and we soaked up the powerful image before us.

"Let's find a place for the picnic," suggested Gretchen.

"Just a minute," said Hans. He leaned forward intently, concentrating on something. "Can you see it?" he asked.

"What?"

"Get closer . . . see?"

The four of us leaned as close to the windshield as the car would permit. That's when Hans blew the horn. "Hans!" cried Olivia. There was an explosion of laughter. To get even, Gretchen snatched Hans' knit cap and passed it around in a game of keep-away. The little car rocked back and forth. A lively beginning for a fun picnic.

I soon learned that the featured attraction of the outing was Hans' homemade rum. There were open-faced sandwiches, a fruit-and-Jello-topped cake, cheeses, breads, and half a bottle of Aalborg schnapps. But the topic of discussion and much anticipation was a half-liter of homemade rum that Hans had "brewed" in the hospital kitchen. It was clear that his reputation as a cook and a resource on the frontier was at stake.

Liquor, they explained, was a difficult commodity to obtain in the islands. To legally purchase spirits you must first show proof that your taxes were paid in full. This, then, set in motion a bureaucratic process that, once completed, allowed you to purchase liquor from local outlets. The price, however, put it beyond most people's means. Most islanders made their own spirits, beer and wine mostly, but Hans had boasted himself into a corner on the homemade rum. For appearances' sake, Gretchen had gone to the SuperMarked to purchase the rum extract. It was on that errand that we had met.

"That was why I had to leave so quickly. Remember, I said we had something brewing?" She laughed outrageously.

We found a level patch of green near the water, laid out the picnic, then sipped schnapps from plastic hospital cups as we skipped stones on the fjord and chatted. There was an unstated realization among the three of them that the rum was going to be a little rough around the edges. But, like committed per-formers before the big show, we psyched ourselves up for the big event.

Hans took the first drink of rum. He raised a toast and, technically, I suppose, we all should have joined in, but we held off and watched in secret as Hans drank. "Ah-h-h," he gloated with a real show of strength. "Damn fine stuff." His nostrils flared and briefly turned a cyanotic blue, then he coughed and stuffed a sandwich in his mouth.

When we saw his color return, the three of us drank and chased it with a sandwich. The artificial rum flavor was crowded out by a slight metallic tinge and uninvited vapors in the nose.

"Good stuff," said Olivia with a cough.

"Good sandwiches, too," said Gretchen with a smirk.

Olivia was the first to show signs of the alcohol when she plunked small stones into everybody's cup. "On de rocks," she said, laughing wildly. She rolled off the tablecloth onto the carpet of spongy green heather. In no time I had worked in an *a cappella* rendition of "Scotch and Soda" and Hans moved from sandwiches to cake, which he served with his pocket comb since we had no utensils.

"Don't worry," said Gretchen with her weight on my shoulder. "It's never been used." Her remark was directed at his balding condition. We ate the cake with our hands to chase down the last couple shots of rum. Gretchen somehow found fun in plucking the grapes and cherries from the top of the cake. She then skipped in a circle around the tablecloth and redistributed them like a playful trainer feeding fish to trick seals. We were drunk.

A chill descended as the afternoon wore on. After talking for a while about how good the car heater would feel, we decided to try it. With arms intertwined, stumbling on everything visible, the big bowl sounding like a tin gong each time it fell, we made our way to the car.

Long legs be damned, I trundled into the back seat with Gretchen. The return trip was also characterized by a different kind of driving. Hans popped the clutch and the little car bounded down the road. The bowl, wedged in the space beside me, tipped back and forth as if on gimbals, and the tires squealed as Hans steered from one side of the road to the other, laughing and glancing over his shoulder to make sure everybody was having fun. As we reached the tunnel, Hans began to gun the engine then let it off, gun it, then let it off, over and over until the little car was lurching fore and aft while he switched the headlights on and off, all of us carrying on hysterically. With heads and shoulders waggling and the lights flashing on and off, our passage through the tunnel was a strangely surreal and erotic escapade.

"Heer comes de big one," announced Hans excitedly. And with it he ground the car to a sudden stop under the falling water at the turnout. The wildly joyous cry of four screaming adults compressed momentarily in the little car then passed through mere steel and glass and clamored down the tunnel. At the same moment Hans sprang from the car and leaped and spun and screamed with flailing arms under the falling water. *"Jeg elsker dig, Danmark!"* He stood under the water with his arms out and his back to the car as the sound of his voice ricocheted and echoed down the tunnel toward the open air.

Then, just as suddenly, his arms dropped to his side and the water falling on the hood drummed a metallic refrain as he returned to the driver's seat, soaked and quiet and emotionally drained. But his comical genius would not be suppressed. His clothes soaked, water dripping from his nose, he turned to us with a contented, quixotic smile and asked, "Cigarette?"

His escapade in the tunnel, however, seemed to have a sobering effect on him. He drove more carefully for the remainder of the trip back to Tvoroyri.

Gretchen's dormitory at the hospital was boxy and only sparingly furnished, but had a nest-like intimacy to it. From the front door, the kitchen, bedroom, and bathroom occupied the right side of the apartment while the rectangular front room filled an equivalent space to the left. A sofa and two chairs were pulled into a small circle around a coffee table near the center. There were no furnishings against the walls, but a large color poster of the *Christian Radiche,* the legendary Norwegian square-rigged sailing ship, hung on the wall between two double window units. On the wall straight ahead, there was a built-in desk and bookshelves and, directly to the right, the double-wide entrance to the kitchen.

Immediately upon arrival, Hans jumped into the shower. Olivia fetched dry clothes for him and, as if choreographed for perfect timing, we all arrived at the sofa at the same time, Gretchen in a cotton housedress, Hans hastily bathed and clothed, Olivia with tea and snacks, and me returning from the SuperMarked with milk for tea.

Conversation over tea was muted. My head throbbed unbearably. Finally, I asked Gretchen in a whisper for an aspirin. She brought out a bottle and all four of us tossed down a double dose. There was a long, quiet lull. I had seen sheep heads in the freezer at the store. I mentioned it. They were a popular local dish, Gretchen explained. There was a little talk between the three of them until they tested the word "aphrodisiac" on me. The sheep heads were said to be an aphrodisiac, explained Gretchen with that lovely mischievous smile.

By ten o'clock, Gretchen and I were lovers. In the afterglow, as we chatted and clung tightly under the bedclothes, her eyes gently closed, her supple body relaxed and ready for sleep, her words, like her behavior, resonated tenderness and affection, but the message changed. She had come to the Faroes to mend a broken heart, she confided. In the future our relationship would have to be Platonic, she explained. This had been an exception. She had lost control. She needed time and space.

The Gretchen that I had spent the day with was gone. This Gretchen seemed all business, yet giving. She promised to help hone my Danish language skills. She also said I could come and go in her apartment as I pleased, that I could spend the night any time. "I don't need a place to sleep," I told her with all the tact I could muster. I was confused and wondering if I had done something to damage our burgeoning relationship.

I had a fourth dream that night as we slept on the sofa. It was more unnerving than the previous ones.

In it I stood on the main deck of the *Marite* and looked to stern as two ships approached at a brisk pace, one to port and one to starboard. As the ships passed just yards away, the *Marite* was totally swamped in their wakes, and, as the *Marite* pitched and yawed like a cork in a curling wake, I watched with disbelief as the *Marite* stood abruptly on end, bow straight up in the air, then sank as swiftly as an iron pike. I then woke up in a hospital.

I must have awakened with a start because it jostled Gretchen. "I just had a strange dream," I told her. She grumbled, tugged at the blankets, and rolled over. There would be no more sleep for me. After repeatedly analyzing the content of this fourth dream, the Capsize Dream, with no meaningful resolution, I got up, dressed, and left, half-worried yet half-elated over having found an exceptional mate. We would work things out, I told myself.

Chapter 8 – Footloose in Limbo

The *Marite* was ready to depart for Copenhagen. The crew had been ready to leave for weeks. The departure hinged on one simple development: purchase of the ship. The skipper's distress over financial issues showed in his eyes and added qualifiers to his replies. It was the Great Unknown.

Days passed in limbo. Soon June passed. As the days went by and uncertainty reigned among the crew, doubts and criticisms arose and tolerance levels fell. Squabbles erupted over petty issues that degenerated into blaming, then name-calling. Every little thing generated a polarized response. Being penniless didn't help.

Initially the influx of freighters had furnished crew members with pocket money. But as spring receded the big push to resupply the island after winter waned. Fewer ships needed unloading and the majority of the work went to students who had returned home for the summer. The net effect was that grown men who were accustomed to self-sufficiency were now reduced to dependency. Allegiances began to shift. "What are you going to do if this falls through?" was the question that repeatedly cropped up. "I don't know" was the usual response.

I was lucky to have Gretchen. Although our relationship had stalled, I recognized that her company and the hope of something better had helped keep me from lapsing into some sort of over-the-counter schizophrenia. Monty, Chris, and Billy subsisted on exploring the island and the activities provided by the *tres amigas*, Monty's term for Larla, Birthe, Frieda.

None of us knew what Taylor was up to. He rarely spoke about his social life but was often whisked away in a little car after supper and somehow returned before breakfast. Clearly he had made friends among the Faroese but none of us were privy to the circumstances. We were not surprised, however, when he showed up at the discotheque one Saturday night with a red-headed jezebel in tow. Taylor could find a girlfriend on the dark side of the moon.

However, a number of unsubstantiated rumors suggested he had had a minor run-in with local authorities. One morning both he and the skipper failed to show up for breakfast. Tellingly, they arrived at the hotel together for lunch. During the meal the skipper briefly reminded us of our ambassadorial roles as Americans abroad.

Early one morning, as I drank coffee at dockside, I discovered Hutch watching from a distance. He stepped forward when he saw that I had seen him. He said "I couldn't sleep so I—" as I said "I couldn't sleep because—." We laughed awkwardly in the mist, then spoke at the same time again, then stopped again.

After a long moment he spoke. "You don't have to explain anything to me, Don." His voice had a distant, defeated quality to it. More so than anybody else onboard the ship, Hutch was alone. He looked at me. I recognized the writhing soul behind the blinking eyes, behind his mask of choice.

We walked together back to the galley. Hutch poured out his soul over three cups of coffee. He had sent for return airfare and was throwing in the towel. I couldn't tell if he wanted me to talk him out of it, take up for him after he left, or what, so I just listened.

He didn't like the way things were shaping up. Apparently the skipper had tried several times to get straightforward information out of Mr. Heflin, but the replies, when they came, were vague, evasive, lawyerly. "It's just no way to run a railroad," he complained. "You just wait, Don, you'll see. If you work on enough of these rust-buckets, you'll see. The goddamn millionaires who own them got rich by screwing every Tom, Dick, and Harry out of every nickel they could. So screwing some sailor out of a buck-two-fifty is just child's play." He swallowed to blunt the emotion that had entered his voice.

I felt like a therapist or priest as I nodded, affirmed, and took his confession. After breakfast he apologized for "dumping" on me and asked that I not mention to anybody about the telegrams between Captain Hofman and Mr. Heflin. I promised.

According to the BBC news on Gretchen's radio, Nixon's attorney and the Special Prosecutor had taken their struggle for the subpoenaed tapes to the Supreme Court that day and a ruling was expected soon. Nixon's presidency could very well teeter in the balance, or so said the commentator. I explained the three branches of government while she trimmed my hair and beard.

As more days passed in limbo, I began to feel a perverse sympathy for Nixon. I detested him and felt America deserved better, yet, like him, my world seemed poised to turn a corner. Everything was on hold, awaiting some pivotal turn of events over which I had no control. I made my way over to the double windows in Gretchen's place and looked outside at the steep slope. I couldn't get my mind off the intertwining events. The dreams. Gretchen's change of heart. The Watergate drama. The growing recognition that my life was out of my control.

Standing there, immobilized by my thoughts, it occurred to me that I had spent a lot of my life staring out of windows with little, if anything, to show for it. My thoughts slipped out of

focus and I retreated inside until I occupied a room in my head
with double windows. I stood quietly and looked out the
windows at myself looking out windows. What I saw was a man
masquerading as a sailor, a man who didn't know himself or the
world, a young man pretending he is loved, pretending his life
is on track, pretending he has no need for pretense.

Gretchen purposefully clunked a steaming cup of tea on the
window sill before me. I turned. She started to say something
but just swallowed as I looked into her eyes. I wanted to kiss
her, to be kissed by her. I wanted her to fill the void in my life.
"Some hot tea, sailor?" she said at last. She wore a faded blue
T-shirt with "Made in Denmark" printed right over a firm, pro-
truding nipple. More than ever I felt alone with my shattered
world of dreams and gnawing uncertainty. I slept for a few
hours, tossed and turned for a few, then trudged through an
early morning fog to the *Marite*.

At breakfast, the skipper said he had an important
announcement and asked that we all remain in the mess after
the meal.

"You got a telegram from Mr. Heflin?" ventured Chris.

"Your questions will just have to wait until the proper
time," answered the skipper.

The eggs and hash browns went down fast. In anticipation
of a substantive meeting with some bantering to follow, I made
a large pot of coffee. Everybody eagerly helped clear the dishes
from the table as the skipper, reading glasses in hand, patiently
chatted with Wally. Finally we returned to our seats.

"I've got a bit of good news," said the skipper to the excited
faces around the table. "I talked with Mr. Hansen last night and
he has agreed that we can proceed with a couple of projects I
have in mind for the *Marite*." There was silence. The smiles

dimmed as the skipper continued. The projects turned out to be a reworking of the space around the chain locker into a berthing area to hold as many bunks as possible and removal of the shelter deck that effectively walled in the stern section of the main deck. He put his reading glasses back in their case without ever using them. "Any questions?"

"No telegram from Heflin?" asked Chris. Like all of us, he felt let down. Having called a meeting for all hands over something that was only relevant to a work party seemed almost … dishonest. If nothing else it showed that the skipper wasn't sensitive to how we all felt. It made him look small. Had he arranged the whole thing out of a need to appear skipperly? If so, the unstated message was that he himself was losing confidence.

The skipper started the Sunday afternoon meal by an-nouncing he had received a telegram from Mr. Heflin. He fussed over his reading glasses in a contrived display of annoyance. "Damn things," he murmured as he put them on. His behavior indicated that it was good news. He unfolded the telegram and read. "Have booked a photojournalist. An administrative delay in final funding should give way to green light any day. Will advise." The skipper beamed with pride. He spoke as he put up his glasses. "Any day," he recited. "The photojournalist is to document the return trip." He struck a familiar posture with both hands flat on the table as he leaned toward us. "We have also discussed the possibility of making a film of the return voyage, but that remains undecided." He stood upright.

"That is the best news I've heard in a while," gushed Hutch. "I'm sick and tired of this start and stop routine." His voice was uneven, emotional.

Everybody returned to the meal. After a short while Chris asked, "So what's on the agenda for this week?"

"Good question," said the skipper. Smoothing his pale hair straight back with his hand, he looked at Hutch. After a moment Hutch said, "How about if we get rid of the shelter deck?"

The skipper looked back at Chris as if he had personally answered the question. The swinging door into the kitchen opened, filling the dining hall for a moment with the sounds of an electric guitar. It gave the skipper a start, "What is that?" he asked, looking around stiffly.

"The Beatles," said Billy. "From *Sergeant Pepper*."

Wally casually leaned forward to see around Chris to Billy. "Did I tell you about my buddy who served a hitch as first mate onboard the Beatles' yacht?"

"No kidding?" said Monty. "You're not talking about the *Yellow Submarine* are you?"

"No, the personal yacht of one of 'm. But I did meet the skipper of the *Yellow Submarine* once. I was down at Huntington Beach, just south of L.A., running a little charter fishing outfit when they were down there filming it." He looked around to see if the skipper was listening. Wally was not aware that the *Yellow Submarine* was an animated film named after the British government's master computer that contains tax files on all of Her Majesty's subjects. However, the fictional pubcrawl that he invented with the submarine captain was more entertaining than the film itself.

Over lunch one day late in July Captain Hofman announced that we would be taking the *Marite* on a shakedown cruise. The short excursion, he explained, would provide a test of the steering and instruments and help him calculate how much ballast would be needed for the voyage to Copenhagen. Things seemed to be taking shape for our departure in the not-too-distant future. He had a clipboard and looked at us over the top of his reading glasses. "In short, gentlemen, it looks like things are back on track." He was happy to have some good news.

"Does that mean we're going to be reimbursed for our air fare soon?" asked Taylor. "I'm tired of mooching off my Faroese friends." Silence ensued.

The skipper took off his glasses slowly, folded them, and slipped them in his pocket. "I've had no fresh news from Mr. Heflin. But I can assure you, Mr. Taylor, that you will be the first to be reimbursed once the funds arrive." The skipper was miffed. Taylor didn't press the point. "We'll have to stock up on diesel," said Wally, looking puffy from a night of reading. The skipper nodded in agreement. His ready consent indicated to me they had discussed it already.

That night, with my hands gummed in bread dough in Gretchen's kitchen, the BBC announced that the House Judiciary Committee had voted twenty-eight to ten to proffer articles of impeachment against President Nixon. Six members of the President's own party had voted against him, and many more were calling for his resignation. Stubbornly, Nixon reiterated that he would not resign under any circumstances. It was also the day I learned to make French bread. While waiting for the dough to rise, I brushed Gretchen's hair one hundred strokes, counting each brushstroke in Danish, "en (stroke) . . . to (stroke) . . . tre (stroke) . . ." She was a resourceful teacher.

The first week in August was a crazy, hectic, dizzying seesaw of nonstop activity and overstimulation. Maybe it was something in the stars, but the moods and morale of the crew seemed to shift from one extreme to another as we struggled amid a confounding array of petty hassles and adversity to ready the ship and ourselves for the shakedown cruise. Still, the skipper was pleased with our progress, and when we finished dismantling the shelter deck he used the occasion to give us a pep talk over supper. This would be our last weekend in Tvoroyri, he assured us.

After the pep talk, I ventured on deck to examine the new look to stern. The main deck aft of the galley was entirely open now. I went over to the intake vents by the galley and looked to stern. A benumbing thought struck me. With the shelter deck bulkhead stripped away, the stern section now permitted a 180-degree view aft. This meant that I could now see to port and starboard with the precise perspective that I had had in the last dream. In fact, I stood within a few feet of the exact spot where I had stood in the dream. My body stiffened as a sense of dread swelled in me. I had never made the connection before, but as long as the shelter deck was in place there was no complete view to stern, no way to experience the Capsize Dream in the flesh. Not totally convinced, I looked around. Another obstacle came to mind: other ships could not pass along both sides of the *Marite* so long as she remained moored. My thoughts raced ahead to Monday's scheduled shakedown cruise. It seemed the pivotal event I had been expecting—and dreading. Would a catastrophe strike during the shakedown cruise?

I went to Gretchen's that night with extra voltage coursing through my nervous system. I needed time to think about the dreams. About the nagging fears in my head that I was losing my mind. If I just had more time, it would all make sense. I longed to share my feelings with her, to say what I thought without sugarcoating it, to demonstrate that I was normal. I wanted nothing more than a relaxing weekend with Gretchen. Instead, I found the kitchen table had been moved to the center of the room and everything was set up for cards.

A wind-tossed rain was on the menu for Sunday, but it didn't dampen anticipation for what was expected to be our last weekend in Tvoroyri. To commemorate the event, Billy administered a satirical benediction over the dishes and napkins, knowing the food would not arrive until after the ship's officers did. "Omnia patria, holy bread and butter, bless my ortho buds and their mudders." The unmistakable sound of Wally's voice carried to our ears from the hotel vestibule and prompted silence around the table until they arrived.

"My ears are itching," said Wally as he sat. He looked to see if the waitress had seen them arrive. "You guys talking about me?" he asked, looking to each of us.

The skipper moved his chair out of the way and assumed his speaker's posture—leaning forward, arms spread, palms on the table. "It would appear that we have a few minutes before our meal arrives so let me pass on quickly our schedule for tomorrow." He stood upright. "Breakfast at six-thirty as usual, then clean-up. All hands report to the mess at seven where the ship's officers will make assignments for the shakedown cruise. We disembark at eight o'clock sharp." He looked to Wally and Hutch first, as if expecting them to fill in anything he had left out, then looked to the rest of us. "Any questions?"

"Why don't we just set a course for Copenhagen?" said Wally. His remark was met with near unanimous approval.

The skipper smiled and nodded. After the murmuring stopped he said, "Just be patient. Our day is coming . . . and soon."

With everybody in good spirits, Wally entertained us with his theory that the use of paper matches—instead of wooden matches and lighters—was the cause of lung cancer. Taylor officiated over the pointless response that paper is a wood by-product.

I awakened earlier than usual on Monday but found Monty already in the galley with coffee going. "The rain woke me up," he said, half-apologizing. "I guess I'm a little excited too. It's like the night before Christmas or something."

Hutch, Chris, and Billy soon arrived and pitched in to make breakfast. Everybody was excited about what promised to be our maiden voyage onboard the *Marite*. But two things forced the postponement of the shakedown cruise: an unusually hard rain and none of our crew could operate the ship's radio. The postponement caused our soaring spirits to plummet.

The rainfall and wind slacked, then stopped by mid-afternoon. This prompted a new round of enthusiasm. By late afternoon Hutch and the skipper had found a boat owner to instruct them on the use of the radio. The shakedown cruise was reset for Tuesday.

That night a BBC political analyst argued that, given Nixon's misuse of the FBI and CIA as instruments for partisan political exploitation, Congress would have to press for impeachment or tacitly allow future presidents to do the same. This would clearly erode the two-party political system and undercut its viability. He further stated that Congress would have to impeach whether or not Nixon prevailed before the

Supreme Court. I fell asleep listening to the radio and slept through Gretchen's return home after a night on the swing shift.

The shakedown cruise commenced on Tuesday as planned, but soon went awry. From his obligatory station at the helm in the pilothouse, the skipper could not direct operations on deck. So those duties were assigned to Hutch. Hutch had organized the crew effectively but with one small oversight. He had presumed there would be fishermen on the adjacent ships to throw off our lines. There were none.

Being the closest free hand at that critical moment, I leaped to the task and, as the skipper warped the ship out, I was left on the deck of the *Azelda T* in the rain as the *Marite* put out. I dashed across the *Azelda T* to the quay, hoping that the skipper would pull alongside so I could climb onboard. But the skipper was not informed and Hutch had turned his energies to the untethered foremast boom.

I waved and shouted frantically from the dock as the *Marite* chugged by. The skipper waved back, apparently mistaking me for a well-wisher. The ship was so close I could see the rain splattering on Monty's back as he coiled a mooring line on deck. I shouted louder but without success. I felt helpless. I also realized that the stage was set for the ship to sink while I watched. In a spasm of fear I averted my eyes, turned my back, then purposefully walked out of town to avoid the hospital. It was a gut-wrenching day of ominous thoughts, aimless walking, and tense rest stops beside the road with my back turned to the sea. Doing it made me feel silly and superstitious, but I couldn't not do it.

The ship returned in mid-afternoon. Naturally, I got the story later about the cruise. To get the feel of her, the skipper had mostly tacked and turned and accelerated and tested the

North Atlantic from varying angles. On several occasions, undeveloped sea legs made for some humorous stumbles. However, the one event that my peers fixed upon was trivial yet somehow summed up the episode for them. Chris described it as the "loose can on deck" episode.

"It was crazy, Dee," Monty told me. "Hutch was pissed about the boom swinging free, really, and wanted to find out who had left it untied. Anyway, he had worked himself into a state when the bucket that protects the winch motor from rain tumbled off and rolled across the deck in front of him. He kicked at it but missed. So he goes chasing and kicking at this bucket until he connects, but the handle hangs on his heel and he's looking like the three stooges minus two and walking around with the bucket on his foot and glaring at us like a rabid animal." Monty vented a laugh but stopped short.

"So what happened?"

"He kicked and kicked and finally kicked it overboard, but by then he was in such a fury that he just kinda threw up his hands. And you know how he gets red in the face? Well, I thought he was going to blow a gasket. I mean, everybody looked the other way. He was so angry you couldn't look because you didn't want him focusing it on you."

"It was like looking at the sun," observed Chris. "You were afraid of burning your eyes."

A variety of moods showed on the faces assembled for our evening meal at the hotel. The deck hands were grim-faced and introspective over the embarrassing shakedown cruise. Wally and the skipper, however, were energized and talked sea lore at their end of the table. Hutch didn't join us for supper. Without him as a link, no communication took place between the crew and the ship's officers. Wally and the skipper were in one world and the ship's crew in another.

I told Hans and Olivia about the shakedown cruise. Hans laughed uncontrollably, rolled off his chair, and tumbled onto the floor, hands clutching his side like an injured man. "It is good ting de Norsemen did not vait for Americans to find America," he said after recuperating. His goading and laughter infected us all. I actually felt better after laughing at the whole thing. Things didn't seem so grave.

Gretchen had to work the swing shift for the rest of the week so it was just the three of us to play Yahtzee and listen to the BBC. The big news was that while Nixon had turned over the tapes, large sections had been erased. The commentator described the erasures as a "death knell" for the Nixon presidency.

After the news, Olivia suggested that rather than mourn Nixon's passing we should celebrate it. He was, after all, a morally detestable figure who was responsible for thousands of deaths in Vietnam. Hans quickly suggested we have a wake when the resignation finally came. He recommended we have *forshoved,* one of the sheep heads I had seen in the SuperMarked, plus his new, improved homemade rum. When Gretchen returned, she sided with Hans and Olivia on the vote. She and Olivia agreed to make dessert and side dishes. I volunteered to make bread, and Hans agreed to do the rest. We agreed upon Saturday night since Gretchen would have the day off.

On Wednesday morning, the skipper asked that I accompany him on a restocking mission to the various merchants. My neck muscles knotted up as we strode through

town. From the skipper's point of view, resupplying the ship
was a given. You have to feed the crew and provide fuel and oil
for the engine. These were operating expenses pure and simple.
But from my perspective, it was like marching before a gallery
of yet-to-be-told victims—the chandler, the SuperMarked,
hotel, and fuel supplier—and each extending a trusting hand to
the skipper and me. We charged the goods and moved on. But I
felt like a thief. For weeks I had told myself that the Plastic Gun
Dream was only a dream, yet I knew all the while that the
mounting debts were real. On this morning the dream had
become a my private unavoidable manifest destiny without ever
leaving my mind.

Lethargy overtook me on the way back to the ship. The
patches of blue sky and sparkling sea seemed a cruel hoax. The
literary rules of the road called for rain. Its absence seemed
tangible. Another kind of payment delayed. A denial of symbolism owed. It was as if our little maritime venture was, in
addition, bilking humankind out of the metaphorical trappings
of loss. By the time we returned to the *Marite,* I felt I had
earned one wet and dreary night. And in the North Atlantic you
can bet that one will not be long in coming.

I couldn't sleep that night. After several fitful tries, I gave
up and wrote the letter I had promised Troy back at the
Balclutha. As a precaution, I asked in the letter if he had heard
from Dalton and had a current address he could send to me.
When morning finally came, instead of feeling exhausted, I felt
energized, watchful, like a man in mortal danger.

I got permission from Hutch to go to the post office after
breakfast. Six local seamen and the skipper were discussing
some matter in Danish when I returned. From what I could

translate and from the skipper's sidebars with Wally and Hutch, it was clear the *Marite* was to be moved. I joined the rest of the crew at the foot of the pilothouse. "We're finally getting out of this place," declared Chris.

"Did we get a telegram from Mr. Heflin?" I asked.

In a brief meeting in the galley, the skipper confirmed that the *Marite* was to be relocated to the other side of the dock. In addition, the port authorities asked our help in moving the *Skarveinur* into our vacated berth alongside the *Azelda T*.

With only a dozen hands to handle the mooring lines on the three ships, the relocating process would require good coordination. First, a fishing boat acting as a tug pulled the *Skarveinur* away from the end of the L-shaped dock and directed it slowly into the sheltered area where the *Marite* and *Azelda T* were moored. Next the *Marite's* mooring lines were let out and she was moved several yards away from the *Azelda T*. The *Skarveinur* was then maneuvered forward until the three ships lay abreast with the *Marite* in the middle. I was on the stern deck with the stern line to the *Azelda T* in my hands as the *Marite* was pushed backwards by the fishing boat from between the two ships. Visually, the two craft were overtaking the *Marite* just as in my last dream. In reality, of course, the *Marite* was moving backwards while the others stood still.

The slow-arriving reality of what I saw paralyzed me with dread. Another dream had come to life and had caught me off guard. Despite the mooring line in my hand, I felt untethered, floating suddenly, horizontal yet standing. A soaked section of mooring line dripping in my hands brought me back. I pulled out the slack, but then stood flinching and blinking neurotically. A soundless voice echoed in my head, "Why is this happening to me?"

I had to fight back. The dreams were wrecking my mental health. I had begun to see hidden meanings in everything. There was nobody to tell. Gretchen had described my dream anxieties as *storhedsvandid*, a scary word connoting big and crazy, and Monty had turned away when he heard my tone of voice.

At the end of the day I made a beeline to Gretchen's place. I was so stressed from lack of sleep and overstimulation that my neck muscles squeaked inaudibly when I turned my head. A long hug, a beer, and a nap would help set things right.

Hans and Olivia arrived moments after I stretched out on the sofa. Had I heard? President Nixon had scheduled a press conference. According to the BBC he was going to resign. The press conference was scheduled for one o'clock in the morning. They had taken the liberty of bumping our sheep's head dinner ahead two days. In fact, the sheep head was thawing in the kitchen sink. I nodded and agreed, nodded again, and collapsed on the sofa immediately after they left.

Gretchen came home with a bag of party goods in her hands. Incredibly, when she pushed the front door closed with her foot, it shook the room sufficiently to loosen the thumbtack holding the left side of the sailing ship poster. As I opened a dreary eye to the world, the poster was swinging back and forth on the remaining tack until, when nearly still, the ship's bow pointing straight up as had the *Marite* in the dream, the other tack came loose and the poster fell to the floor.

"Time to wake up," said Gretchen in a playfully miffed tone. She strode over in her hospital whites and picked up the poster.

The sailing ship on the poster had "sunk" and I had awakened in the hospital dorm. The full realization of what had happened hit me as if I were a tuning fork struck from behind.

Everything was knocked out of focus. For a few minutes the world was a crazy, crushing, confusing, convergence of forces. I couldn't tell if my eyes were closed—even though I saw a smear of colors—or open to a swimming blur of objects and shapes. When I reoriented myself—under an afghan, on the sofa, in the hospital dormitory—Gretchen's smiling face slowly melted into sad-puppy folds of sympathy as she leaned forward to engage my eyes. I wanted to prove to her that I wasn't some wacko with brain-shattering glimpses into the future, but rather a Normal Joe to whom all of this was inexplicably happening.

I sat up. Gretchen smiled perfunctorily as she strode toward the kitchen.

Incomprehensible things were happening inside my head; normal things were happening in the outside world. "Hans and Olivia will be over in a minute," said Gretchen softly. "You look like you could use a shower." She fetched a towel and tossed it in my lap and smiled warmly. "Did you see our dinner in the sink?" she asked with a tilted smile.

I was going crazy. That was the only logical explanation. It seemed impossible that one moment could contain such wildly different experiences. On the one hand I had just witnessed in the real world a highly specific event that I had viewed a month before in the exact same spot but in a dream. And at the same moment I was bathed in the gentle, apt friendship of a woman who freely responded to my emotional needs while shunning the desire that spawned them. The combined effect was dissatisfaction and confusion; utter and complete dissatisfaction; inexplicable confusion. I want, but cannot have. I am, but cannot be. I dream, but . . .

Still, the whole pot of gold—love, adventure, happiness— seemed so close. I ached for Gretchen as she walked into the kitchen, her perfectly contoured bottom swaying under silky layers of white. I wanted to envelope her with my whole being. To pour out my soul to her. To explore her every fold, contour, and mystery. To feel her writhe in my arms. Yet an invisible hand seemed to be leading us in opposite directions. Was my headful of crazy dreams running her off? I groped in the dark for an answer. Did she recognize something that I had not yet admitted? That I had gone over the edge?

The sound of clinking spoons, clunking pots, and the voices of my overanxious friends reached my ears before I had turned off the stream of hot water in the shower. I hurried to join them. Olivia handed me a glass of Hans' homemade rum as I entered the cluttered scene in the kitchen. "It's better this time," she told me. Her hair was up in a bun. She looked different, chubbier.

"Especially with Coke," said Hans wryly. With a slightly soiled white apron and a paper chef's hat set at an angle, he really looked like a chef.

Gretchen hastened over. "Let me show you this." She guided my hand against the stainless steel pitcher that contained the rum. "Still warm," she said with her mischievous laugh and a toss of her head. It felt good to be in the company of such natural friends. My thoughts went back to the *Marite*. I wondered what kind of mood prevailed there. I wondered if they knew that Nixon was scheduled to resign. I made my way into the kitchen to start the bread.

As billed, Nixon resigned at one o'clock am, local time. The commentator, after going through the laundry list of potentially damning evidence, suggested that the deciding factor in Nixon's decision had been the simple matter that he would lose his presidential pension and bodyguards if ousted through the impeachment proceedings. It seemed odd that such a monumental matter could turn on such small stakes. But then I guess a measure of prestige and a few creature comforts is what most desirable things boil down to.

Nixon's resignation was a hard act to follow, but the boiled sheep head made a good run at it. As expected, the homemade rum greased the skids for the big event. But even total stupefaction was not preparation for the sight and sound of Hans sawing the skull in half with a handsaw on the kitchen counter. Worse still was having half a sheep's head on a platter with potatoes and a steamed leek beside it. Rather, it looked like something you'd stumble across while hitchhiking on a dirt road.

Gretchen wedged in beside me and wrapped an arm over my shoulder. "The locals say it's an aphrodisiac," she said. She used her other arm to wave Hans and Olivia closer, and then, with a conspiratorial whisper, said, "But let's eat it instead." We laughed and laughed. She hung a leg over my lap and bit my nose in a drunken display of gaiety. After the humor of her remark faded, Hans and Olivia asked what was so funny. We laughed again and yet again when Gretchen explained it in Danish. And just as the fun had run out and we were left with the unsightly sheep head on the table before us, Gretchen fetched her medical bag, cleaned the sheep's nostrils with a swab, examined the nostrils and ears with a penlight, prescribed two aspirin for a splitting headache, and bed rest for double vision. What a night!

Eventually we ate the sheep head and drank the rum. I woke up late, still wearing one boot, in a tangle of bedclothes and a disabling headache. Hans and Olivia lay motionless under a blanket on the floor beside the table. Gretchen grimaced in her sleep when I moved to get up. It was a rainy morning. I took four aspirins, brushed my teeth gingerly, and trudged down the hill to the *Marite*.

Chapter 9 - Adrift

"Heard the news, Dee?" asked Chris after I made it to the forecastle. He was barefoot and listless.

"Yeah. We stayed up and listened on the radio."

"Not that," said Chris. "Not Nixon. The telegram." He paused, swallowed. "We got a telegram from Heflin. The whole deal is shit-canned." He stood there, nodding his head.

"No shit?"

"No shit. If you don't believe me ask the guys in the galley." He pointed to the duffle bags and suitcases that lay around the compartment. "The skipper is talking with Mr. Hansen right now. So are Hutch and Wally."

We smoked in silence. The aspirin was starting to relieve my hangover but a new and equally oppressive sensation was descending. "So what are you gonna do?" I asked him.

"I don't know." He shook his head, suddenly sullen. "It's over, man." His voice, thick with emotion, seemed to cling to his throat. His eyes slowly met mine. He threw a hand up in frustration.

"It's a heart-breaker," I said. He nodded and strode away, visibly shaken.

The skipper convened a meeting just after lunch and confirmed everything Chris had related. He also explained that Mr. Hansen had made arrangements for the entire crew to move to the hotel, and then to relocate to the hotel in Thorshavn. Afterwards, the *Marite* would be sealed and anchored in the fjord until another buyer came along.

Taylor quickly steered the discussion onto money matters. The best the skipper could do, he told us, was provide each of us with a written voucher stating what we were owed according to the terms of our employment.

"That won't buy a ticket back to the states," said Monty.

The skipper paused and smiled warmly at Monty. "Don't worry. Mr. Hansen and I spoke with the American Embassy this morning and they have agreed to help." The skipper raised a hand to hold off another question from Taylor. "Please, let me finish." He paused to collect his thoughts. "Now, for those who want, the American Embassy will provide air fare back to the states. However, they also will impound your passports and thereby prevent you from traveling until you pay them back. What they prefer doing in cases like this is to find passage onboard merchant ships headed for the states. That way you arrive and receive a paycheck at the same time."

The skipper pulled out his pocket watch. "Hutch, can you take charge one more time? I simply must meet with the chandler and the innkeeper."

"Sure."

There was silence until the skipper left and then another silence. Finally Hutch spoke. "Well, I guess when we signed on for this deal we all knew that this could happen." He smacked his lips and sighed. "And now it has." This, he must have felt, was his last opportunity to address his crew. He seemed to be either choosing his words carefully or trying to contain his emotions. He went on. "As for the question of why we cannot remain onboard the *Marite* until we depart, there are two reasons. First of all, Mr. Hansen wants to get her sealed up and anchored in the fjord as quickly as possible to avoid paying additional mooring fees: there is a daily charge to keep the *Marite* at the dock."

"I'll bet it's not close to the two or three hundred a day it costs to put each of us up at the hotel," said Chris.

"Well," said Hutch in his slow way, his head turning away momentarily. "The other reason is, well, I guess we have made some enemies in Tvoroyri."

His remark stung. There was a silence.

Chris looked around quizzically. "Enemies?" he said.

"How'd we make enemies?" asked Taylor.

Hutch exhaled and mulled over his words. "Well, for one thing we have purchased a lot of things on credit and apparently Mr. Heflin hasn't sent one red cent since the first week."

"That son of a bitch," blurted Chris. "I hope his balls rot off."

Hutch quelled the angry words with an upraised hand. After it was quiet he went on. "And apparently we didn't do so good here, either," he said. "I guess a lot of folks are angry because we . . . I mean . . . some of us . . . or some of you, have been . . . ah, taking liberties with the local female population." His words took forever to get out.

"Haven't they heard about the notion of consenting adults?" blurted Taylor.

"I don't think they were talking about you or Don," said Hutch, but with thinly disguised disfavor. His remark was followed by a dead silence. He looked around. Everybody was waiting for the rest of the answer. "Well, I guess the gossip focused on younger girls mostly."

"Hey," said Monty angrily, "we never touched those girls." He looked Hutch straight in the eye. "And believe me, they did everything but beg us."

Hutch cleared his throat. "I know that. I'm not blind. And I told Mr. Hansen that. And he believes it too. The problem is with the rest of the locals." Slowly the source of the problem dawned on us. The liberties in question had been taken by Billy and the angry "locals" meant Birthe and her family.

With that on the table, there wasn't that much to talk about. The answers to our questions were either decided already or unknowable. The discussion quickly degenerated into a gripe session, then collapsed. Hutch closed the meeting, left, but returned to inform us that a pair of trawlers were entering port.

The skipper and Wally were at dockside watching the *Grimsby Titan I* and *Grimsby Titan II* maneuver up to the dock in a stiff wind. Monty and I watched from the *Marite*. With his jacket panels flapping and his fluorescent hunting cap, Wally reminded me of an obese organ-grinder monkey off his leash as he stood beside the fastidious skipper. Monty noticed it too. "Did you ever read *Of Mice and Men?*"

Wally and the skipper helped moor the first trawler to the dock while chatting with crewmen working the lines on deck. The second trawler was moored to the first, which saved port fees. A short time later, Wally shouted into the fo'c'sle that there was another meeting in the galley with the skipper. "He got some booze," ventured Chris without cheer.

Once there, the skipper apologized for the failure of the enterprise but restated that Mr. Heflin had just never come through as promised with the money. Beyond that, he said he had gotten us together again to share a toast. At that point Wally produced a bottle of vodka from his jacket pocket, somebody gathered cups and we drank until the bottle was empty. Hutch, looking doe-eyed and sentimental, tore the page for Friday, August 9, 1974 off the Danish calendar and asked the skipper to translate the quotation at the bottom. The skipper looked at it, smiled, and handed it to me. "Can you read it?"

I studied it for a few seconds. "It says something like, 'In this world everybody has to reap what they sow, even amateur gardeners.'"

"Very good," said the skipper. "There's nothing I can add," he said to Hutch. It was hard to say who was more pleased, the skipper or me.

The get-together lasted a while longer. When Wally left prematurely, I figured he was heading to the trawler to score another bottle. I stuck my head out the hatch a short while later as footfalls crossed the main deck and caught Wally with my typewriter in his hand. He stopped when he saw me. "Hey," I shouted angrily. "What are you doing?"

"This is my typewriter," he said, but handed it to me as soon as I got within arm's length.

"For Christ's sake, Wally, what's wrong with you?" I snatched the typewriter and scowled. He strode by, seemingly unaffected by the incident. "Scumbag," I blurted, but immediately regretted it.

I returned the typewriter to my quarters, then lingered to consider Wally's behavior. He was totally unscrupulous. A creature with no redeeming social values. Sure, he understood engines and had an intuitive knack for repairing them. Still, after eight months onboard the *Marite*, he had yet to actually do anything but eat, smoke, drink coffee, and run the generator for his reading pleasure. Read, eat, and tell lies. That was his entire life. He was little more than a consumption machine living in a world without meaning.

Taylor cornered me later as we packed. "I've decided to stay here," he said. "I've got a place to stay and Margit says I can find work easily." He closed the lid on a suitcase, zipped it, tossed its twin on the bunk, and resumed stuffing clothes into it.

"I'll bet you could find work too." He stopped and looked over his shoulder. "Can't you stay with Gretchen?"

"Probably," I said. "But she's only here for a few more weeks. Besides, I wouldn't want to test her generosity. She's angry with me right now. And she's got this mysterious side." I surprised myself by saying it. However, it was something that had been on my mind, Gretchen's mysterious side. Most mysterious types maintain it by keeping others out of their world. But Gretchen opened the door to her world as if the source of the mystery was so distant, so deep that it was utterly impossible to uncover.

"Dee, why don't you stay? I'll bet this place is a lot nicer once things return to normal."

"After the ugly Americans leave?"

"Something like that." He resumed packing.

"I wouldn't mind. I like it. But I guess you know that there's only two hours of daylight here in the winter." He nodded slowly, like he had heard it before. "I'll bet it gets pretty dreary."

"So what are you going to do?" he asked. He held a book he had pulled from his suitcase. "Work your way back in the engine room of some freighter?"

It probably was an accurate picture of the merchant-marine option the skipper had worked out with the embassy. "I don't know. I thought I'd talk to Mr. Hansen about work. He'll know. Plus, I've got work with Dalton in Copenhagen."

"You keep saying that, but I don't see you lasting two weeks with Dalton. You guys are total opposites. Besides, you can find work here. Everybody speaks English." He held up the book. *Dharma Bums*, by Jack Kerouac. "Ever read it?" he asked.

"I've read *On the Road*."

"*Dharma Bums* is better. I carry it with me everywhere I go. I read it once a year. It portrays Kerouac's friendship with a wild Buddhist poet in San Francisco," he explained. He leafed into it a few pages and read a passage, his eyes caressing the page like a homesick soldier looking through photographs in his wallet. He closed the book and handed it to me. "You have to return it before you leave."

Seeing the shamble of bags and the misplaced crew upstairs at the hotel that afternoon triggered a bout of melancholy. I dropped off my bags, skipped a last meal with the crew, and made tracks for Gretchen's. Everything had changed in the hours since the late-night celebration with the sheep head. It had been a long, hectic day. I knew she would be at work until midnight so I made a sandwich and a pot of tea in the still-messy kitchen then pulled up a seat by the window. I needed to make a decision: to stay or not stay.

The factors in the decision were as obvious as the landscape itself. I looked through the window to the steep slope beyond. The lush carpet of flower-specked greenery sloped upward over the steep terrain as far as the bed of gravel at the foot of the cliffs. If I stayed, presuming I could find gainful employment, soon Gretchen would leave, as would most of the young people, and I would be left with Taylor and a long, cold, dark winter. Like the view before me, it would be a short uphill journey with flecks of color and then a stone wall. A lengthy stay in the Faroes was out.

The most promising course of action was to get to Copen-hagen where Dalton had guaranteed me work. As much as I hated the idea of working for Dalton, it was my most promising option. In the meantime, I needed to earn enough money to steer my own destiny. Allowing the American Embassy to choose for me would be a mistake.

The next question was how to earn enough money to bankroll the trip to Copenhagen. Staying at youth hostels, hitchhiking, and living on bread and cheese, I calculated that $250 was the bare minimum I would need. I already had $31 toward that amount. With luck, that would cover half the price of boat fare to Copenhagen. The next step was finding work in Tvoroyri. I looked out the window at the green and gray landscape behind the hospital. Eric, Mr. Hansen's son, was the person to ask about local job opportunities.

Gretchen came home promptly at midnight. By then I had tidied up the kitchen. "I guess you heard about the *Marite*," I said. She had made a mad dash into the kitchen.

"And the unpaid bills," she said. She swung open the refrigerator and looked inside. "I'm always surprised at how fast people can change from friends to enemies." She handed me a plate of cheese and bread. "The Faroese are very conservative."

"Unforgiving environments do that to people," I observed. "You stray too far from proven methods and sweet providence disappears."

After we settled at the table I hit her with the good news. "Mr. Hansen needs an extra hand for a few weeks. Until mid-September."

Silence.

She chewed, and chewed, and chewed, then said, "Good." The delay and tone were intentional. She took another bite and after a long moment looked me squarely in the eyes. Her gaze seemed to terminate en route between us, and the swirl of emotions I always had felt around her stilled. She pitied me.

That's what I realized. I had been blind to it and wondered for how long? Was it pity, pure and simple, or pity because I had been so desperate for her affections? Or perhaps she regarded me as a nut case because of the dreams?

"It's really good news for me." I swallowed to clear the emotion from my voice. "I have work in Copenhagen if I can just get there and find a place to stay." She brightened with a show of shared happiness, but remained silent. "Mr. Hansen said he knew of lodgings that would be much cheaper than the hotel."

"You can stay here until then." Having said that, she went into the bedroom. I guess she knew all along what I was angling at.

The big mirror in the hotel upstairs at the turn in the hall provided me with a full length view of myself. It was something I hadn't seen in a while. I had gone there for my bags. The lonely sound of the skipper pecking away on my typewriter in his room conjured up in my imagination the image of some godforsaken foreign legion outpost. I wondered where the rest of the crew had gone. Treading as quietly as possible on the maroon and gold carpet with the duffel bag slung over my shoulder, I was caught off guard by the lanky figure that appeared in the mirror. I could see why Gretchen had rejected and pitied me. What I saw was an adult tatterdemalion with a shaggy, mountain-man beard, long unruly hair, and eyes that studied things just a moment too long. My clothes displayed the weeks of coarse work and hand washing in cold water. I turned to view the backside of my jeans. There was a large, bare spot, the result of sliding down the mountain. My underwear showed.

On Saturday, Monty and I got stuck with returning unused egg powder and bags of flour for a credit on the charge account. It was a demoralizing assignment. At lunch the skipper handed out the letters of recommendation and vouchers he had typed for each of us. After that, he announced that Wally had been taken on as a mechanic onboard the *Grimsby Titan II*. Both he and Wally showed signs of having celebrated the event. The effects of the spirits had put a sunny face on what would almost certainly have been a grey day for them.

We all met at the *Marite* after lunch. A going-away toast for Wally slowly evolved into a sedentary round of drinking in the mess, the liquor furnished by Wally's new shipmates. By mid-afternoon everybody was drunk. Comically, Wally and the skipper had exchanged hats. Wearing Wally's bright orange hunting cap with the ear flaps up, the skipper had the look of an Andy Warhol portrait, as Wally strutted around regaling the merits of his new crew for calling him Smokey.

The afternoon took an ugly turn at Wally's departure time when he showed up again with my typewriter. He returned it without eye contact or a word. His face seemed swollen with emotions as he climbed over the side of the *Grimsby Titan I* to the *Grimsby Titan II* moored alongside. As he turned back to wave with the skipper's hat in hand, he slipped and fell between the two ships.

"My God, he'll be crushed," blurted the skipper, wearing Wally's fluorescent hat.

Instantly, crewmen from all three vessels leaped to the gap between the ships and struggled vainly to keep the two ships from inching together as they rocked and swayed at dockside. A fast-thinking fisherman saved Wally's life when he directed four crewmen to wedge a heavy wooden crate between the ships. A terrifying few minutes passed before Wally was retrieved from a coffin of frigid water and steel and stood shivering on the deck beside us. His reddened eyes, seeing terror in every face, seemed to spin in their sockets like coach wheels. Soaked, humiliated, and with only one boot, Wally followed one of his new crewmen through a hatch to warmth without looking back. Later that night the two trawlers departed.

As much as we disliked Wally for his sloth and bigotry, not to mention the world of fantasy in which he lived and foisted upon others, his departure had a devastating effect on the remaining crew. "I feel like tearing up something," said Monty. It summed up everybody's feelings.

The skipper, looking overworked and disengaged, asked Hutch to make a thorough inspection of the *Marite* to ensure that everything was in its proper place while he went for a final talk with Mr. Hansen.

"Aye-aye, skipper," he said, and with a drunken salute ambled toward the *Marite*.

"How about we go for one last climb?" said Chris. He tipped his head toward the cliffs.

We followed a familiar path to a familiar cleavage in the cliff. However, the threat of rain soon persuaded us to return. The enthusiasm that had always made the mountain climb fun was gone. We were just doing something to distract ourselves. It was nearly evening when we stopped beside the white clapboard church with the stilled steeple clock. "I've got five kroner says I can hit that clock," dared Monty, his arm cocked with a rock in his hand.

"Don't do it," shouted Chris.

"I was only kidding," said Monty, dropping the rock. "But it'd feel good, don't you think?"

The end to Adventures in Time, Inc. arrived on Tuesday the 13th when the *Smyril* departed with Monty, Chris, Billy, and Hutch. Like so many things in the last week, it seemed incongruous to see them wave and just stand at the side rail as she put out for Thorshavn. There wasn't much any of us could do. It seemed an anemic, expressionless way to conclude the whole ordeal. There was no discussion, no purchase of tickets, no confusion, not even someone to check boarding passengers. They just carried their belongings up the gangway and were gone without so much as a hiss of steam or a blast from a horn. I felt terribly alone even though the skipper and Larla were right beside me on the dock. We waved.

"Good-bye, Monty. Good-bye, Chris. Good-bye, Billy. Good-bye," called Larla. She struggled to hold back her tears. "I come see you in America." She zigzagged a retreat among the mooring lines, crates, and bollards along the dock, waving vigorously as the *Smyril* departed. She stopped and waved again as it got smaller and smaller. Finally, she glanced back to the skipper and me, clamped her hand over her mouth in agony, and sped down the dock toward home.

The skipper and I started back toward the hotel. He stopped to knock the ashes from his pipe and restock it. He nodded toward the *Marite*. "I'm already working on new financial backers," he said confidently. He held my gaze then flicked a lighter over his pipe. He puffed a couple of times then said, "You will be here working with Mr. Hansen, so I will know how to contact you when things fall in place." He clapped a hand on my shoulder. "I will be leaving Thursday . . . but just temporarily. I'm going to visit my sister in Copenhagen. I have got to make arrangements for Billy's passage home. His mother is worried about getting him in school on time."

"Sounds good," I told him. My remark was directed at his attempt to find new backers. But, like everything else lately, it seemed disconnected and needed explaining. "Looks like rain," I said after retrieving myself from a long blank stare. But he didn't seem to hear. He was transfixed by the *Marite* before us. All the refurbishing had transformed her. She looked renewed and impatient as she tugged at her lines and rolled gently with the tide. As we walked past the bow, the ship's anchor chain, hanging in a swag from the foredeck to the anchor, reminded me of a pocket-watch chain tucked into a vest pocket. Another grandiose image for Adventures in Time.

We reached the hotel without having said much more. The skipper invited me up for a drink in his room later so we could talk over the business of the new financial backers. "I should know more about how things are going to shape up by then." The remark informed me that he probably was trying to recruit Mr. Hansen into helping underwrite the enterprise.

My job started the next morning. Eric, Mr. Hansen's older son, put me to work in the small warehouse. They wanted to enlarge the entrance so a forklift could pass through. Before the entrance could be refitted, however, there was a half-day's work rearranging pallets of fertilizer—a job that a forklift could do in twenty minutes. It was good, hands-on, unthinking labor. Just what I needed to divert my thoughts.

After lunch, Eric took me to a house near the hotel where I met Heine, a widow with two daughters, who had a room I could rent. She was a devoted mother, a rather subdued woman in her late thirties, who at first glance reminded me of a grade-school teacher. She wore a print housedress, a pair of pointy black-rimmed glasses with little rhinestones in the corner, and seemed to smoke nonstop. She showed me the room, her house shoes swishing over the hardwood floors as she walked. The room was small but exactly what I needed. There was a narrow bed with a window over it, a chest of drawers, a built-in closet, and a four-legged washing machine on casters that was kept in the room until put into service at the kitchen sink. Heine told me I could use the room without charge so long as I kept it clean and did some maintenance around the house. She also invited me to share meals with them but indicated I would have to pay my share. That, too, seemed a great bargain. We shook hands and I returned to the small warehouse feeling triumphant.

After work I went to Gretchen's place to get my belongings. She was at work. Good, I thought, which surprised me once again. In truth I guess her message had finally gotten through the veil of hope I had erected. Regardless, I was happy to have my own place, to have a renewed measure of independence, to have work and self-determination. I looked back before exiting through her door with my second load of bags. The poster had been returned to the wall and everything was just like it was the first time I had been there. Only the nest-like cluster of furnishings in the center of the room carried any emotional trace of the many fun and hopeful nights that I had spent in the place. I wondered if it carried any emotional weight with Gretchen.

The skipper was in his room when I called after supper. And, just like the old days with the glove box in his pick-up, he opened his top dresser drawer, poured vodka from a small bottle into plastic cups, and we drank while he talked about a future onboard the *Marite*. He didn't seem bothered by the claustrophobic little room, but I was. It turned out to be a rather short talk. He presented me with an additional letter of recommendation, hand-written in Danish, a slip of paper with his sister's address in Copenhagen, and over a final toast gave me his rigging belt, tools and all.

I was rightly proud to accept the tools of one of the last men to sail a square-rigger around Cape Horn. Without his saying so, the gift had the feel of a changing of the guard, a passing down from generation to generation. I wanted to ask why he was not giving them to his son but abstained. In a way, I was saddened too. Did this mean retirement for the skipper?

Darkness had fallen by the time I exited the hotel and strode to my new home. Although triple the size of the skipper's room, I still felt claustrophobic in my new quarters. I quickly unpacked and emerged onto the streets of Tvoroyri. The wind had stirred up whitecaps in the fjord and smelled like rain. I had no particular place to go, but felt compelled to do so. By habit my feet turned toward the dock, but that was a dead end street in more ways than one. Other than that there was only the bakery and the Dairy Bar, which I could see was closed. Like a fool, I stood in the empty intersection looking in one direction and then another. The unacknowledged goal was to shake that old unshakable feeling of restlessness, anxiety, unchanneled energy, desire, loneliness—call it what you want—but in the Faroes such plans were usually accompanied by a stiff, cold wind. A reasonable person would have gone home, but I tramped from one end of town to the other with raw nerves exposed to the world before seeing the futility in it.

The sound of Heine and other voices awaited me when I returned. I hesitated for a moment at the door until I had the courage to deal with the ritual of making new acquaintances. Surely this set-up must be as alien to them as it was to me. I opened the back door and entered the kitchen. Heine was at the table with her two daughters. She stood, her chaste face suddenly beaming with pride as she introduced her daughters, Adria and Tilde.

I immediately recognized Tilde, perhaps twelve, as one of the angel-faced darlings who had danced with Billy at the discotheque. Adria was probably sixteen and a ravishing beauty who radiated vitality and innocence. I finger-waved to Tilde and politely shook Adria's hand. I was relieved that no informal gathering of friends had been organized as I had expected when I paused at the door.

"Perhaps you will have some tea?" said Heine. She returned to her seat and gestured with an open hand to the teapot on the table.

I drank my tea in large wolfish gulps while Heine sipped and smoked. After a long silence interspersed with smiles for pleasantry's sake, I asked Heine about the maintenance that was needed around the house. She showed me into her bedroom where a sliding closet door had come off the track, and then a dripping trap under the bathroom sink, a pane of glass over the kitchen sink that was patched with clear packing tape, and a door that was hard to close. Between them the repairs might amount to six hours work. I mentioned that and she said there were additional fix-it projects on the outside. There was plenty of time to see them later. I retired to my room, citing a need to finish unpacking, but found myself unconsciously pacing like a caged animal and wishing that I could go out again without having to pass through the kitchen. I was still awake and a mass of frayed nerves when the rain began sometime after midnight.

Instead of resuming work in the small warehouse the first thing next morning, Mr. Hansen had me join a handful of fishermen in the rain onboard the *Marite* with instructions to tie down anything that could move, batten all the hatches, and weatherproof the winches while the fishermen anchored her in the fjord downstream from the harbor. I couldn't identify him precisely through the rain, but I knew that the slightly blurred figure watching from the dining room window in the hotel must have been the skipper. Onboard, a seven-foot giant of a man called Polen, his hands the size of a bunch of bananas, stood akimbo over the anchor chain as it noisily paid out between his feet. Putting the *Marite* out to anchor was a routine task for the fishermen but a decidedly gloomy one for me. The real heartbreaker was climbing over the side on the rope ladder that Monty and I had made and leaving her like some sort of Sleeping Beauty with only the chug-chug-chugging of the fishing boat's engine to console me as we returned to the dock. The figure was no longer in the hotel window.

The *Kronprins* did not come to Tvoroyri on Thursday as scheduled. Instead, the *England,* a newer liner of comparable size and utility with the same corporate color scheme, made a port call. The rain had ceased earlier, but the air was humid enough that everything still dripped moisture. The *England* arrived late, so it was dark when the skipper and I heard the ship's horn and walked from the Hansens' to the dock with his bags. Monty, Chris, and Billy were coming down the gangway as we arrived. "Hey, hey, hey," I cheered. "Fancy meeting you guys here."

"Captain Hofman?" It was the officer manning the quarterdeck above.

The skipper snapped into a more formal posture. "I am Captain Hofman." He sidestepped Monty, Chris, and Billy, and saluted when the officer met him on the gangway.

"Welcome aboard," said the officer. "We are informed that you are Danish." The skipper nodded crisply and their conversation abruptly changed into Danish. I tried to gather what I could of the discussion while listening to Billy and backing down the gangway at the same time. I didn't get much.

"Let's go to the Konditari," suggested Billy. He had scanned the dock to see if the girls were among the dozen or so gathered.

"Billy," called the skipper, "Monty. Chris." He was alone when he strode down the gangway. "I am the only passenger embarking here. They are running late and want to load my gear and go." He paused near the bottom of the gangway as if suddenly aware of the implications. After another pause, he sort of gathered the four of us into one compassionate eyeful. He reached to adjust the cap that wasn't there. I could feel an uncontrollable quiver in my lower lip. "So," said the skipper, trying to put some snap into his voice. "You fellas just round up my bags and say your good-byes." He took a deep breath like a punctuation mark then extended his hand to me. "I hope to be seeing you in the near future. If not, let this serve as a farewell. I wish you success in whatever you do." I stepped aside so Monty and Chris could get by with the skipper's bags. We said our good-byes on the gangway and I returned to the dock.

"And remember to keep your sense of humor," said Monty. He had stopped at the top of the gangway. The skipper had given the two of us that advice dozens of times. Then the gangway was raised, the mooring lines freed, and the floodlights closed. Steam hissed from an outlet in the hull overhead, a solid blast on the horn announced the impending departure, and the *England* put out for the mainland.

"Say good-bye to Taylor for us," shouted Chris from the gunwale, twenty feet up. I watched until the last pinpoint of light was swallowed up in darkness and then opened the floodgates of sorrow. I sat there for a long time just ventilating my tears and anxieties among the familiar sounds of the seawater lapping at rocks and boats tugging at their moorings. I had invested so much of myself in the success of the *Marite* and now, with its failure, I felt drained, angry, frightened, and unfocused.

When I got to my place a small bouquet of Faroese flowers lay on the doorstep, perfectly preserved in the cold damp air.

138

Chapter 10 – Notes from the North Symbolic Ocean

For a few days following the crew's departure I was benumbed by the change that had occurred in a mere eight days. As a distraction, I put in long, hard days for Mr. Hansen. Staying busy seemed the key to sanity. Still, I was temporizing and knew it. I also knew there was plenty of time for sorting out everything. At this point in time I needed stability.

I knocked at Gretchen's door for three days in a row and got no response. On Sunday I finally found her home, looking pale and listless. The curtains were drawn. Something was wrong.

She had been preoccupied with a gravely ill patient, she told me, who had died the night before. It had hit her pretty hard. I made an effort to cheer her up. She declined the overture and asked to be left alone. After a thank you for the bouquet on the doorstep, I left with the pack hounds of depression dogging my heels.

The streets were empty. I needed to walk as an antidote to the melancholia that seemed ready to descend over me, but instead a curtain of rain sweeping across the fjord persuaded me to dash home. Heine and the girls were out. *Dharma Bums*, the Jack Kerouac book that Taylor had loaned me, caught my eye when I entered my room. I made a pot of tea, stretched out on the bed, and read halfway through it in one sitting.

A tour de force of pure energy and enthusiasm, *Dharma Bums* is an autobiographical excerpt from Kerouac's life as a rambler, poet, and beat generation historian based on his freewheeling encounters with Japhy Ryder, a self-styled poet and Buddhist pilgrim. I felt an immediate comradeship with

Japhy and Ray, the central characters, and realized I was not alone in my impressions and experiences. Others out there had found the world both meaningful and mysterious and sought to unravel it and apply what they learned to their own lives with the same big-footed, youthful clumsiness I had. Knowing that and seeing that they were less than successful in communicating what they felt made me feel better. I had always felt inadequate and apologetic about that. What I saw in *Dharma Bums* was a portrait of myself. I was not the only stranger in paradise. When Japhy and Ray raved about a world alive with meaning, it mirrored what I felt. When they waxed ecstatic over the wild and rugged beauty of a mountain landscape, it mirrored the awe and joy I felt on a Faroese cliff side or witnessing a San Francisco sunrise.

Feeling energized, I donned my raingear and headed for the mountains despite the bewildered expression on Heine's face. It wasn't a soaking rain, I told myself, and besides, viewed in contrast to the brooding grey sky, the wet stone and vegetation would be more intensely colorful than ever. I felt free and vowed to remember how easily I had allowed external circumstances to rob me of that freedom and to dictate how and what I saw in the world, including my self-view. I was reminded of the Hindu parable of the pickpocket who had met a saint, but hadn't realized it because he had only seen his pockets.

I had so wanted to be loved and accepted by a beautiful woman that I had come to see myself one-dimensionally as the person she had rejected. The realization lifted me. I looked skyward into the rain and beyond and felt a sudden invigorating jolt of energy shoot through me. Exhilaration buoyed in me, I felt reborn. I steered my weightless boots toward Kivania, an ancient crater formation the girls had shown us. More than ever I felt like a pilgrim, a seeker of knowledge, a traveler.

As I entered the craggy hollow of the crater, a covey of white cliff-dwelling birds suddenly took flight, circled overhead as if surveilling this intruder into their domain, then returned to their ledge, oblivious to my perceptions. In ancient times, I remembered, the movements of flocks of birds were thought to reveal the will of the gods. On important days the spiritual interpreter, called an augur, would section off part of the sky as a designated sector for omens. This designated section of sky was known as a temple and the interpretation derived from it was an inauguration. As I stood within the stone walls of the bowl-shaped crater, birds on wing overhead, I quietly celebrated having survived the craziness of the last of the dreams and wondered what the future held for me.

Darkness closed in earlier than I wanted, so I headed back to Tvoroyri. In the coming weeks, I spent much of my free time combing the rocky cliffs and rugged peaks of the island. It was my temple. Increasingly, as the confusion that had so unnerved me slowly receded into the past, I recognized that the dreams and the real-life counterparts that had so haunted me were actually signposts for a traveler, signposts indicating that my life was on the right path. Although I didn't know where it would all lead, I did know where I was coming from. When I began journaling in a new notebook on Monday, August 26, 1974, I wrote the starting date in block print at the top and below it wrote "Notes from the North Symbolic Ocean." It seemed an appropriate address for a temple.

A letter from Troy arrived soon after, just hours ahead of a big storm packing fifty-mile-per-hour winds and rain that peppered the side of the house like pellet shot. Like the big

storms earlier in the spring, this one shut down all outdoor
activity until it passed two days later. During the course of that
storm I must have read Troy's letter a dozen times. I didn't
recognize it at the time, but the instructions in that letter were
another signpost that initiated an equally madcap escapade
across Europe and propelled me toward a rendezvous with an
enlightened guru from Tibet.

According to Troy, Dalton was refitting a ship in a small
Danish port. But he had forgotten the name of the port, so I
needed to go to Activ Universite in Copenhagen where a
Canadian named Ray Sanders, a mutual friend to Troy and
Dalton, could steer me to Dalton's current whereabouts.

By the end of August, life in the Faroes had settled into a
predictable pattern. I worked until five o'clock, which coincided
with the last glimmer of daylight at that time of year, then had
supper and talked or read until fatigue overtook me. Most of the
weekends were taken up with household maintenance for
several hours each day. When I had free time, I explored cliffs
or joined Hans and Olivia in sightseeing excursions by car to
nearby villages or fjords. But even that came to a close when
Olivia departed for the mainland with the car one week before
the end of Hans' summer term as cook. We had scheduled a
simple going-away party for the day but ended up working on
the car in the rain. Somehow the distributor cap had been
doused while parked. "It's trying to tell you to stay," Gretchen
told Hans as she held the umbrella and flashlight while he
fussed with the problem under the hood. Hans got it running
again just as the *England* made port with a long blast on the
horn. Refusing to shut the engine off, he drove down to the

dock and waited until told where to park so the ship's loading boom could reach it.

The unexpected car problem derailed our plans for a modest going-away celebration for Olivia. It also fouled up Gretchen's plan to announce that she had extended her tour of duty in the Faroes for ninety days. Olivia and I were shocked, and it showed as the three of us walked in total silence down the hill to the dock where Hans stood watching as the red Saab was hoisted onboard the *England*. Gretchen hastily said her good-bye to Olivia and returned to the hospital.

Hans waited until Gretchen was out of sight then said, "You were smart to leave her when you did." I wondered if he was being magnanimous or just didn't know that she had dumped me. "She is here for only one reason." He paused, searching for the correct word. "How do you say *skinsyge* in English?" he asked Olivia. She shook her head back and forth.

"Jealous?" I ventured, after a moment.

"Ya-ya," agreed Olivia brightly. "*Jaloux*."

"She lovey-dovey to make a doctor *jaloux*," finished Hans. The revelation sent a sickening pang through me, but it helped things make sense.

After the *England* departed, Hans and I returned to the dorm in the rain, where we pounced on the untouched party food and talked late into the night. Half of what Gretchen had told me about herself had been false, I learned, but playfully so, as if intended to amuse rather than deceive. I was sad to see him leave on the following Thursday. He was excited about returning home.

I had given Olivia money the week before to purchase a pair of jeans for me on the mainland and to send them as soon as possible. I had hoped they would arrive with the *England's* return trip, but no such luck. In fact, they never arrived.

At the end of August, Eric and his younger brother Charles, who was home for summer break, invited me to join them on a trip to the centuries-old town of Famjin. It was one of the most memorable of my experiences in the islands. Famjin was nearly due west of Tvoroyri, but, like all trips in the Faroes, the road coursed through a series of steep grades, switchbacks, and every imaginable road type. "With good luck we can find the BBC," said Charles as we drove across a high plateau that contained a small lake. He leaned close to the speaker and turned the tuner knob carefully. The radio crackled and hissed until we topped the ridge and descended into a crater formation and the penetrating voice of Patsy Cline suddenly filled the little car. "I go a-walking after midnight." Charles brightened and sat upright. "It's *Country Express,*" he said reverently. A program of country and western fare on the BBC.

The impact of hearing Patsy Cline, an iconic voice from my childhood, intensified the breathtaking beauty of the village before me. Famjin was home to eighty Faroese and hard-pressed to prove it by my estimation, since it consisted of only six or eight homes and a small church with an adjoining graveyard, all nestled meekly at the foot of the dark sidewall of a volcanic crater with two majestic waterfalls spilling hundreds of feet down the cliffs a hundred yards behind. Eric stopped the car. He and Charles had visited Famjin scores of times but still seemed spellbound as they stood stock-still and soaked up the view and sensations.

The waterfalls, Charles informed me, were fed by the small lake we had passed before descending into the crater. "There are more waterfalls when it rains," he added, pointing south. To the west the crater wall had crumbled into the sea a millennium earlier and some of the fallen stone had been reformed by locals into a small curved jetty that protected a few fishing boats from picture-perfect waves crashing on the picture-perfect shore. One of the houses featured a steeply pitched sod roof that was overgrown by tall grass that swayed rhythmically like green Kansas wheat.

Closer to the sea, two piles of moss-covered stones marked where a pair of ancient stone houses had collapsed and been left to ruin. One of them dated to the tenth century, Eric told me. I walked among the dilapidated walls and tried to absorb whatever I could of ancient Nordic humanity. Still, my gaze kept returning to the little graveyard by the church with its encircling stone wall, Celtic crosses, weathered tombstones, and iron gate.

I stopped at the gate to examine the ancient graveyard. The tombstone inscriptions were in Nordic script, but, like all graveyards, the epitaphs imparted a single message: here lie those who have lived before you but who are now dead. What a splendid place to be buried, I thought. Charles must have read my mind. "Only those who are born here may be buried here," he informed me. I walked over to a stone corner post, leaned against it, and opened my senses to the magical little town with the waterfalls. The air was clear and fresh, the waterfalls glistened white as the water tumbled noisily beyond the church, birds called and slowly described arcs overhead. I inaugurated Famjin as another private temple and looked to the sky for an omen.

"The name of the town has an interesting history," said Eric. He had slipped up beside me as I leaned on the gatepost.

As he told it, hundreds of years earlier the little town was home base for a small band of Vikings who raided villages on neighboring islands and mainland Europe. One day the Vikings returned to find French pirates raiding their settlement. Though outnumbered, the Vikings repelled the French on land, then unexpectedly followed them back to their ships where they overwhelmed the crew, plundered their goods at sword-point, then abducted their women. From the shore, as the French ships departed, the agonized calls of the pirates shouting for their *femmes* in Old French sounded like "fam-ee-un" to the ears of the victors.

An ugly storm struck during the return trip to Tvoroyri. At its peak, the storm packed stiff winds that rocked the car and delivered slabs of rain that forced us to pull over. "This is like a carwash," I told Eric and Charles, as we hunkered in the car waiting for the storm to subside. They had never seen nor heard of a carwash. I explained how they worked.

I learned on the drive back that only two more trips of the *England* were scheduled for the season. The second trip was only twelve days away. After that there would be no scheduled passenger service between the mainland and the islands, neither by air nor sea, until spring, although one could arrange passage on a fishing boat. If I wanted to leave on that last voyage of the season I would have to work all weekend for Heine and hope for decent weather too. I crossed my fingers.

That night, after returning from Famjin and doing my laundry in Heine's washing machine, I had another strange dream. In this one I was standing in the doorway of a large laundromat watching as a roomful of strangers, male and female, ran madcap circles around a double row of washing machines arranged back to back in the center of the room. First they ran clockwise, stopping abruptly in front of me, then they ran counter-clockwise and stopped. Back and forth they ran, always reversing their direction in front of me, and everybody, including myself, was naked. The machines were the old-fashioned front-loading kind with porthole-like glass on the doors that allowed you to watch the clothes and sudsy water slosh against the glass.

I awakened with my heart knocking against my ribs and a kaleidoscope of fears churning in my thoughts. Another dream. The realization arrived in the forefront of my thoughts with explosive force. A strange dream. An ominous dream that stood immobile in my thoughts like a near-death experience from the past, yet still ahead of me, I knew. I conjured up the images and reviewed the unfamiliar faces, all frightened and running before me. I sat up, stared into the darkness, and immediately seized on my action plan: Avoid laundromats. Avoid portholes. Do not linger in doorways. Avoid groups of naked people. I wanted to laugh at the absurdity of it, but could find no humor in it. I was terrified. I had tried to keep the previous dream from coming true, but had failed to stop it. Was this dream unstoppable too? I thought of another item for my action plan: Do not change clothes. A single note of laughter blurted out and reverberated in the dark room. How does one live without changing clothes?

Recalling a technique that Japhy and Ray had used in *Dharma Bums*, I pulled my legs into a lotus position and concentrated on my breath. After a while my thoughts stilled and I focused on the problem. This dream had struck me like a body blow because I associated the dreams with the Marite venture and presumed the dreams would cease with the skipper's departure. I thought I had put all that behind me.

Still, the more I thought about it, the more this dream seemed of the unfinished-business variety. After all, I had washed my clothes earlier, and I had worn the worn-out jeans that exposed my backside and impoverished state. Beyond that, the churning suds related back to the day's storm and the "carwash" scene. The combination of explanations soothed my fears. Plus, I could not imagine any scenario in which the dream could come true. There was no laundromat in Tvoroyri, and no nude laundromats anywhere, I told myself. By midday I had regained my equilibrium and had all but put it out of mind. With only eleven days before departing for the mainland, I had pressing things to do. I needed to work as many hours as possible in those days. The dream could never come true. It was impossible. Totally impossible.

Mr. Hansen was excited to learn that I could cut glass and mend broken windows. He had purchased glass, glazing compound in quantity, and cutters some years before, but without adequate glass-cutting instruction, the stuff had just occupied space in a warehouse. As a result, fixing a broken pane in Tvoroyri required having the proprietor of a picture-frame shop in Thorshavn make a special trip. Mr. Hansen had me drop what I was doing and turn my energies to mending broken windows. I spent two of my final days mending windows. I was delighted I could provide such a valuable service for Mr. Hansen. Plus, mending windows seemed like the perfect occupation for me at that point in time. However, while replacing a glass pane over Heine's sink, the replacement pane accidentally fell, cut my cheek, and required that I go to the hospital for treatment. I was treated by the duty nurse, Gretchen.

"Now look what you have done," she admonished with a maternal shake of her head. "You're the lucky one. It could have struck you in the eye." She bathed and examined the injury with firm fingers. It felt good to have her so close again. "This will take more than a kiss and a Band-Aid," she added with her usual flair for innuendo.

I told her I was leaving on Thursday. She had calculated as much. A handsome young doctor entered the examination room with a swish of sanitary whites and a stethoscope draped over his left shoulder. A flicker of red flashed across Gretchen's face as the doctor leaned forward to look at the cut, a wedding band on his left hand.

"He's a sturdy one," said Gretchen. "He'll survive."

The doctor agreed and breezed out of the room. "I'll bet you're glad to be back on the day shift," I said, just making talk.

"It won't make any difference in a few weeks," she said, searching through the first aid cabinet. "It's dark at four o'clock already."

I received spray-on stitches and a spider bandage. I wanted to tell her that I understood our situation but it was pointless and probably would be painful. The injury ought to heal pretty fast, she told me as we parted company. I thanked her for everything—the fun times, Danish lessons, health care—and departed.

Mr. Hansen paid me in full in cash at the end of my last workday, knowing I would be busy packing and saying good-byes on my last two days in Tvoroyri. He also invited me to supper with the Hansen family that evening. I considered the invitation a special honor. I had only been in their home a few times but recognized the sanctity that family held with him. As expected, it was a formal, almost sedate affair, but with fine china and Mrs. Hansen and Larla bringing food to the table in waves. The menu included the local apricot soup I loved, lamb, potatoes, and vegetables for starters, along with fresh rolls with that incomparable Danish butter. After a brief chat, Mrs. Hansen served up lemon meringue pie, coffee, and schnapps. Classical music murmured in the background from an antique phonograph with a thick and flawless coat of clear varnish. Conversation touched on what was in store for me on the mainland, then drifted to the beautiful fjords of Norway. They encouraged me to visit Norway, and talked at length about a resort they had visited that straddled the Arctic Circle. I told them about Henni, a student friend from Oslo who I had become chummy with in San Francisco, and promised to visit Norway.

The going-away supper that Heine and I created the next day was not nearly as formal nor exquisite in its presentation but was memorable in other ways. For one thing, it was the first time in months that I had cooked a real meal in a real kitchen, so it was more fun than work. Plus, with two of us working on it, we were free at times to join Schuyler, Heine's beau, in the front room where he kept glasses topped with schnapps and served as disc jockey using Heine's 50s-style hi-fi and a lackluster collection of jukebox tunes on 45s. We ate and danced to Ray Coniff and Boots Randolph, talked and drank, and taught young Tilde to do the four-step. By departure time we were all soused and teary-eyed and had played Englebert Humperdink's *The Last Waltz* over and over while slow dancing in our socks in the kitchen. "I hate to leave," I told them when a blast from the *England* signaled fifteen more minutes. I gave Heine, Adria, and Tilde a hug and a kiss and got help from Schuyler and Tilde with my bags.

Taylor was among those gathered at dockside as I arrived. "Where's my book?" he asked.

I returned it and expressed my gratitude. It seemed a fitting topic for our final minutes together. "I think I'll find a Buddhist center when I get to Copenhagen," I told him. "I'd like to learn to meditate, you know, like Japhy and Ray."

The *England* blew her horn to announce final boarding. We shook hands, hugged, then I strode up the gangway. After I reached the top, Gretchen showed up on the quay below. I caught her eye and waved. She waved back, her presence on the quay as radiant as a long-stemmed rose. After another moment she blew a kiss. "I'm sorry I missed you," she shouted through cupped hands. I didn't believe her. In fact, I had the feeling she had waited until I was onboard to arrive.

The ship's captain issued a final blast on the horn. Steam hissed from an opening in the hull below as fishermen on the dock untethered the mooring lines. The *England* was underway. I stiffened with the thought of the uncertainty that lay ahead. On the dock below, Taylor looked to be in a mild state of shock as well. Impulsively I grabbed the lifesaver hanging on the rail before me and tossed it overboard to him. It bounced once on the concrete before he caught it clumsily. The crowd on the dock cheered. The ship's engines were shifted into idle for a few minutes as a deckhand retrieved the lifesaver, and then the ship set out for the mainland.

I dragged all my things to the stern deck and watched as the lights of Tvoroyri receded. *The Last Waltz* played over and over in my head.

152

Chapter 11 – Gordian's Lot

The passage to Esbjerg, Denmark allowed me two-plus days to take stock. My third-class passage on the *England* did not include a stateroom or bed, but I had my choice of the rattan chaises and wool blankets on an upper deck to stern, where I wrapped myself in plaid and reviewed my finances.

The month of work for Mr. Hansen, minus the money for the jeans, passage to Denmark, the farewell party at Heine's, and miscellaneous expenses, left me with more than $120. That was less than I wanted but considerably more than I had on arrival in the Faroes. Plus, I reminded myself, I only needed to make it a few days until I could find Dalton. And though I dreaded the prospect of working for him, I was relieved to be moving on to something new. The mystique of Europe would make my job with Dalton more palatable, I told myself. I pulled the blanket up to my chin and searched for stars in the patches of sky between clouds as the England cruised toward the Jutland coast. I hadn't seen the moon or a star in a long time.

I disembarked at Esbjerg on the Jutland coast with fifty or so other passengers headed toward Copenhagen. From there the trip continued by train. With three bags and a typewriter to carry, I boarded the nearest train car and settled into the first empty compartment. A large man in a three-piece suit with a briefcase entered and sat across from me. Moments later a pale older woman in black entered and sat with her hands in her lap beside the man. Silence followed. I was updating my notes as the train pulled from the station. The man opened his briefcase on his lap and began studying paperwork until a steward came along for tickets. The large man spoke to the steward in

German. The steward turned to me and said something in German.

"I do not speak German," I told him in my best Danish. "I speak a little Danish, a little Spanish, and English."

"You are an American?" the large man asked in English.

The steward examined my ticket. "I'm sorry sir," he told me, "You must go to the third-class car. This is first class."

"No-no-no-no-no," said the man in the suit. "That will not do. He is doing no harm here."

The steward looked to the woman. She gestured for me to remain seated. "Pleeze," she said. The steward nodded and exited.

I apologized for the intrusion. "This is my first trip to Europe. I am not familiar with the train system."

"Oh-ho," said the German. "Then you are an American?"

I nodded.

"I thought so," he continued. "I am becoming quite good at spotting you Americans." He looked to the woman to let her speak. When she repositioned her hands in her lap and lowered her gaze, he turned back to me.

"Where are you from?" I told him and answered additional questions. He pointed to the typewriter. "If you are a sailor, why the scribe machine?"

"I write, too," I exaggerated. That bought a little silence. I turned my attention to the landscape clicking by outside the window but could see in the reflection that the man was studying me. A naturally curious man, I presumed, or just talkative.

The train streaked through a panorama of farms, fields, and forests to Kolding where, under a bright sun, the rail cars were temporarily transferred onto ferries to Middlefart. From there the journey resumed on rails to Nyborg, where the transfer to ferries was repeated. The German had been a boxer in his youth, he told me. Not professionally. But he admired Ernest Hemingway and Norman Mailer. We talked about boxing. My grandfather had been an amateur boxer and a boatbuilder. As the train approached Nyborg, the German's point of departure, he presented me with his business card. His name was Werner Holtz. He owned a small hotel in Hamburg, Germany. He wrote his home phone number on the backside of the card and invited me to call on him if I needed a job. And with that, he stood, kindly waved good-bye, and left to connect with the ferry to Kiel.

I thanked him for the job offer as he rushed from the compartment. His invitation had come from out of nowhere, like a good left hook.

Europe looked to be my kind of place. I had been here for just a few hours and already had a job offer.

At Korsør the rail cars were rejoined with the track for the final run to Copenhagen. With the warm sun pouring in the compartment, I dozed off with my head against the window. The train had stopped and the car was empty when I awoke at the main terminal in Copenhagen.

At the taxi stand outside the station, I sat for a moment in the gathering twilight to look around. The evening star twinkled overhead in the cool, clear evening sky. Straight ahead a large open plaza permitted a sweeping view of the central city. Set against a backdrop of red brick buildings with mullioned windows and tarnished copper spires, the streets, sidewalks, and cobblestoned plaza were a blur of human activity accompanied by the overlapping sounds of cars, bicycles, and feet in motion. After seven months of living on a small ship in a village on a

remote island, Copenhagen both thrilled and frightened me.
Thrilled because the city offered so much to explore; frightened
because my Danish was poor, I was unfamiliar with the city,
and I only had enough money to survive on cheese and crackers
for a few weeks.

Only one modern skyscraper rose above the Copenhagen
skyline. I liked the pre-modern look. In general, the downtown
buildings topped out at ten stories or so and featured red brick
trimmed with ornate stone. I lugged my bags to the plaza and
paused for coffee at a kiosk along H.C. Andersen Boulevard.
The onion-domed entrance to the Tivoli Gardens a block away
glowed like a neon Taj Mahal in the cool night air. Everywhere
I turned I saw a picture of health, prosperity, and smiling people
in motion. Copenhagen looked to be a great city.

I learned about the youth hostel from an Australian student
who asked me for directions to the train station. I pointed. He
gave me the street names at the intersection nearest the hostel. It
was located in a three-story red brick building near the zoo. I
saw no signs but found my way to a vehicle entrance into the
building by following the sound of rock. The vehicle entrance
led to an interior courtyard with large trees and trellised roses
situated around several picnic tables. Small groups of youthful
travelers sat at the tables eating, chatting, listening to music,
and drinking wine. Perfect.

I struck up a conversation with a pencil-thin fellow from
Minneapolis who politely disengaged from a bowl of stew to
talk with me. He had been a guest for the two previous nights
and related the logistics of staying at the place. He told me that
unexpected numbers had been staying because the other youth
hostel in town had closed for maintenance. If I wanted a

mattress I should check in as soon as possible. He also recommended the stew, which smelled like good advice.

A busty blonde in a Neil Young t-shirt and army fatigue jacket stood behind the Dutch door at the office. A sign on the wall behind her declared: ten kroner per night. Next to it was a poster advertising Frank Zappa at Tivoli on September 20th. Without questioning the arrangements, I plunked down the money and got a billet. She sent me to a room down the hall where mattresses and army blankets were dispensed by an American draft dodger with a deep-South accent, which persisted when he spoke Danish to his girlfriend.

Thus furnished with bedding, I found an acceptable bit of floor space to set up house. The sleeping quarters were in what resembled a long, empty hospital wing. I was too late for stew.

Four newly discharged Israeli soldiers arrived late that night. They bedded down near me because the only illumination on the wing was the flashlight I had rigged overhead for reading. The next thing I knew, I was talking with Ben, one of the Israelis. His face brightened when I mentioned that I was going to Oslo to visit a friend. He was going to Norway, too. "Perhaps we can go together," he suggested. He nodded toward the other Israelis. "My friends do not share my enthusiasm for Norway."

We agreed to discuss the Norway trip at breakfast, but Ben didn't show. I waited in the interior courtyard for a quarter hour before leaving. I needed to chase down Dalton's address, which promised to be time consuming. I reread the letter I received from Troy while in Tvoroyri. He had misplaced Dalton's address, but knew that a mutual Canadian friend named Ray Sanders would know Dalton's whereabouts. So Troy's instructions were to look for Ray Sanders at Activ Universite to get Dalton's whereabouts.

The three-story brick building that housed Activ Universite extended the length of a short city block near Oster Anlaeg Park. I entered the heavy oak door without knocking. The large vestibule included a wide stairway to the left and classrooms straight ahead and to the right. The rooms were uninhabited, but furnished with worn chairs, tables, and a portable chalkboard on wheels.

Voices from upstairs caught my attention. I left my bags in the vestibule and went up. A young Danish couple was struggling with an open door at the top. "You taking it off or putting it on?" I asked uncertainly in Danish.

"Off," said the girl in English. I helped them remove the door. Unfortunately neither of them knew Ray Sanders. They were volunteers. I would have to ask Professor Jordan, the headmaster, who was due back shortly.

My new friends were Eric and Michelle. They had been asked to remove all the doors that hung along the long corridor on the second floor. Clearly carpentry was not their chosen vocation. I volunteered to help until Professor Jordan returned.

Eric was the prototype fair-skinned, blue-eyed Dane with a strong nose, wiry body, perfectly manicured hands, and blond hair cut straight at chin level. In keeping with the reserved Nordic archetype, he was direct in manner yet reserved in speech. Michelle, on the other hand, was a natural communicator who spoke excellent, though accented, English, which probably contributed to Eric's reticence. Despite her dark Mediterranean eyes and winning looks, Michelle seemed unaware of her appeal. She was tall and slender, with long shimmering black hair that narrowed into a clasp at her neckline. Full of energy and upbeat, she wore no make-up and made no attempt to beguile. Like Eric and the majority of young Danes I had seen in Copenhagen, she wore faded blue clothing from head to foot.

With Eric and me handling the doors, Michelle departed to make tea. She returned a short while later with a box of pastry and another couple, Philip and Annika. The three of them made a huge pot of tea and when everything was ready, Eric and I joined them in the dining room, which also was being refurbished.

The dining room was large with high ceilings. I stopped in the doorway to look around. Directly to the right of the entrance was a pass-through counter to the sink area on the other side of the wall. Two steps beyond the pass-through a pair of swinging cafe doors led into the kitchen. We advanced to the center of the room and sat at a table. Several other tables and dozens of chairs were pushed and stacked haphazardly against the walls on all sides. The long wall opposite the entrance featured eight tall windows that overlooked the street.

The tea and pastry was as good as the companionship. The four of them were full of questions and goodwill. "Is that your scribe machine downstairs?" asked Philip. Michelle's face brightened.

"The professor may ask to loan it," said Michelle. "He needs one that writes English." She was softening me up. "For one or two days," she added.

"That would be okay as long as I get it back." In truth, it sounded like free storage to me. I had more bags than I could comfortably carry. A short, economical trip to Norway would be burdensome with such a load.

"Really?" said Michelle, with delight. She was doing most of the talking. I supposed she was the most fluent English speaker. "You can trust the professor," she assured me. "You really can." The others agreed enthusiastically.

Trusting Michelle, I loaned the typewriter to the professor without meeting him, then set out to explore the city. By sundown I was exhausted, famished, footsore, and anxiously hastened to the comforts of the hostel, where I ran into Ben. He too had explored all day. He too had been to the army surplus store for a backpack, and he too loved Copenhagen. We found a table in the shaded courtyard and shared a bottle of wine, Havarti cheese, French bread, and talked until dark.

Ben and I became instant friends. For one thing I was drawn to his sincerity. In him I saw a rare combination of compassion and willfulness—attributes that were not ordinarily found together. Like the other Israelis, he had just come from the front line and yearned to unwind and experience a different climate. His focus on Norway was no accident. During World War II, Norwegians had sheltered fleeing members of Ben's family from the Nazis. To demonstrate his gratitude, Ben felt obliged to go to Norway to personally thank them. He didn't have any names, addresses, or even towns; the specifics had been lost or concealed over the years, and he just planned to go there and thank Norwegians.

On Sunday morning I returned to Activ Universite to seek out Ray Sanders. The professor had not been around and no one knew of Ray Sanders or any Canadians. The way things looked, it might be a few days before I learned Dalton's address.

Rather than wait, I called Captain Hofman at his sisters' house. Dalton, he informed me, was refitting two ships at the shipyard in Korsør. The skipper had visited him a few days earlier. He assured me that there was a year of work in Korsør and that Dalton was looking forward to my arrival. I had passed through Korsør en route to Copenhagen, he reminded me.

As for the rest of the crew, Monty had caught a freighter bound for New York out of Rotterdam, Billy had flown back, and Chris had slipped away shortly after arriving in Copenhagen. The skipper was slated to return to the states in a few days. But first he had one more local financing avenue to explore for the *Marite*. "As you can see, I am still trying to get it all together." His use of the slang expression stood out like a banjo solo in a Bach concerto. He probably had picked up the expression from a summer with his son.

The good news on the job front liberated me. I no longer needed to find Ray Sanders, which had been a dead end. I figured I could travel frugally for several days without compromising my plans. That was enough time to visit Henni in Oslo and perhaps go as far as Bergen. She had told me about Bergen while in San Francisco, and the Hansens had added a ringing endorsement.

The Danes like to say that the weather in Denmark is unpredictable for a fortnight before and after the full moon. To me it seemed a waste of a perfectly good expression, for I had seen nothing but beautiful late-summer days and pleasantly cool nights. Ben and I set out for Norway on just such a day. We took the train north out of Copenhagen through tree-lined fields and fleeting glimpses of townscapes embroidered with flower gardens, statuary, and Nordic architecture.

On the ferry across Oresund Strait to Halsingborg, Sweden, I took a long look to stern at Elsinore Castle, the setting of Shakespeare's *Hamlet*. Like scores of others onboard, I seized the opportunity to purchase tax-free tobacco on the three-mile, duty-free voyage between nations. Once in Halsingborg, the train route to Norway was a straight shot north over rolling hills along the coast of Sweden. With a few hours and a repetitious view, Ben and I had plenty of time to talk and even nap.

In Ben I found a kindred spirit. Beneath the handsome olive-skinned face and curly dark hair was a keen mind and a pilgrim. Our discussions, though generally casual to start with, usually evolved into a spiritual debate or a search for meaning. By the time we reached the Norwegian border we had exchanged personal histories and felt like old friends. Ben was going to return to Israel and live on a kibbutz. I was going to see the world and write about it. I told him about the *Marite* and the Faroes; he told me about the hardships and heartbreak of the centuries-old Arab-Jewish conflict.

Evening arrived as we reached Oslo in a light rain. Incredibly, Henni answered the phone on the third ring. She had given me the telephone number two years earlier while a student in San Francisco. "Henni and I lived in the same building," I explained to Ben as we took the commuter train to Kringsjaby, near the university. "You'll like her."

Henni was waiting right where she said she'd be and beamed that bright Norwegian smile all the way back to her apartment. She had just returned from the Canary Islands, where her fiancé lived, which explained the tan. She was more fit than before. We settled into the kitchen where we soon were joined by friends with a huge jug of homemade wine. By midnight, the wine was nearly gone and we had told all of our San Francisco stories. For old time's sake, Henni put Leonard Cohen on the phonograph and we linked arms over shoulders and sang "So Long, Marianne" in perfect drunken harmony.

The party thinned out quickly after midnight. Henni and I ended up on the open balcony for some fresh air. I asked if she had ever read *Dharma Bums*, the Jack Kerouac book. Henni's academic specialty was American literature. She had read Kerouac's *On the Road*, she told me, but no others. "Among scholars he is considered a typist, not a writer," she told me. Undaunted, I told her about *Dharma Bums* and asked if there was an eastern meditation center in Oslo. "The closest one is Activ Universite in Copenhagen."

Her reply knocked me backward a step. Was this another coincidence, or merely a case of leftover paranoia from the dreams-come-true days? Henni returned to her guests. I leaned on the damp handrail and stared blankly at a glistening sphere of light seemingly suspended just twenty yards away. It was a streetlight globe shrouded in mist in the courtyard between buildings, not an apparition. I filled my lungs with the damp, pine-scented air and tried to relax.

Ben appeared with my wine glass. "Why so sad?" he asked.

I reflected on the complicated chain of events that had led me to Activ Universite. "It's a long story," I told him, "and a story that is hard for others to understand." He gestured inquiringly with hands near his ears. I relented. "I guess the easy way to explain it is that Henni told me to go to Activ Universite in Copenhagen, and she is the second person in two days to send me there."

"And this makes you sad?"

"If it was an isolated coincidence it wouldn't bother me. But I have had more than my share of coincidences in the last few months. I'm beginning to feel like a coincidence machine." I didn't know if I was getting through, I was talking fast and

English was a second language for him, but I continued. Mostly I wanted to get it off my chest. I told him about the dreams.

"This is going to sound strange," I concluded, "but I feel like I'm being steered toward something. But I don't know what."

The music from the party suddenly got louder as the door to Henni's apartment opened. We both looked. A couple exited and closed the door. They walked toward the stairs at the other end of the balcony.

"Fate," said Ben. "Is not that your word for it?" I nodded. His English vocabulary was pretty impressive. I had been looking over the rail but turned my gaze to Ben, half-expecting him to laugh off the discussion. Instead, he looked concerned. Perhaps overly so, I thought.

His concern, it occurred to me, may have been calculated to ascertain a traveling companion for a while longer. He had been lobbying for it. Or was it really an honest expression of compassion and interest. I thought it over as he explained kismet, the Middle Eastern notion of fate.

Unaware of my wandering thoughts, Ben continued his explanation. I studied him. He was confident, even-tempered, comfortable with himself. Unlike me, life held no ambiguities for Ben, no perceivable paroxysms of self-doubt, no idealistic visions, no surplus of unanswered questions. "Of course," he concluded, "the whole business of fate requires an all-powerful higher being—a God." He read my face for a moment and added, "I think you are agnostic. Am I right?"

I nodded.

Ben told me about dreams he had had while a soldier assigned to defend the Golan Heights. They were strange dreams that had occurred under stressful conditions. My dreams had been similar to his, he contended. I disagreed. He dreamed and remembered his dreams virtually every night, while I had remembered only five dreams total in my adult life, and four of them had occurred within the last eight months. Beyond that, he had not experienced his dreams in real life months later. In the end, his explanation for both our dreams centered on a set of Iron Age rules that had been dictated from on high. But we had drunk too much wine, which made for a messy discussion. Still, Ben smiled triumphantly. "It cannot happen without God," he stated flatly. He smiled again and then held up his glass of wine in the night air. "Here's to things that cannot be."

Half of the next day was lost to a hangover. Henni and a friend took Ben to the Viking museum after lunch. My plan for the day was to visit the laundromat downstairs. I approached it cautiously, like a foot soldier on reconnaissance, and was relieved to find it empty and much too small to fit into the Laundromat Dream scenario. Henni's reference to Activ Universite had sharpened a suppressed anxiety in me.

The next morning, Henni unfolded her map of Norway on the table over the breakfast dishes. Ben was already packed and ready to hitchhike. Henni's plan was to help him organize his visit. Within two minutes of opening the map, Ben had settled on Hammerfest at the opposite end of Norway as his destination. It is the largest city above the Arctic Circle, Henni pointed out, and he would need special clothing to survive there. To me, it made sense that somebody who had been forced to stand guard in a uniform in the desert for four years would yearn to visit a permanently frozen city in insulated garments. However, Henni wanted Ben to understand what lay before him. "Hammerfest is the same distance from Oslo as Rome," she told him, "and more than half of the journey will be on icy roads. Whole days will go by without seeing a car. Everything is expensive." To Ben, who increasingly seemed willful to a fault, her concerns seemed like perfect reasons to go. At his request, Henni drove him to a good spot on the main northbound highway, where we said our good-byes. Ben and I had known from the beginning that our paths would diverge after Oslo. He had not recognized, however, that he would be in a race to Hammerfest with Old Man Winter.

I headed for Copenhagen early the next morning with a sandwich and apple Henni had packed for me. To save money, my plan was to hitchhike as far as Halsingborg then take the ferry and train to Copenhagen. She took me to the appropriate highway on the outskirts of town. I was exhausted when my journey ended at the Copenhagen train station the following afternoon. I had only one thing on my mind: get to the hostel and sleep. After that I planned to go to Activ Universite for my typewriter, inquire about meditation instructions, then head for the shipyard in Korsør and rendezvous with Dalton. So when the train stopped in the main terminal in Copenhagen, I shot across the plaza and down Vester Voldgade toward the hostel. That is where I ran into Benny.

"Wow! Don!" said Benny with a startled expression.

"Wow!" I said, equally surprised. Benny and I had never been more than casual friends. I had last seen him onboard the *Balclutha* at the going-away party. "What are you doing here?" I asked.

"I've just come from visiting the skipper at his sister's house," he said. "He's leaving for San Francisco tomorrow." Benny was tall and lean and had a habit of moving his upper body in herky-jerky motions for emphasis as he spoke. His long blond hair was longer but still down his back in a ponytail. His eyelashes were several shades darker than his hair. "What are you doing?"

"I just got back from Oslo. Visiting a friend." I dropped my bags and noticed he had no baggage. "So what are you doing? Come over to work onboard the *Marite?*"

He nodded. "I'm down in Korsør. Remember Dalton Ames? The guy who helped us strike the yard on the *Balclutha?*" His words trailed off as I nodded. "I'm working with him."

"What a coincidence," I said, "because that's where I'm headed."

"The skipper said he sent you there. I was wondering what happened." There was a brief silence. "The train leaves in ten or twelve minutes." He looked at his watch. "Make that fourteen." He reached for my bedroll. "I'll help you with your stuff."

"Actually, I have an errand to run first. I was going to spend the night at the hostel then head for Korsør tomorrow."

"The hostel has closed for the season. I found out the hard way." He grinned but didn't explain. "You'll have to go to Activ Universite. That's where I spent the night last night."

"At Activ Universite?" I asked incredulously.

"Yeah. It's up that way near Dag Hammarskjöld Boulevard." He laughed and pointed over his shoulder. "Don't you love all these weird names?" He smiled again.

"You spent the night at Activ Universite?"

"Yeah," he chirped, not recognizing my discomfort.

"It's not really a university. It's one of those centers that teach yoga, astrology, and stuff." He looked at his watch again. "I gotta go. I don't want to miss my train or I'll have to kill a couple of hours until the next one."

"What about the work situation?"

"Oh, yeah, well, we're refitting a couple of ships. A hundred-forty-footer with a steel hull and an eighty-four-foot Baltic trader. It's a beauty."

"So, is there work for me?"

"Oh, sure. Tons of it." He knew that would be a relief to hear. "Things are pretty slow right now, but there's probably a year of work there." He looked at his watch again and began to back away.

"How do I get there?"

He explained and then raised a hand. "Really, man, I gotta go." With that he turned and trotted away, his long ponytail swaying behind him as he weaved through the pedestrians along the sidewalk.

I sat on my bags to contemplate this latest development. Meeting Benny on the street in Copenhagen, half a world away from San Francisco, was only a moderate surprise given his connection with Captain Hofman and the *Marite*. But having him direct me to Activ Universite was an infinitely improbable event. It seemed to be one more coincidence in a recurring string of them. And again, as with the dreams-come-true, it was the time factor that baffled me most. If I had detoured for a water fountain in the train station or even boarded on a different car, I would have missed him. Likewise, if Benny had been detained at one extra red light or stopped to window-shop while killing time before his train, in all likelihood we would have missed each other. In my mind our meeting was not so much a single strange coincidence at work as it was dozens of little ones, and all of them a continent away from home. And what was I to think of the fact that three different people in three different countries had directed me to go to Activ Universite, each for a different reason, while I had planned to go there myself for yet two more reasons—to ask about mantras and to get the typewriter?

I was feeling bombarded by coincidence again. I gathered my bags and headed for Activ Universite at a cautious pace. My thoughts raced there and back several times before I actually arrived.

A pair of travelers stood at the entrance, Canadians, gauging from the maple leaf patches on their backpacks. "It's not open yet," said one to me. "They said to come back after four."

I started to ask if one of them was Ray Sanders, but the sound of voices arrived behind the front door, then it opened suddenly. A muscular young man with short cropped hair and a large neck wreathed with a dozen strands of red yarn pointed to a broken pane of glass on the door. As he spoke Michelle and Eric stepped from behind the door to look.

"Oh! Hello!" said Michelle. Her greeting prompted a pause. She turned to the muscular young man with the red yarn and nodded in my direction. "Kristofer, this is the American who left the scribe machine." He smiled warmly and extended a hand.

"I hobe you have not come for de scribe machine," he said in thickly accented English. "I vas hobing to use it some longer."

"Actually, I did," I said, ". . . come for the typewriter."

Silence. I guessed he was hoping I would extend the loan time. When nobody moved to break the silence, I said, "I was told by a friend that travelers can spend the night here." I was relieved to see Eric and Michelle behind him agreeing.

"Certainly you may," said Kristofer. He bent forward and looked at the two Canadians departing behind me. "And since you are friend of Activ Universite you may come in." I piled my stuff in a corner and turned back to Kristofer's contented smile. "How much longer will you need the typewriter, the scribe machine? Can you finish tonight?"

I knew the answer was "no" from the silent calculation instead of a reply. "I need one more veek, I tink." When I didn't stiffen he added, "I am in middle of some-ting wery important."

I hesitated. "It means I would have to come back to Copenhagen in a week."

"Or you may stay here," said Kristofer. He smiled and looked over to Michelle and Eric. "They say you are good with tools." He looked to them then back to me. He must need it badly to go to such lengths, I realized.

"Vee have a special guest coming in December and vee must have everything ready by then," explained Michelle.

"Do you know how to mend broken vindows?" asked Kristofer gamely. He pointed to the fan-shaped configuration of panes at the top of the door. One of the panes was broken.

"If you have a glass cutter I can fix it in about half an hour," I said, trying not to sound smug.

"Vee have tool. Vee have glass," said Kristofer in a rising tone. He smiled and raised an open arm to me, "and now vee have the master." The three of them enjoyed a smile over the comment and then showed me upstairs into one of the rooms where Eric and I had removed a door last week. Four bunk bed sets had been moved into the room.

Replacing the broken glass took less than an hour. After that I scraped away paint that had been slopped onto the other panes. The door looked much better. Sensing my willingness to help, Eric directed me to other broken panes and said my meals and lodging would be free in exchange for the work I had done. He also invited me to stay at Activ Universite as long as I wanted. It was the closest to a conversation I had had with Eric, and it was in Danish.

Kristofer returned unexpectedly with the typewriter that evening as Michelle, Eric, and I feasted on red cabbage and rice in the dining room. "It sounds like you must need it," said Kristofer. He set it beside my chair. "Copenhagen is a beeg city. I can find one some-vhere."

"No, it sounds like you need it more than I do right now," I said candidly. "I just don't want to lose track of it." I handed it back to Kristofer.

He beamed. "I vil take wery good care," said Kristofer. He patted me on the shoulder thankfully. "Oh, and by the vay, you did wery good job on the door. Thank you." He headed for the door but turned back and said something to Eric and Michelle in rapid-fire Danish.

"Yah-yah," answered Eric. *"Det godt."*

There was silence as we returned to our meal. After a couple of bites Michelle invited me to stay and help them. "Vee have much to do and so little time." I explained my situation but told them I would probably spend some weekends in Copenhagen.

"Then you must come back in December to see the Karmapa," said Eric in an insistent voice.

"Who is the Karmapa?"

"The Karmapa is a wery powerful Tibetan guru," said Michelle looking deeply into my eyes. "Promise you vil come."

A Tibetan guru. I swallowed. There it was! *The* connection. A guru was visiting Activ Universite. My thoughts swirled with

the stream of events stemming from the deck of the *Balclutha*
through the tormenting dreams to this moment, then distilled
into a vision of me sitting cross-legged in front of a guru. My
mind soared with the thought. I recalled the wildly mystical
events documented in *Be Here Now*, the Ram Dass book
regarding his first encounter with a guru. "When the student is
ready the teacher arrives," had been one of the messages in the
book. There will be answers, I told myself. *This* was an answer.

Energized by the meal and news, I engaged Michelle and
Eric in a long conversation about the Karmapa. I wanted to
know everything.

As they explained it, Kristofer, who had once been an
Olympic boxer, had learned of the Karmapa while in India and
had roamed the region for weeks until he had found him at the
foot of the Himalayas in Sikkim. After studying for many
months at the feet of the master he returned to Copenhagen
where he had collaborated with Professor Jordan to establish a
Tibetan Buddhism center at Activ Universite. Since then, the
center had hosted the Dalai Lama and Kalu Rinpoche, both
highly esteemed Tibetan gurus, and had initiated Tibetan
language studies through Copenhagen University.

I had participated in the Transcendental Meditation scene a
few years earlier and had a few stories to share, and had
enjoyed the exotic tales in Alexandra David-Neal's *Magic and
Mystery in Tibet*. Despite our exhaustion, we stayed up past
midnight talking. Before they left for the night I promised I
would help ready the place for the Karmapa whenever I could
break away. And I promised to return in early December. It was
only nine weeks away.

Chapter 12 – The Knot

The shipyard in Korsør was easy to find. Aside from the shipyard and "slips" where rail cars were transferred to and from ferries, there was little else to keep the town on the map. I found Dalton and Benny living on a mothballed passenger ferry moored near the shipyard entrance. Although decommissioned, the ferry looked to be in good shape judging from the paint—solid white with red trim—and the absence of any visible rust or repairs in progress.

I crossed the gangway onto the ferry then searched until I heard voices in what turned out to be the galley. Dalton saw me as I strode up. I felt relieved, as if I had reached a safe haven. True to form, Dalton shook his head piteously and said, "Alas, the trail of tears continues from the Good Ship Lollipop." The remark caught me off guard. I looked to Benny for a clue but got none.

"What? Did the *Marite* crew drop in for a visit?" I said lamely.

Dalton returned to a steaming pot on a hotplate.

"Just Captain Hofman," inserted Benny cautiously. He held up his arms like a boxer anticipating a flurry of punches.

Dalton spun around with the ladle still in hand. "You schoolboys don't know what a captain is," he declared. "Hofman is more like a choirboy than a captain." He fixed his dark eyes on Benny, then me.

There didn't seem any point in arguing, especially since I had yet to secure a job. "What's the deal? Did he run off with somebody's girlfriend or something?" I asked.

"Ha . . . Ha . . . Ha," said Dalton sarcastically. "The man is history . . . and has been for a long time." He stood with his feet spread wide and hands on his hips, a ladle in his right hand. He wore the same black leather jacket that he had worn on the *Balclutha* and his fiery mane and beard appeared unchanged over the months. I wanted to laugh about the ladle but held back.

"How's that spaghetti coming?" asked Benny. He looked at his watch. "Those noodles only need to boil for five minutes."

"Eight," answered Dalton. "And it's pasta, not noodles, dip." He waved his hands in the air in a comical Italian gesture. That was my first clue that the verbal exchange between them was just macho posturing. Everything was normal. The realization was accompanied with a sinking feeling. Here we go again.

The argument seemed over. Dalton lifted some pasta and examined how it drooped over the edge of the ladle. "So, Dalton," I said firmly. "I'm looking for work. You need a hand here?"

"Benny told me yesterday that he hired you already," he shot back.

Benny shook his head in frustration and shrugged. "Baloney," he countered.

"Isn't that what you told me? You said you told him to come down because there was plenty of work. Isn't it?" When he got no answer he turned off the hotplate with a snap of the wrist then looked to Benny. "Isn't that what you said?" He put the lid on the pot and carried it to the sink.

I intervened. "He said he thought there might be enough work for me to get on," I said. "If not, I can go back to Copenhagen. I have a room and board offer there and a job offer in Hamburg."

Dalton hovered silently over the sink. With his back to us it was impossible to read his face, but I think the notion that I might have an option caught him off guard. Using the lid as a strainer, he poured the water from the pasta into the sink. It drained directly into a five-gallon bucket positioned under the sink. He took the pot back to the stove. "Soup's on," he called. He turned to me with a gleaming smile and his charming voice. "Help yourself, Don."

I followed Dalton and Benny to the dish rack beside the sink then over to the hotplate for the pasta. There wasn't much left but I wasn't particularly comfortable about eating with them yet. I was the last to the table. I sat by Benny. Dalton pointed at my plate with his fork. "If we'd known you were coming we'd have made more." His voice was steeped in sarcasm. He smiled that broad muscular smile then stuffed a forkful of spaghetti into his mouth. "M-m-m-m-m," he said with exaggerated pleasure.

I put a forkful in my mouth and violently ejected it. My taste buds were nearly incinerated. Dalton had been waiting for my reaction, I realized, and he exploded into laughter.

"Too spicy?" questioned Dalton with emphasis on the last syllable. He sucked air through his teeth with a squeak. "That's the way we like it, right, Benny?"

"I forgot or I would have warned you," said Benny defiantly. "The same thing happened to me." Dalton laughed with exaggerated pleasure.

I went to the sink for water. "It's in the jug," said Benny, pointing to a five-gallon plastic jug on the counter. The improvised water supply and catch bucket under the sink reminded me of the coarse lifestyle I was re-entering.

After rinsing my taste buds with a glass of water I picked up the bottle of hot sauce from the counter beside the hotplate. "En Djaevel's Hand," it was called. The label included a picture of a caped devil that, given a year's growth of hair, a Charles Atlas body-building course, and a black jacket, would have looked just like Dalton when he smiled. "He even puts that stuff on ice cream," said Benny with undisguised scorn.

Dalton's response was a loud, forced belch.

After lunch, Dalton instructed Benny to go back to work. "Our new man can catch the dishes."

That was how I learned I could stay. When I didn't balk, Dalton added, "Then I'll show him around." As soon as Benny had left Dalton turned friendlier. "Glad to have you onboard," he told me. "If you turn out to be half as good as what I saw in San Francisco I may just run Benny off."

The backhanded compliment helped drain some of the tension from the air, but left me wondering what he would say about me when alone with Benny. It seemed an unnecessarily complicated way to live.

He had me drop my bags in the cavernous main passenger bay then took me over to meet the owner of the Veronica, a three-masted, 140-foot steel "monstrosity," he called it, moored just a hundred yards away. "This guy thinks he's God's gift to sailing ships and women," he warned me, "but he doesn't know shit from Shinola about either. If you don't believe me just look at the ship and the woman he ended up with." He laughed loudly at his comment.

Dalton was a fast walker. I hustled to keep up with him. "His main claim to fame," he told me, "is that he used to be a photographer or lecturer or something for *National Geographic*. He also was cook onboard *Yankee Gale* when Captain

Hightower was at the helm." We rounded a corner along the dock and approached the *Veronica* from astern. "His name is Arvin Arkady, if you can believe that shit, but everybody calls him Ike. His wife, who looks like the Pillsbury Doughgirl, is Mandy."

We weaved among unopened crates and spools of cable wire cluttering the dock beside the ship. "Oh, and she's pregnant," he added. We stopped at the gangway. Given the steel deckhouse and cargo handling masts fore and aft, the *Veronica* looked more like a small freighter than a sailing ship. A tangle of hoses and electrical lines ran up over her gunwales like life-support systems to a patient in an intensive care unit. Splotches of red lead paint intermingled with the ship's aged black and white colors. The long low deckhouse had recently received an add-on aft, which gave the entire stern section an over-weighted look. "Monstrosity" had been a good description.

I followed Dalton up the gangway to the quarterdeck. "Watch this," he said. He stamped twice then slowly ambled to stern along the weather deck. Three steps later an overfed man in soiled overalls emerged from the deckhouse in a swagger. His facial features had a horizontal quality that falsely implied an Asian lineage. With his black ski cap rolled up and a meaty face with pulsing muscles at his temples as he chewed, he reminded me of Jack Nicholson with a two-day beard. His eyes quickly traveled up and down my body and summed me up. "I should have known it was you," he said to Dalton with a controlled voice. He reached out to shake Dalton's hand and then chucked him on the shoulder with a friendly left cross. The crackling sound of nearby welding interrupted the proceedings momentarily. Dalton sniffed quizzically at the cloud of burnt smoke that drifted by and then scowled humorously at Ike. "What's Mandy cooking back there anyway?"

"We all laughed. But I could see Ike already had a rejoinder. "I told you that I eat nails for lunch," said Ike. We laughed a little more. He looked at me with honest, warm eyes and put out a hand. Dalton introduced us. I shook a stubby but firm hand.

"Don and I worked together in San Francisco. He's a good man."

Ike considered that for a moment then said, "Welcome aboard," with a nod.

"Thanks," I said, but his hands were in motion already. He was describing what the *Veronica* would look like once finished. His eyes roamed the sky as he spoke. He had prowled the ports of Europe to find her, he romanticized, and had then sought out the "rigging master par excellence" to outfit her. He plopped a paternal hand on Dalton's shoulder as we meandered around the cluttered deck, never breaking stride in his presentation. "I found the *Veronica* in Porto, Portugal, the birthplace of Henry the Navigator," he explained. Then he smiled wryly to mark a change of tone, "And do you know where I found the rigging master par excellence?" he asked, leaning closer as if posing with Dalton for the cover of *Time*. "In one of the sleaziest bars in Hamburg!" He rocked with laughter and whacked Dalton on the shoulder. "Those were the best two hours I've spent in recent history," he pronounced.

"What about the night you and Mandy conceived?" teased Dalton.

"Oh," said Ike, dismissing it with a brush of his hand, "that took a lot longer than two hours."

Another round of routine laughter gave me the feeling that those precise words had been deployed before. "Ike, you're one helluva man," said Dalton.

Ike pointed a friendly finger at me. "You haven't met Mandy yet," he reminded himself. He turned to stern and shouted "Mandy" then urged me in the opposite direction. "I suppose Dalton already told you about the hydroponic garden," said Ike as we stopped at the main hatch forward of the deckhouse. "It's an idea whose time has come."

"Ike is going to install a hanging garden under skylights that'll be here," said Dalton, pointing. "That way they'll always have vegetables," he added, with just enough disapproval for detection.

"Tomatoes, primarily," said Ike. He looked at me squarely. "Did you know that the tomato plant has not reached much of the South Pacific?"

"I'll be damned."

"Speaking of tomatoes," said Dalton. He took half a step backward to let Mandy enter the group. Ike swept between Dalton and me and formally presented his "bride" with his hands supporting her poised right arm as if in a regal procession. She was both chubby and pregnant but radiated intelligence and confidence like a high school valedictorian. She seemed on the verge of a blush at all times but managed to mask it with a beguiling girlish smile. "Hi there," she chirped. She was the picture of contentment in her white apron lightly dusted with flour and bits of dough. She cornered Ike. "Okay big boy. Where did you put that recipe?" It was like "Ozzie and Harriet Go to Sea," I told myself. Ike shook his head ironically like a man who has had his cover blown, then surreptitiously pulled the recipe card out of his back pocket and passed it to her with contrived stealth. Ike and Mandy Arkady. They seemed the happy couple. Overflowing with love, warmth, tenderness, and, most of all, pretentiousness.

After a whirlwind tour of the *Veronica,* Dalton steered me toward the gangway. "About fifteen minutes is all I can take of those two," he said out of the side of his mouth as we headed down the gangway. He looked back to make sure they hadn't heard.

"Are they always that . . ?" I paused in search of the right adjective.

"Fluffy," said Dalton derisively. "And need I say yes? But in this business, Don, you don't turn down work if the money is right. Jobs are too few and far between."

The *Apollodora* was at the opposite end of the shipyard, tucked away in a corner. Of the two vessels the *Apollodora* was the more promising sailing ship. A wooden ship from stem to stern, it was clear she had been somebody's proud possession. "The *Veronica* is going to be a monstrosity by the time Ike is through with it. But this one will be a crown jewel," said Dalton. As he told it, a Polish family had worked the Baltic trade routes for the last thirty years with the *Apollodora.* The new owner, a meticulous Dutchman with aspirations to make the *Apollodora* the official training vessel of the Royal Dutch Navy, was a purist who insisted the refitting be of the best modern materials and maritime standards, yet be historically authentic. "That one will put a little money into my bank account," he said, pointing to the *Veronica,* "but this one will add stock to my reputation. It will also generate more jobs in the end." He paused purposefully and then added, "And who knows, maybe you and I will be partners by then." He looked at me solemnly and then smiled amicably.

More than ever, I was suspicious of his motives, but I smiled agreeably, then followed him aft to the helm where we sat in the tiny wheelhouse and discussed the terms of my employment. It was pretty straightforward: an hourly wage, keep track of my own hours, and keep separate tallies for the two ships. And while the money wasn't a living wage, Dalton pointed out that lodging on the ferry was free, there were no taxes, and I could come and go as I pleased. "And one more thing," he emphasized with a smile stretched tightly across his face, "it's the only game in town."

I gave him my best go-to-hell smile but secretly enjoyed the feel of the ship swaying under my feet. Dalton slapped my back and pulled me hard against his ribcage. "You're too nice a guy to hold a grudge, Don." But he dangled my name in the air for a moment too long. That, combined with the visage of red hair and the gold teeth trapped in that huge smile made me feel a little like I had just sold my soul—and cheap.

There was another letdown when I got back to the ferry to settle in. The ferry had only two small staterooms, which were already taken. That meant the only place for me to lodge was in the main passenger bay. I looked it over. It was an open bay about half the size of a basketball court and with less ambience. There were red cushioned benches against the sidewalls that ran the full length of the compartment fore and aft. I tried the light switch. It controlled six rows of neon fixtures overhead. With the switch on it was high noon on a cloudless day. With the lights off it was natural light from sixteen portholes. I switched the lights off and toted my gear all the way forward to port near Benny's stateroom. I stretched my sleeping bag over a section of red Naugahyde cushions, ousted the life jackets from under a nearby section of bench, and stowed my gear.

182

I paused on the bench seat to take stock of my new home. It was quiet in the huge compartment. Sitting in the corner at one end, I felt small and insignificant as if viewing myself through the wrong end of a telescope. I had experienced the same reverse perspective while overlooking the vast Atlantic Ocean from the towering Faroese cliffs, but there I had felt inspired, in awe. Here I felt exploited and vulnerable.

Come nightfall, Dalton invited me to join him and Bruce for a beer at a local pub. Bruce was an American who worked with us but who lived with a local girl. With his long flowing hair, moustache, and goatee—all curled at the ends—he resembled Wild Bill Cody in a black leather captain's cap. I declined the invitation. No presentable clothes. Plus, I was down to my last few dollars. "Just got here on the bones of your ass, eh?" said Dalton with malice.

"We all did," Bruce told me as they left.

With his door open and a Yes tape playing with the volume up, Benny filled me in on Bruce. "He's got a girlfriend named Marta." He licked his lips as he described her.

"Is he a merchant marine?" I asked.

"No." He laughed. "He worked at a T-shirt shop in Berkeley." Benny didn't seem interested in the subject. He sang along with the music in-between my questions, bouncing in and out of his room to adjust the volume as different songs came and went. "These guys are so-o-o-o good," he regaled when the first side finished.

A guitar and sheet music lay on his bunk. "I didn't know you played," I remarked. He nodded and reversed the tape.

Halfway through the second side he removed the cushion from the narrow bench in his room, lifted the hinged cover and gingerly pulled out a green canvas tote bag. His movements were slow and cautious, like a priest handling sacred objects. From the bag he produced a shoebox and then carefully removed four stuffed mice and a stuffed rat. Each was mounted on a small square of cardboard and labeled. He spread them on his bunk. "Not so long ago I would have given my eye teeth for this one." He held up the rat at eye level. It was brownish grey and about sixteen inches long, including the tail. The label read *Rattus Norvegicus.* It was ugly and menacing. Two teeth leaned out from the bottom of its pointed snout like yellowed tombstones. Cotton stuffing protruded from the empty eye sockets. "That's the one responsible for spreading the plague," he said. He admired it briefly then returned it and the others to the shoebox. "It hasn't been all work and no play," he stated with a smile.

The tape ran out as Benny stowed the shoebox. The display of rodents had reminded me of why our friendship had never evolved. A zoology student at the university, Benny was smart and friendly and generally likeable, but time spent with him was always as bland as a bright and shiny third coat of beige paint.

"Do you think you might stick around for a while?" he asked. The persistent squeak of the ship's bumpers rubbing against the dock was the only sound, and his question seemed to hang there in the silence, simple but full of implications. It acknowledged the desperation of being here in the first place, and the Herculean tolerance needed to put up with it day-in and day-out.

He must have taken it for a snub when I didn't answer immediately because he started whistling the Italian Swiss Colony Wine TV jingle over and over. I was struck by the strangeness of it and also reminded of the goofy little be-bop ditties that Popeye used to sing in the cartoons. It made me think about his question all the more. There had been a beseeching quality to it, and after a moment I realized how utterly alone he must feel. In every instance he was the odd man out. Dalton treated him like a whipping boy, and Bruce probably ignored him. Benny didn't do himself any favors by correcting their grammar and referencing things he had learned at the university. A formal education was a distant ambition in this crowd. So, besides the desperation of the situation itself, Benny was desperate for a friend. He knew I would be much more civilized with him than Dalton.

"Sure," I answered at last. In him I saw a mirror image of my own longing for companionship. As much as I hated to admit it, Benny and I weren't that different. I had more experience at it, that's all.

For work, Benny and I spent our days on the *Veronica*, stripping rust from the hold with non-sparking brass hammers, scraping tools, and facemasks. We chipped and scraped all day at a thick layer of rust that coated the hold up to eye level. Our hands were a patchwork of broken blisters, scuffed knuckles, and cracked fingertips. Rolling out a string of lights every morning and rolling them up at night made us feel like miners working a seam of coal, and at day's end our clothes and bodies were layered with a thick coat of dust, including a circle of mud-like mascara around the edges of our eyes.

Refurbishing the hold was an ugly job, but, reconciled to it, Benny and I pushed hard to complete it in a couple of weeks. Once finished, we added up our time and Benny took it over to Ike to get paid. An hour passed before he returned with the checks. Ike had inspected the hold and was pleased with the work but felt he needed to "review our hours" before paying us in full.

I looked at my check. He had withheld $50. That was two days work at a slave's wage. "What does 'review our hours' mean?" I asked.

"Let's make sure the checks clear before we ask," Benny suggested. We had been penniless for a week. As we passed the grocery story on the way to the bank we decided to buy food rather than confront Ike. Once again, a new pair of jeans would have to wait.

After weeks of washing my clothes in the shipyard shower, I summoned the courage to do laundry with Benny at the local laundromat, located in the basement of a building in the old district. I scouted it and decided it was safe. I put on my worn-out Levis in the bathroom and tossed my good ones in the washer. We had the place to ourselves, except for an old woman who stopped in to read notices on the bulletin board.

Benny left on an errand. I ended up staring out the window and reflecting. Dalton had been out of town for almost a week. The relaxed atmosphere that prevailed onboard the ferry in his absence underscored the amount of tension he deliberately injected into our world. The more I thought about it, the more I despised him for it. In fact, I was ready to leave. Dalton was a bully who, like many bullies, operated in the space created by other people's civility. The never-ending verbal one-upmanship that was supposed to pass for wit, intelligence, machismo, or whatever also rubbed me the wrong way. I saw it as aggression and nothing else. But, as Dalton had pointed out, this was the only game in town. I could stay here and earn a little money or go to Copenhagen and work for room and board.

The lifestyle, people, and work at Activ Universite would undoubtedly provide a healthier environment, but I had to face the reality that it took money to live and the money in my pocket would quickly disappear if I did not earn more along the way. With the accompaniment of sloshing suds and tumbling dryers at my back, I set my sights on meeting the Tibetan guru in December and vowed to see as much of Europe as possible.

Dalton returned without fanfare. On Friday night, he invited Benny and me to join him for a beer after work. "I've got a couple of split-tails for you to meet," he told us.

He took us to an upstairs bar downtown. We were into a third beer before Della and Rhoda arrived. They paused at the entrance until they saw Dalton's huge frame stand in the semi-darkness, then walked toward us. Heads turned as they passed. Benny and I stood too. "Only an hour late," said Benny. He held his watch out for my confirmation, but my eyes were on the two girls coming our way. They both were adorned with blonde hair to the waist, glow-in-the-dark smiles, fine bodies even from a distance, and seemed happy to be joining us.

Dalton waved them over eagerly. "Beautiful women are never late," he informed Benny out of the side of his mouth. "The sooner you learn that the sooner you'll find one." He pulled chairs out for the girls, then sent Benny for beer.

"Good of you ladies to grace our table," said Dalton. Benny returned with the beer and Dalton introduced us. But it was clear beforehand that Rhoda, a real sizzler in boots, tight jeans, and a Day-Glo top with rhinestones, was with Dalton. Della, a quieter, unadorned beauty, had, in all probability, come along to see what Americans did for fun on a Friday night. "It's amazing what a couple of beautiful women can do for a dreary table, right boys?" said Dalton imperiously.

"Like moonlight in a cave," I quipped.

"Vee got stuck in frondt of de house," laughed Della. She spoke good English with an accent. "De tires ver spinning in mud." She laughed nervously and spun her fingers to demonstrate.

"Papa had to pull us free with de tractor," said Rhoda.

"It rains so much in Denmark, don't you think?" asked Della.

"We only got a dab," said Benny, sounding like somebody's grandmother. It was the alcohol. He was not accustomed to three beers in one night. As if aware of the impression he had made, he tried to repair the damage. "But the rain in Spain falls mainly in the plain." He laughed feebly.

Dalton ran a fingertip around the rim of his beer glass. "You'll have to excuse Benny," he said. "He got a letter from his mom last week and his feet haven't touched the ground since."

The girls frowned as they sipped their beer. Rhoda said "Don't be so mean" to Dalton in a gently scolding voice. Dalton rubbed her back.

There was silence. Everybody took a drink.

"This is like 'Silence is Golden,'" tried Benny. "You know, the song." He hummed a few bars and swung his finger like a conductor. It didn't amuse anybody. He looked down into his unused glass. "Guess I better go while I can still walk," he announced with downcast eyes, and then left.

We had another beer, and then the girls drove us back to the ferry, the four of us squeezed into the cab of their father's farm truck. Dalton and Rhoda went onboard with erotic sparks flicking between them. Della wanted me to show her the *Veronica* and *Apollodora* in spite of the drizzle.

We strolled around the shipyard hand-in-hand, chatting quietly among the sheds and ships and mud. She knew a lot about sailing ships. "All Danes do," she assured me. "It's in our blood."

Before leaving she invited me to dinner at their farm in Skaelskor for next Saturday. I was delighted to accept.

Della picked me up in the truck on Saturday as scheduled. She seemed a different person in the daylight. I tried to identify what it was but could not pinpoint it entirely. For one thing she looked more like a farm girl as she shifted through the gears and raised her voice over the sound of the engine. I watched her facial expressions as she drove and spoke. Sensitive, responsible, lively. I didn't want her to discover me studying her, so I looked outside. The sun briefly peeked out from between grey clouds that hung belly-down among the buildings downtown. By the time we got onto the open road it looked like it could go either way—sunshine or rain.

Skaelskor was just ten or fifteen miles down the coast on a wide smooth road that coursed through well-groomed farmland. Della was proud of the area and provided a farm-by-farm account of who lived where and any noteworthy history. Her family in particular had inhabited the same piece of land for hundreds of years. Around Skaelskor their farm was known as the *"Maelkevejen,"* the Milky Way, because it had been a dairy in earlier generations. A long straight driveway led up to the large, two-story, white stucco farmhouse huddled among two barns and two work sheds.

"Leeks," she said as she indicated the field on the right as we drove by. She carefully avoided a huge puddle that occupied half of the area between the farmhouse and the barn. I knew without asking that it was the puddle they had got stuck in. The signs of their struggle were still imprinted in the dried mud around it.

With an hour of daylight remaining, Della showed me around the property. The farm was divided into four square sections by two dirt roads that crossed at right angles amid the farmhouse, barns, and work sheds clustered at the junction. The large puddle occupied the spot where the roads crossed. The two fields to the west were planted in neat rows, leeks in front and Brussels sprouts behind. The east section behind the house was pastureland and the one in front was fallow. They owned a tractor with implements, a milk cow, chickens, and two bird dogs that followed happily as we walked along the north-south road.

A small travel trailer parked beside the road behind the house halfway to the back of the property caught my eye. I stopped to look it over. The rounded, stainless steel exterior gleamed dimly beneath years of dust and inactivity. Grass had grown high around the wheels. Della was surprised that I was interested. To me, it looked like a perfect retreat. "Vee used to take sommer trips to France and Italy in it. That vas many years ago." I opened the door. The elegant wood paneling and cabinetry reminded me of the captain's cabin on the *Balclutha*. The amenities included a working kitchen, toilet, dining table with benches that turned into a short double bed up front, and a bench seat that made into a bed across the rear. It was well organized and inviting despite its size. I didn't have an inkling at the time that it was destined to be my home more than once, and I would draft the first few chapters of this book on the dining table.

After examining the trailer, we walked another two hundred yards to a boat dock situated on a narrow channel that ran east and west and connected Skaelskor to the sea. The channel delineated the back of the farm. There was another dock on the opposite side of the channel where a small boat bumped against the tide. On the bank behind it was a large black and white sign for boaters that read Langsom Fart, which literally meant proceed at a "long-some speed," or Go Slowly in Danish.

Before dinner, Della showed me around the house. It was huge, with perhaps fifteen small rooms including kitchens both upstairs and down and two bathrooms. The original house, hundreds of years old, was only two rooms, now used for storage only, with a ceiling at eye level.

The tour didn't take long. We joined Della's mom in the kitchen. She was a short woman who was divided by a belt into upper and lower bulges. She had glassy blue eyes that kept track of everything. She spoke no English but positively glowed with admiration when I struck up some small talk in Danish. She bounced in and out of the kitchen, looking like Santa's wife, with overloaded platters of heavenly food.

The father was a character, too. I wondered how he stayed slim with a culinary wizard for a wife. He was a sturdy man with a weathered face permanently imprinted with the wrinkles of a contented soul. He proudly sported what was probably the only cowboy belt and buckle in Denmark. We talked for hours about the farm, sailing ships, and Denmark. He invited me back as his wife tugged him upstairs.

Della returned me to the ferry around midnight. I was dizzy from too much homemade wine. The last thing I needed that night was another party, but that is what I got when Dalton returned at three in the morning with three girls. "Wake up boys," he thundered as he entered. "Gotta little surprise for ya." He switched on the lights. I felt terrible, almost nauseated, and was in no mood to entertain. He was drunk. The three girls watched from the entrance as I rolled out of my sleeping bag and dressed. Dalton strode arrogantly by and banged on Benny's door. He had a phony, paste-on smile and a stubborn set to his eyes. "You can stop beating your bishop. Come on," he said with a haughty laugh. He opened the door and switched on the light. Benny sheltered his eyes and complained. Dalton backed out and gestured toward Benny for the girls. "Any takers?" The girls laughed uncomfortably. "He's got a damn nice set of stuffed rodents," he said abusively. The girls meandered over. "Show 'm the goddam things," he demanded drunkenly.

Benny pulled on his pants and tried to exit but Dalton blocked the doorway. "Show 'm that big rodent," he bellowed. He laughed uproariously. The girls twittered. Dalton violently pulled the top off the bench in Benny's room and reached for the tote bag.

"I'll show them," said Benny coldly, his eyes downcast. He fetched the specimens and shot a resigned expression to the girls. I think they felt as badly about Dalton's crude behavior as we did. They spoke very little, laughed nervously, and nursed the beers in their hands.

"This is all I got, girls," said Dalton. He pointed to Benny and me like a used car salesman down on his inventory, then wrapped an arm around the one at his side. Her tongue flashed between her teeth. "Dee, go get the beer. It's in the floorboard." He kissed the girl in a dramatic display.

I went for the beer in my bare feet. One of the girls followed. "Sorry," she said sympathetically in Danish. "Vee did not know that you sleep." I tried to be gracious but doubt that I was. We took the beer in. The party had relocated to the galley.

Dirty pots and dishes cluttered the table and countertop. My nausea increased. Benny was telling the girls about the mice. The girls were bored. They wanted to go back to the pub. When Dalton ignored them they tramped out. He followed angrily.

"Nighty-night, boys," he cooed as he departed.

"I hate that son of a bitch," said Benny, his lower lip trembling. He packed his specimens and returned to bed.

The next day was grim. Rain. No work. Nothing in the cupboard. But I had a lot of time to think. I was angry with myself. To think I had once looked forward to this place as an opportunity. Now I wanted to get out as quickly as possible. I thought about the farm in Skaelskor. Della's father had invited me to help harvest the leeks if I needed extra money. Della assured me that he had been serious.

I was down to just a few dollars. So was Benny. It was time to "review my hours" with Ike.

A confrontation with Ike over money wasn't something I was looking forward to while nursing a headache. I trudged over to the *Veronica* anyway. He was cleaning a small accordion at the galley table. We chitchatted for a few minutes—that was Ike's way of doing business—before I asked about the money he had withheld. "It was fifty dollars even," I told him. "That's two days work."

There was a moment of silence as my question cleared the air. Then Ike said, "See this little fellow?" He pointed a thick finger at a single cylindrical fingering button on the instrument. "I had to make that myself from a block of wood. You can't get parts for these." He was rightfully proud of his work. "If you'll give me a few minutes I'll have it back together and I can play you something." He hadn't looked up.

"Really, I just need to review my hours so I can collect the rest of my paycheck." I held out the notebook that listed my hours for the work in the hold. "I'm broke. Benny's broke. We don't have anything to eat." I paused to give him an opportunity to respond. He didn't. "Benny will probably be over to collect the rest of his money pretty soon. We're both down to nothing."

Ike didn't seem to be paying attention. Instead he swabbed around the fingering buttons with a Q-Tip, looking from time to time to see if I was watching. I didn't know what to do. After a few minutes of swabbing he toweled the instrument clean and then slipped his hands into the hand straps and squeezed off a few notes. For the first time he looked me in the eyes. "Any requests?" He moved a safe distance from the tabletop. "How about 'Sloop John B?' I guess you know it was immensely popular years before the Beach Boys came along." When my expression didn't change, he looked at me like a professor disappointed to see that a student wasn't taking notes.

That indignity aside, he started to play. His eyes wandered around the perimeter of the galley as if he were reading sheet music from the crown molding. He was swaying and the music soon smoothed out into the familiar melody. "We come on the sloop John B," he sang, "my grandfather and me. Around Nassau town we did roam." His body rocked gently as he immersed himself in the music, his voice round and full and clear.

I guess I was in a state of mild shock. I didn't know what to do. The music filled the little galley with an air of merriment and camaraderie and Ike was singing wonderfully, entranced by his own voice, and I couldn't help but feel confused and exploited. Finally Ike finished the shanty with a broad smile and pushed his ski cap back on his head with a telegenic flourish. "I like a good song," he said in an appreciatory tone. "How about you? Ever try singing? I'll bet you'd be good at it. It's good for your soul, my friend."

"I couldn't carry a tune in a bucket," I replied.

He laughed at that one. And he laughed about it a little longer and then said, "That was a dandy, Don," then laughed about it some more. He was stalling and he knew that I knew.

I opened my book to the appropriate page and slid it to his side of the table. The muscles in his face slowly gathered into a stern expression. I had defiled the splendor of a magical musical moment with my infernal talk of money. He now seemed hurt. Could a few measly dollars mean that much? his face seemed to say. "I don't know how to say this without seeming petty," he said stiffly. "But there are a number of spots that need more stripping." He set the accordion on the table between us.

"That's fine. We can fix that easy enough. Like I said, we need all the work we can get."

There was silence as Ike picked up the notebook and studied the times and calculations.

"Just show us where the spots are and we'll take care of it." I smiled, having finally got down to brass tacks.

However, Ike expected us to do the work on our own time. I reminded him that we had agreed to do the work on an hourly basis. He insisted that the work was on a contract basis. "You are working for Dalton, not me," he insisted.

"Dalton's contracts are for the rigging work only. This work was in the hold. Side work," I argued. I reminded him that he had paid Benny and me for the work in the hold, not Dalton, and that the money being withheld was so he could "review the hours," which indicated a negotiated wage, not a contracted amount.

"It's all the same work, Don," said Ike gently. "It's just one ship." He paused darkly. His specious argument wasn't holding. He shook his head with injured dismay. "We all used to be like one big family around here." He smacked his lips and shook his head again.

The insinuation that I somehow had ruined things infuriated me, but I held fire.

"You guys are just going to have to wait until Dalton and I can sort out these details."

"This doesn't involve Dalton. He does the rigging. It's between you and me and Benny."

Ike looked at his watch then shared a warm smile with me. "Did you know that Mandy had a premature labor pain last night?" He stood, inched nearer and said, "Any day now," as he winked. With that he scooped up the accordion and tucked it into a maroon drawstring bag. "I've just got to get over to the welder's hut and check on a few things." He zipped his overalls up to the collar. He was ready to go. "Let's you and I get together on this mess after Dalton and I clear a few things up, okay?"

It was a pure power play. He had expected to confuse me with contract versus wage talk. When that didn't work he had to resort to the reality that I could not force him to hand over the money. It was the sort of ugly practice that had spawned international maritime labor laws. "Okay," I agreed bitterly, "but I can't wait too long. And neither can Benny. We are broke."

Ike threw his hands up to signal that I had pushed things too far. "Alright already," he shot back in an irritated tone. He then stepped through the hatchway and waited with additional irritation for me to exit so he could close the hatch. I left feeling

I had exploited his benevolence. He had successfully reshaped the simple request into a case of blaming the victim. I vowed at that moment to never do business with Ike again.

Back onboard the ferry I slumped into a state of depression. The only way to get Dalton to intervene or help would be through flattery or by bargaining away something—and then there was only a slim chance. When I did ask, in fact, Dalton laughed it off with, "That's between you and Ike. You can leave me out of it." He was en route to the office telephone with me on his heels. "What are you going to do when he tries pulling the same crap on you?" I countered. He waved that off without slowing down. I watched him swagger down the gangway and wondered how much of his disinterest was really disinterest. Was Dalton going to do the same thing when it was time for us to collect payment from him? The more I looked at the situation the more it resembled a den of thieves.

Frustrated, I dragged myself back to my corner on the ferry. I was tired of bumping heads with Dalton, tired of all the double talk from Ike, and tired of having angry thoughts inside my head all day. Things just weren't working out. Dalton turned everything into a masculine drama just to aggrandize his world, I supposed. Ike was probably as broke as Benny and me but living on credit. All the talk about being a partner had turned out to be just so much hot air.

I went into the galley to stir up a cup of coffee and consider how to turn things around. The galley was a mess. Benny and I, responsible by decree for cleaning up after meals, had cleaned the galley after breakfast. Dalton had come through since then and trashed it. The table was littered with dirty dishes, a cigarette was snuffed out on a plate, a coffee filter full of wet grounds had been plopped on the counter directly above the trash bucket, and four egg shells and a pan caked with fried egg had been tossed into the sink. It struck me like a body blow. "What am I doing here?" I asked myself out loud. I needed to return to Activ Universite. The signposts had pointed me there. If my life had meaning, that is where it pointed. It also seemed clear that the path back to Copenhagen passed through the leek fields on Della's farm.

I called Della from a pay phone in Korsør to see about work. She said yes and volunteered to pick me up.

"Gonna be a bean sprout?" was Dalton's response when I told him. He had been raised on an Iowa farm and hated anything to do with agriculture. It wouldn't have surprised me if he had told me to take all my stuff because I wouldn't be welcomed back. But he didn't. Instead we talked frankly about the financial pressures facing Bruce and Benny. According to his contract with Ike, he would be paid for the present work only after the foremast was stepped and rigged. "That looks to be six weeks away," he estimated. "Benny's getting a steady trickle of money from home and Marta's supporting Bruce. It's a good thing . . . I can't support them. Something's got to give," he said ominously. The upshot was that my work on the farm would take the pressure off. It would be beneficial for all parties.

Della's family welcomed me like a son. I chose to stay in the travel trailer near the channel instead of an upstairs bedroom. My days were spent in a shed attached to the barn where I readied leeks for shipment to the market. It was a simple routine of shucking, trimming, rinsing, bundling, and boxing the onion-like vegetable. There were enough to keep me busy for a few weeks. I took meals with the family and spent evenings adding notes to my journal and reading every English language book in the Korsør library—mostly Hemingway, Fitzgerald, Steinbeck, James, and Nabokov translations.

Surprise of surprises, after supper one night Dalton called to see if I was coming back. "We need you, Dee," he insisted.

"This sounds like a Trojan horse," I suggested.

Dalton sighed heavily over the line. "You want me to get down on my knees? Is that it?" There was no sarcasm, no bite to his reply. He explained that he and Ike had talked over the contract arrangement and the financial problems for all hands. They had set a deadline of November 8th for stepping the foremast. That was only three weeks away. "We need you back."

Somehow I expected everything to be different when I returned to the shipyard. Nothing had changed.

Regardless, Bruce, Benny, and I delivered. So did the shipyard. The foremast and the rigging were ready for fitting by the deadline but progress was halted on two fronts. First, Ike felt the steel mast ought to be painted before being stepped, the nautical term for erecting a mast. "It'll save time and money because it's easier to do while on the dock," he argued. Dalton argued that the steel needed to "cure" before being painted and that any savings would be insignificant in comparison to the potential for "trapping subsurface rust," if the mast was not properly cured. In truth, they were arguing over who was in charge.

The second squabble centered on the tradition of placing a silver dollar under the foot of the mast before stepping it. Dalton insisted it be a silver dollar or the Danish equivalent. Ike had planned on using a Kennedy half-dollar. Like the argument over painting the mast, Ike's choice of coin was probably a ruse to buy time, since he would never defy such a storied tradition.

Between that and the birth of Arvin Arkady Jr., our money was out of reach. I also knew I would not be reimbursed any time soon for food I had purchased for the three of us from my farm earnings.

With no paycheck forthcoming until the mast was stepped and rigged, Bruce, Benny, and I were caught in the middle. When the war of words continued unabated, I called Della's father once again. He was happy to hear from me. There were several days of work remaining.

The work and serenity of the farm were good for me. On the second day back, Della hand-stitched a patch over my bare-bottomed jeans. I felt liberated. That night I sat before a candle in the little trailer and reflected. This stint at the farm represented my last best chance to earn enough money to travel. With a month before the arrival of the Tibetan guru, I could just squeeze in a three-week visit to the Mediterranean coast. After that, the Brussels sprouts would be ready for harvest. Just thinking about it made me feel better. The signposts were pointing my way again.

I decided on a dramatic course of action: I was going to hitchhike to the Costa Brava in Spain. It was time to put misery behind me. I had enough time and money, and plenty of curiosity.

The last of the leeks lay bundled and ready for market a few days later. I stared forlornly at the half-filled crate that represented the end of the work as if it was the final page in a book I didn't want to end. I was reluctant to let go, to set out again on my own. But it was something I had to do.

On Friday afternoon Rhoda returned from Odense where she attended art school. She had a week-long break from classes. Naturally, that called for a party on Sunday night at the farm, the night before my departure south.

Claus and Lenora, local friends, were the first to arrive. Benny, Bruce, and Marta arrived socially late. Benny brought his guitar. Bruce had four beers. They were all in high spirits. I cornered them in the dining room to get the scoop on things at the shipyard.

Little had changed. The foremast had not been stepped. Dalton had given them a small advance. Ike was stalling, or so Bruce guessed. Dalton speculated that Ike was having to wait for money from the states. However, things were starting to move on the *Apollodora*. Dalton was in Rotterdam meeting with the owner. Apparently he had characterized my choice to work a second time on the farm as a defection. His duplicity was maddening. "But he specifically stated that we could come and go as we pleased," I reminded them. "He even agreed it would be beneficial for me to work here, and that was one week ago."

"You know how he is," said Bruce. "Typical Gemini. Runs hot one day and cold the next. Drives me crazy." He tweaked his moustache as Rhoda looked in, then left.

"I'm going to talk to Ike tomorrow," I declared.

"Won't do any good. He'll just tell you that we are working for Dalton and not him. And when it comes to rigging work, it's true," said Benny.

The subject was put aside for a minute while Lenora brought in some wine. "Everybody is vondering vhere you are," she said to the three of us.

"So what are you guys gonna do?" I asked as we meandered toward party central.

"Tough it out," said Bruce stoically.

"My folks are sending me money," said Benny. "They call it tuition." He put his guitar case on the chair beside him and opened the lid.

"Do you think I'll be welcome back?"

"Sure," answered Benny over his shoulder. He was unpacking his guitar. "Dalton always needs people to shit on."

The party lasted until sun-up for most of us. Everybody was loud and rowdy and drunk on homemade wine. We had consumed large quantities of food and drink, and danced and reveled all night. At one point somebody accidentally knocked over a tall bookcase. It fell on Rhoda and me as we played backgammon on the sofa. Fortunately, there were no serious injuries, but a sharp pain to my forehead was ominous. My immediate thought was that I had been struck by a small potted cactus that occupied a spot on an upper shelf. Instead, I had been burned by my own cigarette when the hand I raised to block the falling bookshelf was flattened against me. The small round cigarette burn was located right between my eyebrows. "A third eye," laughed Bruce drunkenly. "You look like some kind of swami," he chided as he pointed to the burn mark on my forehead.

202

Chapter 13 – Dreamwork

Three days after taking the ferry from Korsør to Kiel, Germany, I stood on the outskirts of Orange, France, watching a cabbage boil in a dented metal pot over a campfire. The pot belonged to Daniel McHarg, an American student-traveler from Boston, who had "found" the cabbage in a nearby garden while I purchased bread and wine in town. Although famished, I declined a share of the cabbage. Daniel regarded the purloined cabbage as providence. I saw it as petty theft.

Daniel was headed for Gibraltar from Scotland, where he had apprenticed for four years to a bagpipe master. Like me, he had little money, and his worn clothes and belongings testified to the hardship of travel on foot. He responded with a hoot when I told him my plan was to hitchhike to an uninhabited stretch of beach along the Costa Brava where I could immerse myself in Shakespeare until time to return to Denmark to meet the Tibetan guru. "You must have a lot of money," he said.

His remark surprised me. I had chosen the Costa Brava over other Mediterranean destinations because I had read that the cost of living there was low. "Why do you say that?" I asked.

"It's like the Riviera or something. You know, real expensive."

Truth is, I hadn't researched the Costa Brava at all. What I knew had come from a spy thriller novel Wally had loaned me in the Faroes. In the book the good spy had gone to the Costa Brava to let his nerves mend following an especially unnerving tour of duty. Unbeknownst to him, his arch enemy had tracked him there. According to the book, the Costa Brava was a stretch of sunny beaches and backwater fishing villages that had yet to be discovered by the dissembling throngs that migrate to the

Mediterranean coast in the winter. Alas, I had been seduced by fiction.

Having acknowledged I had no plan, I agreed with Daniel that a Spanish beach would be perfect for my Shakespeare retreat. Spain was cheap, sunny, and nearby, he assured me, plus traveling was more fun with good company. We toasted the road to Barcelona with the last of the wine, then tried for the remainder of the day to hitch a ride at the entrance to the Avignon toll road. No luck. We wanted to hitchhike as we walked, but pedestrians were prohibited on the toll road. At sunset we pitched Daniel's tent within sight of the road and built a fire, then chatted into the night over bread, cheese, sardines, and wine with Orion the Hunter wheeling slowly overhead and Daniel strumming familiar tunes on his guitar as we talked.

In the morning, four nuns beat us to the good hitchhiking spot sixty yards short of the toll road entrance. After a few luckless hours for us and the nuns, Daniel and I put on a display of retreat for the tollgate keeper then circled around out of his sight and returned to the toll road a few miles beyond the entrance, free to walk and hitchhike at the same time. To celebrate our successful stratagem, we uncorked a bottle of morning wine and took a few breakfast-sized swigs. Soon we were dancing and singing along the road to Avignon, looking like Dorothy & Company promenading down the Yellow Brick Road. But instead of poppies, before us lay miles and miles of vineyards and orchards. "Keep On Trucking" was written in the clouds overhead as we drank and walked and sang.

A chauffeured Mercedes-Benz without passengers provided our only ride between Orange and Avignon. The chauffeur, an inscrutable Arabic gentleman in a dove grey uniform with matching cap, dropped us a few miles short of Avignon without ever having said a word.

After enduring a night of rain in the tent in a field outside of Avignon, we entered the ancient city the next day with steam rising from our damp clothes, which comically looked like auras when backlit by the sun rising over the rampart walls. Daniel was ecstatic about the steam auras and declared us the Wetback Popes in a city that was home to a number of defiant popes in the 14th century. With no money for tourist activities, we explored the ancient structures of the city and strode down to the Rhone River to examine the remains of the Saint-Bénezet bridge. We learned from a tourist pamphlet that it was built in the 12th century and parts of it had collapsed shortly thereafter. Even so, the elegant arched structure was celebrated throughout Europe because of a popular song that romanticized it. As we departed Avignon on the new bridge across the Rhone we paused to study a settlement of a few hundred Gypsies living in tents, lean-tos, and battered vans under the bridge.

From Avignon we traveled westward into desert-like terrain to Nimes, where a rising curtain of black smoke and roaring engines advertised an auto race from a mile away. We paused for a short while in the main business district to watch the noisy grand prix racers screech around corners and wow the crowds, then turned back to the business of the road.

The highway skirted Montpelier, Bezier, and Perpignan as we trekked into higher elevation towards the Pyrenees and the Spanish border. We realized after hours of walking and chatting that the closer we got to Spain the fewer motorists we saw going our way. We split up to improve our chances of getting a ride, but walked for two days straight nevertheless. We slept one night in huge concrete sewer pipes that had been placed beside the road awaiting excavation and installation crews. Sitting cross-legged among the pipes on the sloping, sandy landscape with a small campfire crackling, Daniel played his guitar and sang, in order, every song from Cat Stevens' *Tea for the Tillerman* album before darkness and exhaustion engulfed us. He was an accomplished musician and obviously loved his work.

The next day began with a grueling trek up a winding road carved out of a rocky landscape of overlooks, canyons, and ridges built upon rough, house-sized boulders and upthrusting stone. The two-lane road parted to form a median as it approached the Spanish border, and the space between the divided lanes formed a wide diamond-shaped median. A plain brown wooden building occupied the center of the median and seemed part customs house and part barracks for the soldiers who manned the checkpoint shacks and the black- and white-striped barricades that were raised and lowered to control vehicles in both directions. A uniformed soldier strode straight toward us as we approached the building. He signaled for us to drop our bags and step back while growling similar instructions in Spanish.

We automatically presented our passports for inspection. He glanced through them roughly, tossed them on the gravel beside our bags, and began pawing through my bags. He counted the money in my billfold and tossed it back in the bag with a snort. I told him in clunky Spanish that I would receive additional funds via Western Union when I reached Barcelona. He snorted at that too and turned to Daniel's gear, which included two large bags and an acoustic guitar in a case. He unzipped the largest bag. A polished wooden drone from Daniel's bagpipe popped up through the opening. The soldier sprang backward a step and studied the instrument with an astonished expression. He looked to Daniel, back to the instrument, stood abruptly, pointed, and said, *"Toca."* Daniel looked to me as if he had just been handed a death sentence. "Play," I translated with less authority. Daniel looked to the soldier, who repeated the command.

Smiling now, Daniel retrieved the bagpipe, strapped it over his shoulder and slung the bag under his left arm. He then began blowing air into the mouthpiece as he pumped the bag with the upper part of his left arm. Moments later the reedy sounds began to emerge and he organized them into a melody. Half a dozen soldiers with drawn rifles bounded out of the brown building toward us. Their grave expressions melted into smiles as they pulled up beside their comrade. Daniel began marching in place in time with the music, no doubt the celebrated "Seventy Ninth's Farewell to Gibraltar" piece that had inspired his trip to Spain. A handful of men in civilian clothes came around the building and joined the roadside audience.

"Grab our stuff and follow me," Daniel told me hurriedly, skipping a few notes. With that he began marching in a small circle around the group as I casually collected our bags, draped some over my shoulders, and clutched the rest in my hands. Feeling like an overloaded camel, I joined Daniel as he marched in larger and larger circles around the group, still belting out that famous song, until he simply strode forward toward the checkpoint shack, the two of us marching in lockstep, backs straight, heads erect.

The soldiers at the checkpoint raised the barricade as we neared and grinned gamely as we marched through. The road began to slope downhill and we noticed as we marched that the lane on the opposite side of the median was lined bumper-to-bumper with produce trucks parked along the shoulder. The drivers clustered near their trucks in small groups smoking, talking, and applauding as we marched into Spain. The line of trucks and drivers stretched down the winding road for several miles. I learned from a driver who gave us a beer that the produce trucks had to wait until midnight to enter France.

Exhilarated over our fantastic entrance into Spain—yet exhausted and dehydrated—we spread our sleeping bags under a bridge in the dark and fell asleep to the comforting sound of a babbling creek. We woke up beside a filthy creek with inches of dirty foam coating the water's edge on both sides and decided without discussion to skip a creek-side breakfast. Within a few minutes we caught a ride all the way to Barcelona with a British couple in a small recreational vehicle.

Despite the head-turning power of Gaudi's architecture and the Old World attraction of this ancient port city, four days was all I could tolerate of Franco's Spain and Barcelona. Armed soldiers patrolled vacated sidewalks and scowled menacingly as we passed. People withdrew in fear as we approached. Eye contact was unthinkable. The food was bland. I had never before felt so threatened, never felt such sympathy for a people, and never before realized the potential for violence embodied in an unhappy teenager in uniform with a machine gun.

We camped in an orchard on the outskirts of town until realizing that camping might land us in prison. We both felt compelled to move on. Daniel continued south toward Gibraltar and I turned north toward Copenhagen, toward a rendezvous with a Tibetan guru.

That night I slept in a haystack on a small farm at the foot of the Pyrenees and departed hastily in the morning at the behest of a snarling dog. An hour up the road I stopped at a picturesque roadside cafe for coffee. Daniel and I had found it closed on our trek into Spain days earlier. Encouraged by a thin column of smoke rising from the chimney, I hurried past the Jeep parked in front, found the door ajar, and strode right in.

A gruff voice bellowed *Quando?* as I entered. *Quando*, I recalled, meant "when." I froze. Between me and a bar along the back wall stood several tables with chairs stacked on top. I blinked to help my eyes adjust. Three men stood to the left at the extreme end of the bar. The morning light illuminated the area through a doorway behind them, silhouetting the bar and the men. Two men wore shiny black patent-leather hats with winged brims. The hats marked them as the dreaded Guardia Civil, Franco's Gestapo. The third was an old man with a white towel draped over his left shoulder and shaving cream covering his right jaw and neck.

The officer standing nose to nose with the old man shouted *"Dice me," tell me* in Spanish. The old man cringed in fear. I cringed in sympathy. The other "black hat" stood with his back to me. They hadn't noticed me. Slowly, I inched backward. My pulse raced, the hair on my neck and arms tingled.

The old man murmured something and struggled to swallow. I took a backward step toward the door. The interrogator standing nose to nose with the old man suddenly jerked his knee into the old man's groin. The man doubled over and cried out in agony while crumbling slowly to the floor. The other interrogator hammered a fist into the old man's ribs as he sank, which spun him as he crashed to the floor, toppling a barstool. A dry soundless scream clawed at my throat as the barstool clattered to rest under a table. I took another backward step to the doorway.

Bending closer to the old man, the first interrogator shouted something about *dinero* to the crumpled, gasping man. He wanted *money*. The old man shook his head and sputtered something incomprehensible while trying to cover his face and ribs with his arms. The "black hats" exchanged sneers and moved closer.

I backed out the door and shot across the road, my gaze fixed over my shoulder, torrents of hot blood roaring in my neck, clicking in my ears. I was an animal in flight.

Soon I realized there were no "black hats" in pursuit. I ran, nevertheless, until exhausted, and then walked with heaving lungs, an ear tuned for the distinctive sound of a flathead-four Jeep engine. A few minutes later a battered white Peugeot rounded a curve. I stepped into the lane and waved manically. The car pulled over and I gratefully jumped in. With a screech of rubber and four power shifts, we were soon up to highway speed with The Doors playing at high decibels. Miguel turned the radio down long enough for us to exchange cordialities then jacked it up to high. By God, I was moving now.

Slowly the tension drained away and I let out a sigh of relief. My instincts told me to report the attack to the police . . . but the "black hats" *were* the police. More than ever I realized the forces behind the repression in Spain, and I wanted out. I looked to the driver and wondered how he put up with the ugly realities of Franco's Spain. He caught me looking, smiled, turned down the radio again, and cocked an ear. I asked for his destination. "Bezier," he answered, then turned up the radio. Bezier was just beyond the Pyrenees in France.

What a crazy world, I told myself, as we cruised over the arid, mountainous terrain. In a single morning I had incurred a sojourner's heaven in the haystack, witnessed a brutal beating, and fled at sixty miles per hour like a coward with a rock n' roll soundtrack. As my adrenaline level subsided, a blue mood descended. Last year at this time I had been a night watchman in San Francisco. Where, I paused to wonder, would I be at this time next year? All that change, and yet, had anything really changed? I stared blankly out the window. The landscape flowing outside the window had a hypnotizing effect. My body felt relaxed but my mind was tensed. The question came again. Had anything changed? No. The restlessness was still there. So was the longing for a woman, for community, for meaning. So was the uncertainty.

I camped in a vineyard outside of Bezier and awoke to a cloud formation of mares tails moving in from the sea. To sailors the high cirrus clouds signaled an impending change in weather. A distant flock of birds in flight hung noiselessly in the distance to the south. Another temple. I watched the birds until they disappeared, wondering what was in the future for me. Would a change in weather coincide with other changes? Would the gods reveal their will? My empty sardine can from last night's supper, I noticed, had been moved ten or twelve feet during the night and licked clean. What noiseless nocturnal creature had visited during the night?

Within an hour I caught a ride with a man who was either named Belgic or was from Belgium. Our conversation didn't develop beyond that. The journey retraced a winding, two-lane road that Daniel and I had taken only a week earlier. And so, when I caught sight of the sandy, tree-covered hillock east of Montpelier where Daniel and I had camped one night, I asked Belgic to stop. He seemed puzzled by the request but pulled over.

The hillock was not so sunny and warm as the Costa Brava beach I had envisioned from my improvised bunk on the ferry in Korsør, and the tumbling waves along the coastline were many miles away, but it was close enough to that vision to satisfy my half-baked travel plans. So I fashioned my small green tarp into a suspended tent-like roof among a stand of saplings and stayed for two days while I read *Hamlet* and meditated. A plan within a plan.

I used the last few hours of sunlight on day two to focus on my situation. Obviously Dalton's ship-refitting contracts involved a year or more of work, and he had invited me to stay and work for him. So that would stabilize my financial situation. The key deciding factors, however, were whether or not I could tolerate the abusive environment that he maintained and if I could trust him and Ike to honor their financial commitments. The alternative? Going straight to Activ Universite to see if I could find some kind of employment through that connection.

My thoughts wandered forward to the rendezvous with the guru, then backward to the crazy events that had led me to Activ Universite. The dreams. The coincidences. I had convinced myself that they were spiritual signposts communicating that I was on track for a rendezvous with an exalted spiritual teacher. Or was I deluding myself? Was the signpost interpretation just a coping mechanism for a frightened and lonely sojourner? My own private superstition?

I pulled out my notebook. It was time to put to rest all the anxiety and mystery of the dreams and coincidences. I leafed to a blank page near the back, divided it into five sections with horizontal lines, and entered in chronological order the five dreams with space for notes under each one. An hour later I had synthesized my thoughts into manageable summaries.

Burger Joint Dream—Had dream in Oklahoma, came true fifteen months later in San Francisco. The dream: Freighter chugging by, viewed in chef's hat through back door of burger joint.

Mystery: How could I know fifteen months in advance that I would witness a passing freighter through a doorway while wearing a chef's hat and working at a grill near the bay?

Balclutha Capsize Dream—Had dream in San Francisco. Unfolded in two parts. The dream: Monty, Chris, Taylor, an unknown crew member, and I watch as *Balclutha* capsizes in a narrow channel and crew abandons ship and swims to the shore. At shoreline the five of us pull the five of them to safety through openings between large rocks. The rescuers and survivors are the same people. Part 1) Monty, Chris, Taylor, and I all "abandon" our jobs on the *Balclutha* to join the *Marite* adventure. Part 2) Monty, Chris, Taylor, myself, and the unknown crew member (skipper's son), assist ourselves in climbing through rock crevices along a mountain ledge overlooking a fjord in the Faroe Islands.

Mystery: How could I know months in advance that I would stand among large stones overlooking a long narrow channel and assist crewmates climbing through rocky openings? And how could I know that one of them would be a complete stranger?

Plastic Gun Dream—The dream: While purchasing tobacco at the local store, I hand the blue tobacco packet to the skipper and it turns into a blue plastic gun.

Mystery: Having this dream come true in the grocery store, which involved the skipper's help in stalling for time, allowed me to meet Gretchen—a meeting that provided the hospital connection needed for the next dream to come true.

Capsize Dream—Unfolded in two parts. The dream: I watch from the *Marite's* weather deck as two freighters pass at high speed, with the *Marite* in-between, and their wakes cause the *Marite* to sink, stern first; then I wake up in the hospital. Part 1) occurred on the *Marite* in slow motion. Part 2) occurred in Gretchen's hospital dorm room.

Mystery: How could I know in advance that these things would occur? Astonishing details: I did my best to keep the dream from coming true and failed. Impossible for Part 1 to come true until two changes in the material world occurred: the *Marite's* shelter deck was removed, which occurred many weeks after having the dream, and a change in Gretchen's working hours.

Laundromat Dream – Dreamed that I stood in a laundromat doorway as a dozen or so nude people repeatedly ran around a row of washing machines, running clockwise until they reached me at the door, then running counter-clockwise until reaching me at the door, reversing direction each time they reached the doorway where I stood. Virtually impossible, but it could come true.

I studied the notes with a renewed sense of bewilderment. The same unnerving questions and anxieties arose yet again: How could I have known about the reality depicted in the dreams in advance? How, when doing so violates one of the fundamental understandings of human nature: that it is impossible to know today about a specific incident that will occur weeks or months from now?

At the simplest level, one could argue that the *Balclutha* Capsize Dream was simply a good guess, a good subconscious guess of the sequence of events that would happen when the project received a green light, and that I then lived to see it come true. But would such a lucky guess in San Francisco ensure that the appropriate group of people would all meet on a rocky landscape overlooking a blue channel and unwittingly re-enact the dream event months later? And how does one repeat that kind of performance four times in eighteen months with different dreams, different sets of people, different settings, and all intimately linked to an evolving set of real circumstances unfolding thousands of miles apart? I felt like a coincidence factory.

And what about the Laundromat Dream? I worked my imagination to envision a way in which it could be realized, and recognized that avoiding nude gatherings, laundromats, and washing machines was the key to maintaining my sanity. It was all so sensible, so sane.

After revisiting the same mysteries and the same plot-stoppers for a while, I took my anxieties on a stroll across the arid landscape. The sun hung over the Pyrenees to the west and in a short while would dip below the horizon. Was it Friday or Saturday? I pondered that for a moment. I could check my journal, I knew, but wandered afield instead to the arbitrariness of such things. How had such distinctions been made? I recalled from my Danish lessons with Gretchen that some of the English-language days were named for Nordic gods –Odin's day, Thor's day, and Frig's day. But what about the quantification of time? How were those distinctions made?

Some of the divisions were obvious. It takes a year for the earth to revolve around the sun; a month for the moon to revolve around the earth; a week for each quarter of the moon's revolution; and a day for the earth to rotate 360 degrees relative to the sun. However, the smaller divisions in time were not obvious at all. Why was a day comprised of twenty-four hours rather than thirty-six or one hundred? Had some king or queen commissioned this work? And the more radical question: does the ability to divide and track time mathematically really provide an accurate illustration of time itself? Does 36-24-36 describe Marilyn Monroe? It's obvious that time can be parsed and tracked into infinitesimally smaller or larger increments, but do such distinctions help us understand the nature of time? Like so many things that are considered basic scientific facts, they seem based on the presumption that mathematical crunchability trumps all other forms of understanding. My thoughts slipped back to the broken clock on the church steeple, the dreams, and the irony of working for Adventures in Time, Incorporated. The ability to add, subtract, divide, and multiply days and weeks and years could not explain the journeywork required to create such a profound reflection of my situation.

As long shadows began to stretch across the spare landscape, I returned to the relative comfort of my hillock with the improvised tarp roof suspended shoulder-high among the saplings. From a distance it looked like a miniature house. I paused to enjoy the image. It was my faux-Costa Brava beach house, and the distant swishing sound of cars on the highway was the beckoning surf of an imagined Costa Brava coastline.

I sat in the sand near my green-roofed "house" and pondered the power of mathematics. In essence it is comprised of two functions only—adding and subtracting—since multiplication is a way of aggregating individual addition functions and division is a way to disaggregate them. From this I took away two appreciations.

First, that, despite the dualistic limits of such a system, applied mathematics was responsible for so much of what we know and do and experience in the world, ranging from tapping the power of the atom even before we could see it, to placing humans on the moon, recording music for posterity, eliminating polio, and making all of it repeatable through a universal language.

Second, that if a dualistic system based on addition and subtraction only could describe the world with such accuracy and diversity, then the actual world must be many, many times more nuanced and complex. And though I lived in the world of air flight, recorded music, and medical wonders, I knew there was much more out there to experience than we can see or imagine.

Having gone through the entire catalog of dreams, coincidences, puzzles, and shopworn circumlocutions, I was looking again at my own version of Gordian's knot, my own tether connecting the material world to the spiritual world. And though the conversation in my head did not answer the questions, going through the exercise was a comfort, a test of my sanity when increasingly I felt like a walking talking coincidence machine. It was my shelter in an inexplicable world. My house. With nightfall closing around me, I organized my belongings under the tarp roof, brushed my teeth, and climbed into my sleeping bag. The sand conformed perfectly to my body.

Feeling content, I set out for Denmark the following morning. Five days would be plenty of time to hitchhike there.

One ride later, on a curve overlooking a valley outside Remoulins, I crossed paths with a bedraggled youth kneeling in a flattened spot among tall weeds beside the road where obviously he had slept, ten feet from passing cars. He reeked of stale liquor and seemed stricken by illness. He struggled to stand as I approached, his hair and clothes gnarled and dirty. He tried to walk, a hand extended to me. I stiffened when we made eye contact. My pulse and breathing raced. The scene put me in mind of an illustrated story I had read in the fifth grade about how Prince Siddhartha had encountered a stricken person along the road. Having been sheltered from such suffering by wealth and royal decree, the incident motivated the prince to give up his royal estate and embark on a search for meaning. I looked into the troubled eyes of the young man by the road. He seemed disengaged mentally and emotionally, numb, a dying old man somehow inhabiting a young man's body.

An urge to help him overwhelmed me and a swarm of feelings swept me back to the maddening days of dreams and inexplicable events. Much like those days, I was at a loss to account for my emotions or a reasonable explanation. I steadied the struggling youth with an outstretched hand as he took a step toward his fallen beret. He mumbled gratefully. I picked up his dirty beret and handed it to him. He dropped it. I picked it up again. He was a pathetic and bespoiled figure, but I wanted to help.

The two of us stood beside the road fumbling with the beret when the sound of an approaching vehicle caught my ear. Although supporting the haggard youth, I stuck out my thumb as an old delivery van with the word "Frit" scrawled on it rounded the curve, pulled over, and gave us a ride. One minute we were beside the road struggling just to stand, the next we were in a van cruising along a winding country road in the south of France.

Again, I was at a loss over what to do. After a brief exchange of words in French between the stricken youth and the driver, the youth slumped into a heap with his back against the sidewall. The driver smiled at me. He was tall and lanky, with disheveled hair and a nose like the ski jump at Innsbruck. I instantly liked this friendly and animated fellow and, except for the nose, we could have passed for brothers. I sat on the right front wheel-well and retrieved my notebook. The driver smiled more broadly and asked something in French. I explained that I spoke a little Spanish and Danish, or English. His face brightened.

"American?" he asked. I nodded.

"I am Jean-Paul," he told me, with eyebrows peaked and a thumb pointing to his chest. Then he pointed at me and said, "Jack Kerouac?"

The remark caught me off guard. Jean-Paul saw the change in expression on my face and added, "*Dharma Bums*" in accented English.

His remarks swung like a wrecking ball through the shelter I had created to house my wounded world. I shrunk inside myself, lost focus, and flinched as the words swung back through. With just four words I had been stripped of a place to hide my inexpressible fears. I looked to Jean-Paul for a clue. He laughed outrageously, slapped the steering wheel, and briefly ran off the road because of it. His remarks had had the same impact as one of the dreams, but without the weeks-long time lag and bed rest. Inside, my mind felt exposed, unprotected. Electricity pulsed beneath my thoughts. Hot gases flared in my stomach. Survival impulses pushed all else aside. I felt like a gladiator awaiting my clash with the lions. Outside, it was a lovely day in the South of France as I recorded it all in my notebook.

At Remoulins, Jean-Paul stopped in front of a bakery and let the haggard youth out. The hour's rest appeared to have done wonders for him. Jean-Paul asked if I wanted a ride to St. Etienne. That was near Lyons, a hundred miles or more north, I recalled. He indicated with hand gestures that it was many miles away. *"Oui,"* I answered.

The road from Remoulins to St. Etienne follows the west bank of the Rhone River valley for long stretches. The two-lane road wound through postcard-quaint villages and over landscapes charged with natural beauty and freshly rinsed earlier by sporadic morning showers. "I love the smell of soil just before a rain," I told Jean-Paul, then sniffed with an exaggerated motion. He understood perfectly and fluttered two fingers under his nose.

Our view to the east covered a mile-wide expanse of the Rhone River valley. Because the road followed the valley rim hundreds of feet upslope from the river, we also had an eye-level view of the underside of the rain clouds in the valley. As we slowed, the sun suddenly appeared and a rainbow arced over the shining river below. Jean-Paul voiced an "Oo-wee" at the same moment I cried "Wow." Jean-Paul was doubly pleased at having his private tour enhanced by the rainbow. As we proceeded north, the rainbow remained ahead of us on a parallel track.

Beyond Pont St. Esprit and Meysse, tiny towns perched on the rim overlooking the Rhone, and the river provided another glimpse of her charms with a bigger, broader rainbow. As we wound along the rim road, a second rainbow winked on and off over the first one. Jean-Paul pulled the van over sharply and quickly scrambled onto the roof. I followed him, and we stood there in the sunlit rain as the two huge rainbows glowed magically on the opposite side of the river. The whole valley radiated with a misty auric glow that reflected on the surface of the broad river below and lasted for a quarter hour.

Speechless and wet, we drove to St. Etienne, the squeak and swipe of the windshield wipers lulling us all the way. On the outskirts of town Jean-Paul steered the delivery van onto a side road to show me an overpass with a graffiti message emblazoned across it in French. He stopped the van directly beneath the overpass and, with the engine running, scrambled onto the roof, kissed the fingertips on his right hand, then patted the graffiti affectionately. Moments later we were back in the van heading north again. I glanced out the rear window at the graffiti, wondering if it was his handiwork. It reminded me of a graffiti message on an Oakland underpass that I had seen a year earlier, proclaiming that "the only difference between a common man and a king is a bath and a hot meal."

The two rainy days I spent with Jean-Paul and Ilsa, his Danish girlfriend, rejuvenated me. Jean-Paul was a sculptor. Ilsa was a fiber artist and a willing translator. Their rooftop atelier on an old building near a St. Etienne commercial district was just a short walk to an art museum with one of Monet's *Water Lilies*. Jean-Paul, who was scheduled to exhibit some work there in the coming weeks, bullied the doorman into admitting me for free, claiming I was his apprentice.

That night I had my first-ever taste of crepes. A rainstorm with lightning provided a light show through the louvered skylights on the east as we listened to Louis Armstrong and talked halfway to morning about art, France, Americans, and music. Ilsa turned one of her hand-woven wall hangings into a beautiful shoulder bag for me. Jean-Paul joked about "Muscatel," the haggard youth by the highway. The youth's affliction, I learned, had come from a magnum of cheap muscatel.

After breakfast and a bath the next morning, I felt like a king. Before leaving I laundered my clothes, which permitted me to wear my good jeans. The patch that Della had added to the worn-out jeans was stripped off in the washer and the hole in the backside was larger and more frayed than before. At departure time, Jean-Paul took me to the edge of town on the road to Lyons. "Good luck, Japhy Ryder," he said in clumsy English. He turned the Frit-mobile around and headed back with a wave. Japhy Ryder was the Buddhist poet in *Dharma Bums* who had departed for Japan at the end of the book.

I managed to stay ahead of the rain on the first day. After a drunken night with hippie squatters in an abandoned cookie factory near Dijon, I took off in the wrong direction the next morning, then took a shortcut on a secondary road to get back on track. I wandered lost along farm roads for hours. Finally, I was given directions to the highway from a farmer having lunch on a checkered cloth beside his tractor in a field. Crows watched from fence posts by the road as he sketched a map in the dirt.

The rain caught up with me in Orville, a village with only a handful of dwellings. Caught in a downpour, I sought shelter in an abandoned roadside gas station. I had pulled off two boards nailed in an X over the doorway and taken three steps inside before realizing I was walking in wet concrete. I backed out and hurried through the village in the drenching rain. A mile or so beyond, I saw a tractor sheltered under an open shed just forty yards from the road.

Totally soaked and chilled to the bone, I scrambled over the barbwire fence and slogged across the field to a spot beside the tractor. The rain drummed on the metal roof. Half a minute later, after gathering my bags at my feet, I wiped the rain from my face and suddenly realized that the "tractor" was a full-grown, snorting angus bull with breath that smelled like fermented vegetables and horns that glistened like sickle blades. I bolted across the muddy field in one explosive heartbeat, heaved my bags over the fence, then scaled it and jumped. I landed in the ditch, my feet stuck in the mud, but momentum sent me forward anyway. The terrifying yet comical event left me on all fours in six inches of running water in the ditch. My backpack had tumbled onto the road straight ahead. My sleeping bag was in a puddle to my right. The bull had not moved.

So much for being at the right place at the right time.

The rain let up as I rinsed the mud from my clothes in the water puddled on the road. I could live with the drenching, the humiliation, and the mud stains on my jeans, but the thought of having to use a laundromat under these circumstances suddenly overloaded every neuron in my brain. I was in no condition to do battle with a laundromat.

A saint at the wheel of a two-ton Mercedes truck hissed to a stop beside me. The driver, Fritz, a spontaneous German with a walrus moustache that covered his entire mouth, was eager to help and spoke good English as well. He turned the heater to high and talked about how soon we'd be in Mannheim as he shifted through the gears. I fell asleep shortly after warming up and slept until awakened at a truck stop outside Mannheim. I changed into my worn-out clothes in the truck and stuffed the dry but mud-stiff clothes into my wet backpack, which made a matched set with my wet sleeping bag.

For reasons unknown to me, Fritz found a ride for me to Hamburg. I thanked him profusely before exiting with the new trucker. He didn't offer a name as we shook hands beside the cashier stand in the restaurant. He already had a passenger, he told me, as we avoided puddles in the huge, hard-packed gravel lot on the way to his truck. A young, dark-complexioned girl sat in the passenger's seat. Her name was Maria. She scooted to the middle of the bench seat. The trucker had picked her up near Freiburg, he explained. She was going to Hamburg.

Only the driver and I spoke for the first part of the journey. An intermittent rain kept the wipers busy. With gentle coaxing in my limited Spanish, I learned that Maria was from a small town near Valencia and was headed for Hamburg with no particular plan or contacts. Almost certainly she was short on money. She had escaped Franco's Spain. That probably had been the extent of her plans. She seemed neither excited about her achievement nor concerned about the many uncertainties that lay ahead. The driver confirmed my impression with a shrug. He had seen it before.

We reached Hamburg just after midnight. The driver dropped us in the port district. We thanked him and climbed down into the cold night air. At first, I naively thought he had let us off there because of my connection with ships or because that was his destination. But as Maria and I ambled uncertainly along a street of sailor bars and girlie shows, it became obvious that here was where most of the prostitutes plied their trade. The driver had known. That was Maria's plan. Or not her plan so much as her lot. It was the price of escape. She was attractive and would be much more so with some provocative clothes, an updated hairstyle, a little make-up, and a cute little umbrella, which I now saw were deployed as portable advertisements by her competitors on the street.

The anger rose in me. I cursed Franco for all the ruin and devastation he had caused. I had run away when threatened before but there was no threat this time. I needed to do something. We stopped in front of a garishly loud discotheque with hundreds of blinking light bulbs so I could find the business card of the German businessman I had met on the train across Denmark. Perhaps he would give Maria a job. I found the card. Werner Holtz. Hotel Verein.

The hotel was smaller than I expected and close to the port district, but it was well kept and respectable despite the nightclub a few doors down. The young man at the desk straightened his posture when I asked for Mr. Holtz by name. He arrived at nine o'clock daily, he told me, and "No," he didn't think they needed any domestic help. I took the cheapest room he had. The young man obligingly exchanged my francs into marks at the rate posted in the newspaper, and promised to hand-deliver my note about Maria to Mr. Holtz. Maria and I then retreated to an all night eatery we had passed earlier and had a hot, cheap meal.

I wanted to explain to her that dignity was a universal human right, but I didn't have the Spanish vocabulary for it. Besides, she was worn out. Through all of this she had maintained the sad blinking eyes of the helpless. Nothing seemed to get through. Her life in Franco's Spain had not equipped her for such distinctions. The world happened to her; she had no control, no power.

We returned to the hotel and parted company in the lobby with the clerk watching suspiciously. She was shocked and maybe offended that I was not planning to spend the night with her. I left her standing on the ornate maroon and tan carpet with her belongings rolled in a gray blanket under her left arm, the key in her hand, her right hand extended to me, still sad and blinking, and having had her only tangible source of gratitude devalued. She was as powerless to compensate me at this moment as she was in all other matters.

A cold reality awaited me in the streets. My pocket money was down to the exact price of the ferry from Keil to Korsør. It was after three in the morning, a few snowflakes were arriving on a raw north wind, the Keil highway was miles away, and there was only an occasional car on the road at this hour. If I did not catch the ferry at noon I faced the dismal prospect of waiting another twenty-four hours under the same conditions. I stopped at the cafe where Maria and I had eaten earlier and asked for directions. I had covered two blocks along that route when a man who had been in the eatery pulled over in a Volvo station wagon with fogged windows and gave me a ride. A full-fledged snowstorm was unfolding when we reached Keil at 6:30 a.m.

Soon things would be different. In just two days I would be meeting a Tibetan guru. The thought sent a shiver up my spine. What if he could read my mind? What a mess he'd see. Or was everybody this lonely, restless, and confused? What would I say? If given one question, what would I ask? Who am I? What is consciousness? What does it all mean? And what about my dreams? How was it possible to know something was going to happen before it happened? I inhaled deeply and exhaled. And again. Soon the mantra arose. *Om mani padme hung.*

The ferry arrived on time, discharged her passengers and automobiles, and lay serene in her berth, rising and falling on gentle swells. With sunlight glittering on her brightwork and flags aflutter, she looked like a ship bound for some uncharted new land. Instead, it would take me to Korsør and the depredations of Dalton's world . . . but only for one night. Just long enough to collect my money and launder my clothes. Who could say, maybe I would go to Tibet after that.

228

Chapter 14 – Dharma Déjà Vu

Benny sat alone in the galley onboard the ferry. His mood visibly brightened as I passed through the hatchway. He had been alone for a week, he confided, and was on the verge of quitting. He had other complaints. Dalton had gone to Sweden, there had been no work for two weeks, and he had had no contact with Bruce. The foremast on the *Veronica* had been stepped shortly after I left, but Ike only had enough money to cover the shipyard bills.

We vented our anger until late evening. Plans to wash my clothes in the shipyard showers were dashed by the padlocked door. Dalton had the only key on weekends. With nothing going our way, we ate spaghetti pasta topped with margarine and went to bed.

Hutch's warning about no-pay ship owners echoed in my mind as I strode up the gangway to the *Veronica* to confront Ike the next morning. Technically, the work I had done on the foremast before the trip to Spain had been for Dalton—Ike only owed me the $50 he had withheld for work in the hold—but I was desperate. The others had been given an advance, and I needed one too.

The walk to the *Veronica* had given my anger time to galvanize into cold, objective logic. I was ready to spar with Ike. Instead, Mandy answered my knock and invited me in to see their new baby, Ike Junior. I spent a little time admiring him and chatting with Mandy, then left. Ike Senior was on an errand, she told me. They were leaving as soon as he returned.

Benny had said it was a dead end. He was right.

An hour later I had left a note with the Activ Universite address for Dalton, bid farewell to Benny, gathered my things, and struck out for the highway to Copenhagen. I tied a Faroese sweater by the arms around my waist to cover my underwear showing through the back of my jeans. Ike and Mandy drove by as I exited the shipyard gate. Ike gave the horn a friendly beep, waved, and smiled gaily, but had no intention of stopping. Through the back windshield I could see Mandy protest. The brake lights came on and the Volvo stopped. There was a brief exchange, then Ike slowly backed up until beside me.

"Quite a load you got there, Dee," he observed. "Can we give you a ride to the station?"

I threw my stuff in the back then hopped in beside the baby in a car carrier in the back seat. "Thanks," I said. "It's a lot to carry." Mandy radiated with the glow of motherhood.

Ike promptly launched into a story about the porters who had carried his gear on an Amazon expedition. "Those guys could run all day without breathing hard," he narrated, dragging the story out with anecdotes. "You've heard about a second wind?" he expanded. "Well, these guys had third and fourth winds that kicked in while fording rivers and climbing mountains. The monumental irony is that they requested payment in American cigarettes." He looked over his shoulder to see if I was enjoying the irony. We both knew that it was a diversionary tactic. He had paused, however, on the wrong topic—a workman's pay.

I asked for the $50 or an advance.

They were on their way to Copenhagen, he explained, to have it out with his accountant. The accountant was to blame, had prohibited them from spending money until January. "The guy says I'm too soft, Don," he said with soft-eyed sincerity. "Says I have to keep a tighter rein on our accounts." He put on a victim's face and assumed an injured tone. "He's taken my checkbook away."

I knew better. The extravagant modifications to the *Veronica*, the skylights and deckhouse add-on, were vanity additions. That was the truth behind his deception. Ike had bought a stodgy freighter and was trying to make it look like a sailing ship. Hence, the unbudgeted vanity modifications had been given priority over essentials, and contracted workers like Benny and me, who did not have a shipyard or the clout to enforce payment, were being stiffed to help pay for them.

Passing the blame also camouflaged his total disregard for our needs. It cloaked the ruthless egotism that fueled the deception. Recognizing this made me angrier. Ike was a fraud, a charlatan no better than a two-bit crook. To him, Benny and I were something akin to serfs, put here by a providential world to ensure he could achieve his plans. My only advantage lay in Mandy's link. She was probably ignorant of the true nature of their financial difficulties, and Ike would not want her to know that she was an unwitting accomplice in the scheme, that she was grist for his machinations as well.

Ike stopped to drop me at the train station. He looked physically ill when I explained that, like them, I was going to Copenhagen but didn't have a penny. "Oh," said Mandy giddily, "then we can give you a ride." Ike's white-knuckled grip on the steering wheel did not correspond to his magnanimous smile.

The drive to Copenhagen gave Ike time to promote the merits of the around-the-world voyage planned for the *Veronica* next year. Like the venture, he had sold "apprenticeships" to students. Much of his presentation underscored the nutritional benefits that hydroponic tomatoes—to be grown under the skylights—would add to their diet. "It is an idea whose time has come," he proclaimed for the umpteenth time.

When I brought up the withheld $50 again, Ike feigned shock. I explained that Benny and I were totally broke and had no safety net. He changed tactics, asserting that he had no petty cash. The featherbedding shipyard workers had cleaned them out, he explained. The shipyard had charged an arm and a leg for the changes. He was full of excuses. Mandy nodded in agreement.

Ike's disingenuous account of the difficulties tipped the balance. I told them that I probably would not be back and that Benny was going to quit. Ike pulled the car over for a talk. Without cheap labor there would be more delays and more financial problems. He shut off the engine. Cars and trucks sped by as he blamed the problems on inflation, shipyard delays, and the demands of greedy suppliers. Everybody but Ike, it seemed, had contributed to the financial problems of the enterprise. In the end he offered me the job of cook for the around-the-world voyage. He had heard I could cook. Aside from the captain, he noted, the cook would be the only paid position on the *Veronica*.

The job offer seemed too good to be true. I wondered if he planned to offer it to Benny, too. More than ever I distrusted him. Still, the opportunity was too good to disregard. Or was it a ruse to keep me working so he could bilk even more labor out of me? I would have to decide if a trip around the world on the *Veronica* would be payment enough.

Ike let me off near the Little Mermaid Park in Copenhagen. Activ Universite was a short walk away. I could make it there by dark.

The "We Open at 4:30" sign had been removed. I entered and dropped my bags in the vestibule. A lot had been done since my last visit. A fresh coat of paint adorned the walls and trim and the oak stairway had been refinished. The tables and chairs in the upstairs dining room had been arranged in a sideways-H configuration. The room was crowded with travelers.

The overhead lights in the east end of the room were turned off and a documentary on acupuncture was showing on a TV that had been wheeled in. On the screen a Chinese woman lay on an operating table with a small surgical curtain erected like a fence over her torso. On the upper side of the "fence" the woman nibbled orange slices and chatted with a nurse while below it doctors performed a Caesarian birth with only needles to anesthetize her.

I sat next to a pair of American girls. Like me, this was the first time they had ever heard of acupuncture. "Can you believe it?" asked the brunette. She was the high-energy type with a knee bouncing under the table, black hair in a single thick braid that almost reached her waist, and huge blue eyes that roamed gamely among the faces in the crowd. "I've learned more about sex in one hour in Copenhagen than I did in twenty years in Texas." She chuckled and looked to the girl beside her.

"There was a sex education program on before this," explained the other girl. "I'm Amy, by the way, and this is Beth." Amy was tallish and slender, with long, limp blonde hair that hugged her skull. Her gentle blue eyes seemed to embrace the world rather than look at it. She had a few freckles, a lovely oval face, and slender hands that were propped under her chin as she spoke. "I can't wait to see what's on next."

The documentary concluded and the viewers noisily discussed the high points. The voice on the TV announced that a movie was next. I translated it for the girls. "A German film," I told them. It made a good impression. If I was lucky, they wouldn't notice my ragged jeans.

The lights came on. A dark-haired beauty with a perfect Coppertone tan appeared at the doorway. From the back of the room a strange low growl rumbled. It had come from a haggard young man with a flattened gaze who sat with his back to the corner, legs spread provocatively, and his eyes pinned on Coppertone. Obviously annoyed with the growler, Coppertone joined us.

"That guy's a sicko," said Beth to the girl. "He did the same thing to us. He's Danish, too," she added with a condemnatory tone.

"Scary, I'd say," said Coppertone. She tossed her long brown hair over her shoulder as she sat. A natural beauty. Tall, sleek, large breasts, wide mouth with perfect teeth, and an unaffected, gliding gait.

"Did you notice he's cut out the crotch of his pants?" said Amy with a curled lip.

Everybody looked briefly. The young Dane growled again and waggled his legs. The crotch had been cut out and he wore no underwear. Clearly this was a very disturbed person, but no less disgusting because of it.

"You speak Danish," said Beth, suddenly inspired, "go ask him to leave." The other girls agreed.

The young man sat up slowly as I approached, then began rocking back and forth nervously. His name was Steig, I found out, he lived in Christiania, an abandoned military garrison in Copenhagen that had been overrun by squatters a few years earlier. He growled because he liked girls, he told me. Up close he seemed a greasy, pathetic, loner with no conscience. I felt as if I was sitting beside the hard rock bottom of human depravity.

I returned to the girls and imparted my impressions. The moment I finished Beth sprang to action and within a few minutes had spread my account around the room. Her behavior angered me, made me feel dirty, as if I had instigated it. Amy apologized for Beth's rumor-mongering. "She can't help it," she said. I left.

I found Eric and Michelle later, at the end of the hall inspecting a loose handrail on the back staircase. I joined them just as Professor Jordan ascended the stairs. I had heard his name dozens of times, knew that he had founded Activ Universite, but had never met him. We shook hands. Eric told him in Danish about the typewriter and the help that I had provided. The professor looked from Eric to Michelle to me, then nodded approvingly. He asked in Danish if I liked Copenhagen. He was fifty or older, bald with wispy grey hair over his ears, bushy eyebrows, pale blue eyes, and wore an old pinstripe suit that he must have purchased when he was thirty pounds slimmer. He had been described to me more than once as an absent-minded professor, so I wasn't surprised when he just strode away from us without a word, seemingly contemplating something more substantive than an introduction.

We snickered about the professor's departure. He was a grand old gentleman, they told me. Their soiled and paint-spotted dungarees indicated they had personally done a lot since I had seen them last. They paused from the press of work for a chat. To my relief they informed me that the Karmapa's schedule had not changed. As a reward for all of their work, Kristofer had put them in charge of refurbishing the building. I volunteered to help and asked to stay through the Karmapa's visit. Michelle answered with a question, "Can you paint?"

The refurbishing effort, they related, was on track but behind schedule. They needed help. The two large bathrooms were due a facelift over the next few days. I volunteered to tackle the basement bathroom. The rest of the basement was scheduled for cleaning and re-organizing, but that was the last job on the list. As the workload had backlogged over the weeks, the volunteers had been compelled to extend their working hours a little later each night, and to work a seven-day week. Eric and Michelle, I noticed, seemed more mature. The weight of responsibility had displaced the air of serenity that hadn't worn that well on their youthful faces anyway.

My motives for redoing the basement bathroom had been only half honorable. Being penniless, the basement showers looked to me like a safe place to do my laundry. As the person responsible for refurbishing the bathroom, I would control the work schedule—and the door key. By mid-afternoon on the following day I had everything ready. I taped a Closed sign on the bathroom door, retrieved my clothes, then locked myself in. I quickly stripped and, using a mop bucket, began hand-washing my clothes on my hands and knees with two showerheads directed on my body. My body needed cleaning, too. I sloshed the clothes in the bucket of sudsy water, smiling as I recalled the bull in the muddy field in France. From the safety of Copenhagen it was almost funny. I let the water run inside the jeans, then repeated the whole process to make sure they were clean. I was so focused that I failed to hear the footfall on the stairs and the turn of a key.

Two female volunteers entered the bathroom. Embarrassed to be caught washing clothes in a bucket on my hands and knees in the nude, I must have blushed. But they hadn't looked long enough to notice. Rather, they promptly stripped and hopped under the showerheads to my right. Suddenly I was washing clothes in the nude beside two naked women. My thoughts raced backwards in time from the muddy field in France to Jean-Paul's, and back through the Korsør laundromat, Oslo, and all the way to Tvoroyri until I relived that moment, sitting tensed and sweaty on the edge of the bed in Heine's house, nervously weighing the significance of the Laundromat Dream that had just awakened me.

A riot of useless thoughts rushed to the forefront. With great difficulty, I hauled myself back to the present, only to confront the absurdity of having just recalled in chronological order my last several trips to a laundry. More craziness. I shook my head vigorously, hoping to clear it. This is not the dream, I told myself. But the implications of both moments, both experiences slowly settled in. I was washing clothes among naked people.

This wasn't supposed to happen. I had worked so hard to prevent it. An indignant anger arose in me. I have control of my life, I wanted to shout, but didn't. Instead, I summed up the situation: three nude bathers in a basement bathroom was not the same as a frenzied crowd running back and forth in circles around a bank of washing machines. The dream had not come true.

Still, a claustrophobic loss of freewill seemed to descend over me, as if I was cornered but didn't yet know it. The mix of similarities and incongruities between the nude bathers and the Laundromat Dream confused me. If the entire dream had come true, I would have been better prepared to deal with it. Or would I? In truth, I would never have washed my clothes in the shower if it had resembled the setting in the dream. I had carefully scouted each laundromat since the day of the dream in order to short-circuit the possibility of it coming true. And now, as with the previous dreams, the Laundromat Dream had come true, or partly so, even though I had worked to prevent it. And, as before, it had the feel of fate.

I rinsed the jeans quickly and got busy on the rest of the clothes. Feeling out of place and half-paranoid that a naked crew would suddenly arrive with a bank of portable washing machines and start running madly in circles, I nevertheless relished glimpses of the inviting loins and breasts so near. I indulged in the nude bodies beside me yet tried to concentrate on the dirty socks in the bucket. Halfway through two other girls entered. Not Buddhists. One was Coppertone. They promptly stripped and took the two showers to my left. I felt the first stirrings of an erection as steamy pinkened flesh moved in and out of my field of vision while I squeezed the suds from the socks. Coppertone seemed to relish my dilemma and as I stood to rinse the last of the clothes at the shower head, she gently thrust her bosom outward and lathered those rounded, firm breasts with luxurious caressing strokes over, around, and between, her eyes turned away.

I adjusted the hot water to cold. My body shuddered, my imagination shrank.

The girls, I noticed, were chatting gaily back and forth as if I wasn't there. I stared blankly at the drain. My mind strained for answers. Was this another dream? Was this really happening? I gathered my wet laundry and retreated to the dressing area near the sinks. I watched through the shroud of steam as the girls lathered, rinsed, fussed with their hair, and chatted gaily.

From that distance, my thoughts cleared. Although the nude bathers had not corresponded to the dream imagery, the incident had felt like a close cousin to the dream. By appearances, my efforts to keep the dream from coming true had resulted in a distorted rendition of it. Feeling sapped, I quickly dressed and wove my way through the cluttered basement to the boiler room where I draped the laundered clothes on the insulated steam pipes leading in and out of the boiler. The clothes would dry quickly in the hot space.

I ran up the stairs. Eric, Michelle, Kristofer, and the professor were gathered outside the upstairs bathroom. They were in good spirits. Kristofer stepped across the circle and plopped an arm on my shoulder. He smelled strongly of garlic. "Kan you help with kooking tonight?" he asked in a Scandinavian lilt. "It vil be a beeg crowd."

I nodded yes. Activity would take my mind off dream-related matters.

Kristofer's eyes twinkled. The four of them seemed to share the same smile. "He vil make a good Buddhist, you think?" He compressed my lungs with a friendly side-by-side hug. "Vee also learn that the Karmapa vil stay tomorrow at the center in . . . how do you say it, cone-iquette?"

"Con-necticut," said Michelle. "The Karmapa is staying one more day in Con-necticut, so vee have more time."

"Perhaps to Friday," said Kristofer. "Vee see. First vee do prayer tables." He released his arm from the hug and draped it around my neck as if we were dear old friends. He explained that others could work on the bathrooms, that my carpentry skills were needed for making a dozen small prayer tables for the lamas traveling with the Karmapa.

In the discussion that followed, I learned that Professor Jordan owned two other buildings at the intersection where Activ Universite was located. For a workshop, I was to use the vacant building diagonally across the street. Before departing, Kristofer reminded me that I was needed in the kitchen to lift heavy pots when food was ready and, if possible, to help manage the crowd. The two volunteer cooks were new and had limited English skills, he told me.

"It may get crazy," added Michelle. "We get a lot of hungry and impatient travelers."

Eric and Michelle escorted me to the building where I was to build the tables. It was a smaller but nicer three-story red brick building with stone trim around the windows and a fluted pillar at the corner that embellished a recessed entrance. The street-side exterior was standard plate-glass windows on the north and east sides, which were covered on the inside with brown craft paper. Once inside, Eric found the circuit box in the back and switched on the toggles. The three of us looked around.

The interior was dressier than I expected. The walls were covered with a textured jute wallpaper and trimmed in dark hardwood. Most of the ground floor was taken up by a large split-level dining area that would have wide views of the intersection if the paper was removed from the windows. The split level divided the dining area into a large and small section separated by a hardwood partition that reached table height on the upper level. Access between the two areas was facilitated by a double-wide ramp hugging the north wall.

The long galley-style kitchen followed the south wall of the upper area and included a walk-through storeroom that connected to a windowless workroom in back. I never visited the upper floors, but the high ceiling on the ground level was clad in pressed-tin tiles and appointed with three rows of hanging cut-glass light fixtures spaced at twelve-foot intervals. "This would make a great coffeehouse," I pointed out. "And with minimal effort."

They saw it too, but indicated that the professor seemed totally disinterested in the building. However, their words faded into the background as a vision of transforming this space into a coffeehouse arose in my mind. Given the steady flow of travelers to Activ Universite and its educational and spiritual role in the area, a coffeehouse seemed a natural companion enterprise. The idea expanded in my mind as we worked our way toward the workshop.

The large area just inside the front door would accommodate fifteen or more tables and offer a broad view of the immediate vicinity and Activ Universite through the two large, plate glass windows. The smaller, raised area shared only a short section of the northern window, but that made the upper section ideal for small tables and intimate diners. The kitchen was equipped with restaurant-grade appliances and featured a long "prep area" counter outside the kitchen door.

Eric led the way through the storeroom, covered in wall-to-wall shelving, to the workshop. I could live in the workshop, I realized as we entered. Apart from two worktables and a tall bookshelf loaded with tools, the only thing in the room was a long roll of carpet against the wall. I could borrow a bed frame and mattress from the basement across the street. It would be a simple life. I could write during the day and manage the coffeehouse come afternoon and evenings. In my imagination I added ferns on chains from the ceiling in the front area and a small platform up front for musicians and poets. "Does the heater work?" I asked Eric. I could make it fly, I told myself. I could be happy in Copenhagen. I felt giddy with the idea as Eric handed me the front door keys.

The hostel guests had been let in before we returned to the Universite. I checked in with Hedda and Margrit, the two Buddhists who had volunteered to cook. My excitement over the coffeehouse idea made me eager to help. They were just getting started but already were besieged by people entering the kitchen to ask when supper would be ready. The crowd was rowdy, I had noticed, when I walked through the dining area. I made a "Staff Only" sign and taped it beside the swinging doors.

By size alone, the dining room crowd was loud and disorderly. I passed the word that supper would be ready in an hour or so. Beth and Amy helped put out dishes and flatware. The crowd thinned initially, but a steady stream of travelers kept entering the kitchen with the same question, "When will the food be ready?" The noise level in the dining area rose as the crowd swelled to forty or more. Michelle had said it might get unruly.

I returned to the dining area to announce the estimated time for supper. A strange pimpled English youth, probably in his mid-twenties, pulled me aside for a private conversation. He rambled for a minute through a handful of subjects before acknowledging that he had been instructed to monitor the Karmapa's visit by St. Patrick. He spoke fast and nervously and smelled of sweat and bile. I tried politely to extricate myself, but he wouldn't have it. To ensure that he did a proper job on his mission, he told me, "they" had installed a microphone in one of his molars and implanted a transmitting antenna in his skull. As a result, every word that he spoke and every word spoken in his presence would automatically be transmitted to an underground facility in Ireland that was organizing the second coming of Christ. I tried to break away politely, but he placed a gentle hand on my arm. When I abandoned courtesy and turned to leave, he asked if I could spare some change. He didn't seem to care when I told him I was broke.

Steig returned a short while later. Beth and Amy, like agents of contagion, whisked from one group to the next informing the crowd of the perverted Dane in their midst. An Aussie body builder with a *femme fatale* on his sleeve became the counterpoint of interest as the message circled the room. Trouble was brewing. I could feel it. I tracked down the professor to enlist his authority. I explained the situation with Steig as we ascended the stairs. The professor sized up everything and waited. Two girls entered. On cue, Steig bayed low and spread his legs. An instantaneous silence broke over the crowd. Steig's baying hung in the silence like an unwanted odor. He waggled his legs. The professor walked over casually, hands tucked into his suit coat pockets. He spoke softly to Steig. A murmur swelled in the crowd. The body-builder inched closer. Finally the professor gestured politely toward the door, where I stood. A tense moment passed, every ear and eye attuned to the confrontation.

Steig started for the door, but wheeled suddenly and punched the professor in the stomach with a rapid-fire series of short jabs. The crowd snapped upright. Jaws dropped, followed by a collective gasp. All eyes were on Steig and the professor. Steig punched him again. A dozen cartoonish blows that brought to mind a boxing kangaroo as he delivered them.

The second set of blows sent the professor scrambling to the left around the H-shaped configuration of tables in the center of the room, with a stampede of people in his wake. Everything seemed to shift into slow motion as the entire crowd circled to the left toward the door like tottering penguins. Steig sped by in front of me, stopped the crowd, and punched the professor several more times in the stomach. Amazingly, the crowd fled around the tables in the opposite direction, again, heading for the door where I stood. My thoughts collapsed as my eyes followed them first left, then right. And each time, Steig intercepted them and reversed their direction. Back and forth, all in slow motion, tippy-toeing like penguins.

The Laundromat Dream!

I shuddered.

The dream! That haunting image was right before my eyes! A chill descended over me as if a cloud had suddenly blocked the sun on a winter day. My body stiffened, vibrated rigidly, my heart hammered out of control, the sound of blood pulsing through my body engulfed my senses—thum-m . . thum-m . . thum-m . . thum-m—while the crowd ran one way then the other, back and forth, a delegation of wind-up creatures, with Steig's rapid-fire blows reversing their direction each time they neared the door. Whole minutes seemed to pass with this discombobulated slow motion scene unreeling before me. My throat was entangled with squeaking air instead of cries of disbelief. I had no will, no place to go, no place to hide. Suspended in time.

Hedda pushed me from behind. "Do some-ting," she implored.

I stumbled forward and raised a hand. "Stop." The crowd stopped and reversed its field. I repeated the command when they arrived from the other direction. "Stop." The crowd reversed its field again and now Steig jabbed me in the stomach with the same feather-light blows while half the crowd squeezed through the doorway behind me. The rest ran back around the tables. The next thing I knew Steig was mindlessly swaggering back to his chair in the corner. The room was empty except for the two of us, and eerily quiet.

The scene had dissolved as quickly as it had materialized. My shoulders slumped, my arms fell limp, I followed myself out into the hall, totally drained and disoriented.

A silent pandemonium was underway in the hall. Frantically people darted up and down the corridor, staring blankly, flitting in and out of doors like an overdone scene in a Charlie Chaplin movie. Beth tottered up to me, her anguished face inches from mine. "It's all my fault," she spewed uncontrollably, tears squirting in arcs onto her cheeks. "The Karmapa won't come. Everyone will hate me. I wish I was dead." She did a mechanical about-face and, still sobbing uncontrollably, rejoined the frenzied traffic in the hall. Everybody seemed unaware of their behavior, except Hedda, Margrit . . . and me.

The front door opened downstairs followed by the sound of hurried feet ascending the stairs two steps at a time. I hoped it was Kristofer, but a uniformed policeman with a kind Nordic face arrived instead. The professor arrived several steps behind him. They quickly buttonholed Steig. A lively discussion ensued with the policeman confronting Steig with an accusatory glare, but then defending him more and more as the argument progressed. In the end nothing was accomplished and everybody except the policeman gave in to exhaustion. The small group of onlookers that had gathered beside me at the doorway ambled to their bunks in the sleeping rooms. Steig had slumped into his chair. The policeman and professor Jordan took their discussion downstairs. I gathered my gear from under my bunk and took it to the workshop across the street.

The workshop was cold and the air slightly polluted with settling dust, but it was away from the craziness. I spread my sleeping bag onto the flattened carpet roll and stretched out on it. Even before I closed my eyes the madcap scene from the dining hall sprang into my consciousness. I tried to focus on the significance of it, but my thoughts ricocheted instead among the images and the bizarre behavior. A few months ago, unfolding dream events of this kind had been enough to drive me to the brink. This time they seemed different, instructive in some undefined way.

I painstakingly corralled the dream-related events into a single visual collage going all the way back to the night in the Faroe Islands when I had the dream in my room in Heine's home, and slowly three thoughts emerged from the knotty sequence of events. First, another dream had come true. And it was by far the strangest and most complicated yet. Second, I realized once again that I was supposed to be here. Like the Capsize Dream, this one had come true in two parts in spite of determined efforts to prevent it. Third, why had everybody behaved like robots except for Hedda, Margrit, and me?

Of the three, the last one was the most curious. Had the other people actually behaved like robots or had I just perceived it so? Steig's punches to my stomach had been empty, meaningless blows. That was factual, not imagined. Likewise, the professor had not been injured or even bothered, it seemed, by the body blows. And what to make of the wildly surreal run-around-the-tables scene? And Beth's behavior in the hall? Her tears had actually squirted in arcs! Her movements had reminded me of the wooden figurines on fancy Swiss clocks that emerge on the hour from a door, strike a bell, and return through the door. The entire incident had had a strange quality to it, as if people's will and judgment had been temporarily suspended.

I had no answers. Only questions. Radical questions. Can this thing called "consciousness" or "mind" really arise out of mere flesh and blood and bone? Do "thoughts" really consist of miniscule electrical charges coursing through a network of tiny flesh pathways? Is it possible, as some scientists maintain, that humans are merely huge lumbering survival machines for genes that surreptitiously steer us along courses that best assure their own transmission to the next generation? According to that interpretation, the experiences that we regard as life are really experienced, controlled, and directed by microscopic entities that dwell in our bodily fluids and combine with similar entities of the opposite sex to emerge as the next generation. To me, this view seemed like cognitive overkill, an expert opinion, but one that failed to take into account the interdependence of all things. It seemed a one-dimensional interpretation of a multi-dimensional thing. The case of a pickpocket who missed out because he only saw pockets.

I studied the pressed-tin ceiling tiles overhead, searching for an explanation in the cold, unheated room. I slipped under the sleeping bag, noticing for the first time that my breath condensed as I exhaled. What a strange day. I still felt a tremble when I reflected on the nude bodies and the bucket of soapy water in the basement showers, the slapstick scene in the dining hall, Beth's robot-like manner, and the unrobotic arc of her tears in the hallway. It all seemed so real and surreal, both worldly and otherworldly at the same time. However, I slowly recognized that the unfolding of this latest dream included a huge comfort factor not experienced in the earlier dreams: other people had experienced it with me. That, I realized, was the difference I had felt earlier.

Once again I revisited the year's dreams in my mind. In three instances I had told Monty about the dream, but the come-true parts had mostly consisted of my own personal experience. The big exceptions were when Monty pointed out that an unknown crewmate had arrived on the *Marite* with the skipper, and when Monty was beside me on the rocky ledge overlooking the *Marite* and fjord as we linked hands with our crewmates, including the "unknown" crewmate, and lowered them through the crevice as happened in the first capsize dream.

Having dozens of people involved in the basement shower event and the crazy dining hall scene was a game-changer. I had not experienced it alone. After months of trying to explain to others the real-life connections to my crazy dreams, the craziest of them all had come true and parts of the unfolding drama had been experienced by others, by friends. I could compare notes with Amy and Beth.

I tossed aside the sleeping bag and made haste for the dining hall. Halfway across the intersection I remembered Hedda and Margrit. I had agreed to help them. What if the craziness had continued?

An unnatural stillness hung over the dining hall. The tables that had served figuratively as a bank of washing machines earlier were now occupied by travelers in mid-meal. Others filled chairs along the walls, plates on their knees. Hedda and Margrit had enlisted a pair of friends to help in the kitchen. They smiled at me in succession—one, two—when I entered. An arpeggio for my wounded inner self. There was understanding in those smiles. I had not been alone. They had experienced it as well. Hedda shoved a plate of food at me with a steadily widening smile.

I sat next to Amy and some other Americans who had been in the crazy incident earlier. "You all right?" asked Amy in a bemused tone. More confirmation. I couldn't help but chuckle. In some ways the incident had been comical. Everybody had seemed so helpless. "That Steig is one weird critter," she continued. "Trevor says he's going to deck him next time he shows up."

"Who's Trevor?"

She nodded toward the Australian body builder. "He's got a black belt in karate."

"He won't need it on Steig."

Beth, who had been talking with the others, scooted her chair over until the three of us sat knee-to-knee. "That's gotta be the wildest afternoon I've seen since David Lebow's party at the lake," said Beth in an overloud Texas voice. "Did you tell him about Lebow's party?"

"No," said Amy. "He just got here."

"You're gonna, aren't you?" asked Beth. She turned to me. "It was the wildest party, let me tell you."

"It was wilder for some than others," said Amy ambiguously. She turned from Beth to me. There was pain in her soft blue eyes. "Somebody put something in the punch. Mescaline or something. Everybody went bonkers, that's all."

"And jumped buck naked into the lake," added Beth. "How could you forget the best part?"

Amy shrugged. "It was a good party. Lebow's this rich friend of ours. His folks own half the drycleaners in Texas or something." She seemed disinterested in the topic. I had the feeling she wanted to compare notes but Beth's arrival had derailed it.

"You feeling all right?" I asked after eating a little.

Beth answered for her. "You mean did we get our dancing shoes stepped on this afternoon?" she asked. "Then, yes. If you're asking if we survived with our pride intact, I'll give you a definite maybe. But if you're asking 'Was this as wild as Lebow's party?' then the answer is an unqualified N-O." She jutted her jaw at me to demonstrate her conviction.

I looked again to Amy for an answer. She confided that she was all right. She had been shaken by the episode, I could tell, but this was not the time to talk about it. I looked over the other faces in the room. A few small groups chatted quietly. Mostly people ate in peace with their eyes on their plates. There was a big contrast between this roomful of subdued expressions and the loud and unruly crowd that had preceded the Steig incident. That change, however, was not evident in Beth. If anything she seemed more anxious, more superficial, downright obnoxious. And that is what I saw reflected in Amy's behavior. She seemed embarrassed for her friend. Amy seemed to have been humbled by the experience. She wanted to distance herself from Beth for a while at least.

"You going to stick around for the Karmapa?" I asked. "Kristopher got a call from Connecticut. He'll be here in a week."

I asked Amy but Beth answered again. "I guess we can hold out that long," she responded. She looked to Amy for agreement. "But we can't stay too long. Right, Amy-girl?"

"We're due back in London on the eighteenth," explained Amy blandly. "But our return flight to the states is after New Year's."

"I ain't gonna miss Christmas," said Beth steadfastly. "'Tis the season to be jolly. Tra-la-la-la-la . . . and get a new car . . . I hope." She seemed off balance and frightened, but intent on concealing it behind a gay facade.

I helped Hedda and Margrit clean the kitchen. Margrit hummed as she worked. The sound of a contented woman soothed my soul. I wanted to follow her home.

For the next few days I worked on the prayer tables. The distance from the others and hands-on work had a healing effect. Eric and Michelle dropped in a couple of times. Plus, I took meals at the kitchen and joined the Buddhists for tea. I asked about the Steig incident at one of the teas. A devotee with a shaved head described it as instant karma. Everybody in the group had something to contribute. Their explanations added up to something like this: prior to a spiritually enlightened being's arrival among the uninitiated, there often are crazy encounters. The craziness, they explained, was a spiritual summation of sorts, an expression of a condensed version of one's karma.

A student of psychology or group dynamics would likely describe the phenomenon as a group regression, I responded. To the Buddhists my remark muddied the water. It unnecessarily injected Western values into a discussion that was universal in scope. I was talking psychological behavior. They were talking spiritual being. I was talking ego. They were talking mind.

An analogy from a Brit named Gellner offered another perspective. He was a quiet, unassuming youth about my size with clear, deliberate speech, and a propensity for solid eye contact when he did speak. Like many of the Buddhists, he had closely-cropped hair, confident yet downturned eyes, and a straightforward though humble demeanor. He compared the chaos of the Steig incident with the confusion that would necessarily arise if ten converging rivers were to meet at one point. Initially there would be chaos, but the converging waters inevitably would settle in accordance with the laws of gravity into an ordered state, be it a whirlpool, a lake, or a river running to the sea. Western psychology, he continued, described the flotsam and chaos at the point of convergence. What the Buddhists were trying to explain were the universal conditions that underlay the event itself—the laws of gravity and hydrodynamics, in figurative terms, or karma in more specific terms.

"But aren't you now injecting Eastern values into the discussion?" I said critically.

"No." He shook his head succinctly. "Western culture has no concept or terms for karma, just like English has no independent term for paprika. If we are to discuss paprika in English we must use the Slavic term and the universal characteristics of the flavor."

Kristofer, who arrived at the tail end of things, wanted to know why we were discussing paprika instead of working. He listened intently to a recap, thought for a minute, then agreed with Gellner. He characterized the Stieg incident as the final equipment check before making a summit assault on Mt. Everest. Kristofer was a true believer.

From other discussions I learned more. The Tibetan Buddhists had distilled from Buddha's teachings a unique path to enlightenment, known in the West as Vajrayana or tantric Buddhism, that centered on compassion but employed visualization techniques and advanced aspects of yoga. By working for the enlightenment of all sentient beings instead of just themselves, countless Tibetan Buddhist practitioners had demonstrated over the centuries that one could achieve enlightenment in a single lifetime. However, a distinguishing characteristic of compassion-based Buddhism was that before an enlightened practitioner actually took the final step into nirvana—that is, to free oneself from the cycle of birth, life, death, and rebirth—they would be reborn over and over under highly favorable circumstances in their next lives, circumstances that allowed them to recognize their Buddhist background early and resume their pursuit of universal liberation. The most accomplished of these practitioners are known as *bodhisattvas*. Over the centuries, many of these accomplished masters learned to predict when and where they would be reborn. At an opportune time years before their deaths, these masters would share information about their next rebirth with their spiritual peers at the monastery, who would then use the information to retrieve the reborn master while still a child and return him to the monastery. The 14th Dalai Lama and the 16th Karmapa were two such "living Buddhas" and enumerated as such because the Dalai Lama had predicted his rebirth fourteen times and the Karmapa had done so sixteen times. In fact, the original Karmapa, Dusum Khyenpa, was the first to predict his rebirth in the 12th century. And his 16th reincarnation—Rangjung Rigpe Dorje, the 16th Karmapa—was scheduled to arrive at Activ Universite on Friday.

I flashed back to the roadside encounter with the haggard youth in France and how it had reminded me of learning Buddha's story as a fifth grader. Did this mean I was probably a Buddhist in a previous life? I asked Gellner as the group headed back to work. "You are a twice-born Buddhist," he stated in crisp Queen's English. "Everybody in this building is, I assure you."

I tugged my eyes away from his steady, blue-eyed gaze.

The prospect that the forty or so travelers gathered at Activ Universite were all reborn Buddhists was a disquieting one. Not so much for what it said as for what it implied. If pressed, I would guess that at most twenty or thirty of them would describe themselves as Buddhists. Like me, many had read about Buddhism informally—countercultural topics were in vogue—but few would call themselves Buddhists. Most were probably non-practicing Christians or, like me, spiritual seekers drawn here out of curiosity. Implied in Gellner's comment was the notion that we were all Buddhists in a previous life but did not yet know it. Implied was that some guiding principle or hand, reaching across time and over generations, had unconsciously steered each of us to this ephemeral rendezvous with a master of compassion and reincarnation. From Gellner's point of view we were not drawn here so much out of intellectual curiosity as we were unconsciously awakening to our Buddhist roots from a former life. And that unseen hand on the helm, whether it be a monotheistic God, self-perpetuating genes, or a collective unconscious, was the real life force, the real entity that takes on and thrives beyond the flesh.

Wow! Now that was heavy. I took a minute to let the thoughts blend. They seemed tailor-made to explain my dreams. If this life force could reach across lifetimes to influence and awaken mortals to the eternity in which they already lived, it could easily reach across a span of several months to manipulate the dreams of one soul-searching pilgrim from San Francisco.

Gellner's steady blue eyes came back into focus. He softly placed a hand on my shoulder. "Don't get bogged down in too much intellectualizing," he cautioned. "It's pointless. Just let things happen. Open up. Only those capable of loving the world are capable of understanding it."

I finished the prayer tables and helped carry them across the street for painting. The basement and downstairs bathroom had yet to be refurbished, and only a few days remained before the Karmapa arrived. I followed Eric and Michelle to the dining room to attend a planning meeting. It quickly evolved into a gripe session. The big complaint was that the basement was full of junk because the professor was averse to throwing away anything. His permission was needed before anything could be discarded. "Even a broken teacup," complained one volunteer. The problem was that the professor didn't have the time or inclination to cull through the stuff. The volunteers asked Eric and Michelle to intervene. They agreed to talk with the professor. I tagged along.

We found him in the sauna, basking in the nude with Coppertone. The two reclined expansively on benches on opposite sides of the sauna as if engrossed in some sort of spiritual happening. To preserve the heat, the professor asked that we step in and close the door. It was an awkward scene, the two of them reclining on benches in the nude at the opposite end of the small sauna, while three of us waited for an answer, fully clothed on a bench by the door in the stifling heat.

As agreed, the professor came to the dining hall half an hour later. He headed straight for Eric and Michelle. Coppertone was with him. She sat across from me, one table over. With Eric, Michelle, and the professor talking in Danish, she put out her hand to shake. "My name is Linda," she said, "but I prefer Brigitte." We shook elegantly.

"That's a nice name," I told Brigitte, while acknowledging to myself that she would always be Coppertone.

My response seemed to go right past her as she scanned the ceiling. Again, I got the feeling she was looking the other way to allow those around her to indulge in her beauty. My eyes strolled from her neckline over her face. Her skin had a moist, well-toned quality that complemented her soft brown eyes, slender arching brows, lending an unadorned elegance to her passive face. She had a way of cocking her head that made her long dark hair stand out from her neck—even now, when it was damp at the scalp. I liked it, though some might say it was a haughty posture. "Are you one of the Buddhists?" she asked, though clearly not interested.

In light of Gellner's remarks, I considered the question beyond a comfortable interval and then answered. "Not really. But I'm attracted to its organic metaphysics."

She looked me in the face for a moment and pondered my response before replying, "Just here to see the Karmapa?"

"More or less."

"You don't sound too sure about it," she remarked as if that irritated her.

"My life has been pretty chaotic for the last few months," I said. She would view the remark as unmanly, I knew. But there was no point in making manly advances on Brigitte. She wasn't interested in me.

"You must be smart to have learned Danish so quickly," she said without preamble. "I have been here for almost three months and only know a handful of words."

"Where are you from?" I asked.

She stood without answering. The discussion with the professor was over. Michelle had an I-told-you-so look on her face as the professor and Brigitte departed. "He promised to help us with the basement in the morning," Michelle informed me. My eyes followed Brigitte and the professor out the door. I wondered what she saw in the professor? Was he wealthy?

When the professor failed to show up as promised the next morning, we postponed the basement clean-up for a day. On Sunday morning, when he still had not showed, Kristofer reluctantly declared that the basement be locked and declared off limits. In effect, it amounted to sweeping the problem under the carpet, both practically and figuratively.

Kristofer arrived at the morning tea break with the aura of good tidings around his smiling, well-scrubbed face. The Karmapa had left the U.S. and was en route to the Karma Ling retreat in Sweden. A swell of excitement swirled around the dining hall. Faces brightened. Conversations quickened. Kristofer spontaneously hugged those beside him and then restored order. He waved off all questions but promised to keep us better informed about the Karmapa's movements. It would be easier now, he explained, since it no longer involved transatlantic phone calls. There was a lot to do in the meantime. A second coat of paint was needed on the third floor. The windows needed cleaning on the outside. A good seamstress was needed in the shrine room. From now on the kitchen would have to be cleaned meticulously after each meal.

The rain had stopped by Monday morning, but the threat remained. Word that the Karmapa was just a hundred miles away had made the rounds, and suddenly there were new faces among the Buddhists and guests.

Increasingly, the growing number of hostel guests made it more difficult to get them to leave the premises each morning so the clean-up crews could work without interruption. Guests routinely asked for an exception to the rule and Kristofer, Eric, and Michelle routinely told them no. However, the professor did grant a few exceptions. Unfortunately, somebody noticed that the few who were granted an exception were either practitioners of eastern religions or beautiful women. When word of this circulated, a very insistent group led by an English couple, Phil and Eva Humphrey, presented a petition with dozens of signatures to the professor, alleging discrimination against non-Buddhists. In a confrontation in the dining hall, they accused the professor to his face of being anti-Christian. He folded without a fight, which was viewed as an admission of guilt by everybody involved. To those of us readying the place for the Karmapa, the development meant the remainder of our work would take place in a perpetual crowd.

At Monday afternoon tea, Kristofer announced that the Karmapa was at the Karma Ling retreat in Sweden and would be in Copenhagen on Wednesday. A hush erupted into a roar of excitement. A tangible state of exultation filled the room. Kristofer let the joyful noise continue unabated for half a minute, then clapped twice forcefully. The noise ceased. There were some important new requirements for the Tibetans, he continued with urgency in his voice. The Karmapa and his retinue would require separate toilet facilities.

This meant the downstairs bathroom and basement would have to be cleaned afterall. The professor had not been seen in two days, which meant that everything in the basement would have to be moved to the building across the street. There was a hush as the logistics of time and labor sank in. We had a little more than a day to move everything and refurbish the basement spaces.

The informal meeting turned into an organizational session. I volunteered to join the sauna-cleaning team, then handed over my keys to the building to Eric and Michelle. I didn't want to watch my coffeehouse dream sink under the clutter of the professor's junk. Besides, moving the junk to the workshop seemed to me like another version of sweeping the problem under the rug.

By mid-afternoon the team had disinfected the interior of the free-standing sauna and nearly finished vacuuming the narrow space between the sauna and basement wall when the vacuum cleaner died with a scary spark and a loud pop. We were half a minute from having the basement clean-up done. I was carrying the vacuum cleaner up the stairs to the dining room for repair when Eric and Michelle caught me from behind. Their faces lit up like searchlights. "Grab your coat," said Eric with irrepressible glee, "you are coming with us."

"Where?"

"To see the Karmapa in Sweden," blurted Eric in good English.

Twenty minutes later we were on our way in the back of an orange and white Volkswagen van belonging to a Dane named Anselm. The strands of red yarn around his neck indicated that he and Sara, a petite blonde beside him, were veteran Buddhists. They sat in front. Eric, Michelle, Gellner, and I were in the back. Much of the passenger space was taken up with camping gear so it was crowded, but I felt in good company.

260

Chapter 15 – The Buddha and the Pickpocket

I expected high spirits and animated conversation on the drive to meet the Karmapa. Instead, solemn introspection prevailed. Gellner, who appeared to be Anselm's old friend, spent the entire journey meditating cross-legged on the floor, a thumb working in small clockwise circles through his prayer beads. On the bench seat beside me, Eric and Michelle followed Gellner's example but with occasional verbal exchanges. Up front, Anselm engaged Sara in periodic chats that never got to my ears due to engine noise in back. Left to myself, I defogged my window with my coat sleeve and looked for comfort in the landscape moving by outside.

We took the northbound highway out of Copenhagen to *Helsingør* and from there across the Oresund Strait by ferry to Sweden. The back of the van was cold, and wind whistled through the louvered side-windows. Surprisingly, the southern tip of Sweden had been blanketed with a foot of snow during the past week while Copenhagen, less than ten miles away, had received a light rain. I stared pensively out the window as we motored over the gently rolling Swedish countryside. I tried meditating but was too anxious to stay focused. In a short while I would be face-to-face with a Tibetan guru. What do you say to a guru? Do you nod, bow, or shake hands? Do you ask penetrating questions about the nature of time and being? Did the Karmapa even know English? I hadn't inquired. I had so much invested in this meeting, yet knew nearly nothing about what to expect or what to do.

I looked again to my colleagues for conversation. Except for Anselm at the wheel, they all seemed inwardly focused. I regarded each of them again, then puzzled over how our lives had converged. I hardly knew them, yet they had made room for me on this special encounter. I felt like Gordius in a Volkswagen. Like so many times in the past year, I had been at the right place at the right time. Sometimes that had meant trauma, sometimes joy, but in each case it had inspired wonder. Had it been just plain luck or had it been Gordian's lot, an oracle's handiwork? The guru's handiwork? The Buddhists would regard my good and bad fortunes as the result of karma. After all, according to Gellner, everybody positioned to meet the Karmapa was a twice-born Buddhist. I was predisposed at birth to become a Buddhist. But why was I in the advance party to meet the Karmapa, while many veteran Buddhists awaited his arrival in Copenhagen? Why did I feel out of place . . . instead of special?

In part, my anxiety stemmed from the realization that, like countless millions of people before me from countless civilizations over countless generations, I was looking to an exalted person from a different land to answer my unanswerable questions. Was I savior shopping? As a master of time travel and reincarnation, the Karmapa could explain how I could dream about something that would not actually happen for weeks or months. Increasingly the dreams and the Karmapa had become linked in my mind, especially since the Laundromat Dream had come true. More than I wanted to admit, coupling the dreams with the Karmapa felt like desperation. As the van slowed and then turned from the two-lane highway onto a narrow icy farm road leading over more snow-covered hills, my anxiety level shot up. I strained to see beyond the horizon through the windshield, but only saw more hills and the road that lay ahead.

We reached the Karma Ling retreat at dusk. The retreat facility consisted of a white woodframe farmhouse and a small red barn nestled among a few bare willows in a hollow where three snow-covered hills met. As we approached, the warm light from the farmhouse windows painted broad swaths of gold over soft folds of snow, like sunset over a serene ocean. The resplendent view furnished a warm finale to what had been a cold trip.

The area around the farmhouse and barn was crowded with twenty or so cars parked at odd angles. Anselm parked and killed the engine. The sound of chanting monks swelled as we hurried from the van across the snow to the barn. Anselm stopped at the door to listen. "We're lucky," he whispered in Danish. "It just started." He pressed his palms together under his chin, bowed solemnly to each of us, then entered.

The sound and smell of a monastery poured out of the open door. Inside, a makeshift foyer had been fashioned from hanging tapestries. The floor was covered with shoes. I doffed my boots and followed my companions through a part in the draperies. The floor in the small barn was crowded with fifty or so people sitting cross-legged. Without hesitating, Eric and Michelle bounded gazelle-like into the gathering of bodies and bounded again and again until they found sitting space along the left side. They repeated a prayer gesture three times with their hands, bowed reverently, and sat cross-legged. I followed their example but remained at the back for a wider view.

The interior of the barn, perhaps fifty by thirty feet, had been transformed into a cavalcade of color by numerous deity paintings framed by silk borders on the walls and drooping canopies and lanterns overhead. The congregation on the floor faced the Karmapa, who sat cross-legged in the middle of a raised platform directly in front on the opposite side of the barn. A dozen or so lamas sat at his left chanting, four of them poised to play ten-foot horns that extended into the crowd.

I concentrated on the Karmapa. At first glance he seemed young, perhaps thirty, as his dark-complexioned face revealed no obvious cues to his age. But the more I focused the more I decided he could be forty or older. He wore a simple maroon and gold monk's robe and sat in a nest of cushions and fabrics. Like the rest of the gathering, he seemed totally focused on the ceremony. Occasionally he accompanied the chanting with a handbell or a small hand-held drum that produced a sharp sound with a snap of the wrist.

I closed my eyes to absorb the layers of sound. The deep, rhythmic chanting formed a baseline that was accentuated at intervals by a crescendo of handbells, hand drums, and cymbals. When the big horns joined the crescendo, I opened my eyes. Their deep bellowing hovered entreatingly at first in a low register that carried the ringing handbells and clashing cymbals, but then rose as a flourish of smaller horns joined the composition with mid-range notes that fluttered to a new crescendo.

The sounds, smells, and spectacle stimulated my senses, and, as the volume of the music swelled, suddenly the Karmapa held a black, gold-trimmed headpiece that he raised to eye level, examined momentarily, then placed on his head. He steadied the headpiece with an upraised right hand, his round Asiatic face absorbed in extreme concentration.

I looked again to the four big-horn players, their backs against the wall as they worked through another undulating movement and then returned to the entreating strain. There was so much to see—the Karmapa, lamas, horn players, devotees, the ornamentation—but my gaze kept returning to the black and gold headpiece perched precariously on the Karmapa's head: the Vajra Crown.

One of the Buddhists at the Universite had told me about it. Said to be created from the hair of 10,000 spiritual protectors called *dakinis*, the Vajra Crown had been presented to the first Karmapa in the 12th century and was only visible to highly accomplished spiritual masters. A visible facsimile of the crown had been given to the fifth Karmapa to benefit those seeking his blessings. This was the facsimile. According to the Buddhists, anybody who viewed the Vajra Crown was assured of highly favorable circumstances in their next rebirth. According to devotees, it etched an indelible image in the mind, one that would re-appear at the moment of death. Could it be true, I wondered? I looked around at the crowd. I was the only person looking! Everybody else seemed to be meditating.

When the coronation part of the ceremony ended, the Karmapa removed the headpiece to his lap in stages and attending lamas returned it to an ornate hatbox. Additional prayers and readings followed for most of an hour. Finally, a trio of lamas outfitted the Karmapa with a maroon headpiece with long trailing panels that draped over his shoulders, and presented him with objects on a tray that he blessed. The crowd rose to their feet in unison and migrated to the right front of the platform, lining up for individual blessings, I soon realized. I caught sight of Eric and Michelle. She swooned back and forth as they pressed forward.

A handful of children received the Karmapa's blessings first, then romped and frolicked as if the barn were a playground. The blessing ceremony progressed slowly although there were only fifty or so in attendance. I watched from near the end of the line as each devotee received a brief benediction from a lama at the corner of the platform. From there devotees proceeded to another lama who sprinkled water on their heads, then to the Karmapa who bestowed a blessing, then to a final lama who tied a strand of red yarn around each person's neck. Although the ceremony took place in a very relaxed manner, the process had an assembly-line efficiency to it.

Like everybody, I fingered the strand of yarn on my neck and circled it with my fingertips until I found the prayer knot that had been added by the Karmapa. After receiving individual blessings, devotees mingled in a contented state, chatting in whispers. Old friends exchanged hugs. Kristofer and Anselm, like many others in the gathering, had dozens of red strands around their necks. When the last blessing had been bestowed, everybody kneeled and then bowed as the Karmapa exited amid a musical flourish from the horns that signaled the end of the ceremony.

Anselm had the engine running and the van turned toward Copenhagen when I climbed aboard. Silence prevailed until we returned to the paved road. Everybody seemed in a trance.

"Where's Gellner?" I asked, suddenly realizing that he was missing.

"He vil return with others," answered Anselm over his shoulder.

Michelle had started to answer but paused. With her eyes on mine and lips poised to speak, she continued. "The Karmapa is the most powerful man in the world, don't you tink?"

The comment startled me. I had been reflecting on the experience and had reached a different conclusion. The ceremony had been exotic and even mesmerizing at times, but from a spiritual and emotional point of view I had been disappointed. I had expected the encounter to furnish answers. I had wanted confirmation that my foreknowledge of dreamed events had been the Karmapa's doing. Instead, I had taken part in an exotic ceremony.

"It was a wery special group. Vee are so-o fortunate," she added. I nodded in agreement and wished that I had been so moved.

The drive back to Copenhagen passed through the same frigid air with the same engine noise, scenery, and alone-together solitude, but the cold and noise were no bother, and the aloneness and scenery never entered my thoughts. Instead I reflected on the different experiences that Michelle and I had had. A simple explanation came to mind. Perhaps I had not experienced it as intensely as others because I had been focused, like a cub reporter, on the mundane details of the event. My focus had been that of the pickpocket who met a Buddha but didn't realize it because he had only seen his pockets. In my case, I had been distracted by the additional seduction of opening a coffeehouse. A few days would pass before I learned that I was missing out. By then I recognized that I was in the presence of an amazingly powerful being and that my life was poised for big changes.

Things were hectic around Activ Universite on Wednesday morning. With the Karmapa due by day's end, the building was packed with a hundred or more people, which meant a gathering in every room, corridor, and doorway. I was asked to join an emergency crew formed to refurbish the basement bathroom that had been left undone first when I was asked to build the prayer tables, and second when the basement full of the professor's belongings had been placed on the do-not-touch list.

The crew of eight were mending, sweeping, mopping, stripping, window-cleaning, disinfecting, and painting all in the same room at the same time.

In mid-afternoon, Michelle sent word for me to repair the vacuum cleaner if possible. A light bulb in the sauna had burst and scattered glass over the benches and decking. A short time later a phone call from Sweden indicated that the Karmapa wanted to use the sauna when he arrived. I pondered the improbability of that coincidence in the dining room as I opened the vacuum cleaner housing and spread the two halves on the table. A wire needed to be spliced, which would require black tape from the basement.

I hurried. When I returned with the tape, a gold-colored booklet titled *The Living Buddha* lay beside the vacuum cleaner. The moment I opened it, I recognized from the drooping lower-case "p" that it had been produced on my typewriter. This had been the project that had required an English language type-writer. A vicarious pride swelled in me. Thumbing from front to back it contained sections on the Buddha, Tibetan Buddhism, the Karmapa and Kagyu lineage that he headed, and a section on repression in Tibet. The second half of the booklet featured a glossary-like series of explanations on taking refuge, dharma, sangha, meditation, karma, enlightenment, emptiness, and more. Now I understood why Kristofer had taken so long to write it. The subjects would be difficult enough in one's mother tongue.

Emptiness was the first section to catch my eye. Despite a misspelling and an untutored English style, his explanation helped clarify the concept. He described emptiness as the state of mind achieved once the barriers of belief and attachment have been dissolved through meditation and purification. Attachments included assumptions about the nature of the world, the validity of our perceptions, and the belief in an independent self. It sounded like the Buddha all right: If you want to understand the world you must give up the world. In particular I liked the description of emptiness as "occupying your mind." In the West, the Buddhist concept of emptiness is commonly misinterpreted as nihilism or an assertion that the world is meaningless.

I paged forward to the dharma section. Dharma means both the Buddha's teachings and the Buddhist path. Dharma is rooted in existence and action, not in belief. That, too, was news to me. Like many Americans, my understanding of dharma had come from Anglicized renderings of Zen Buddhist principles from Alan Watts and literary portraits like Kerouac's *Dharma Bums*. I had always taken dharma to mean truth, which is how it commonly is translated into English. But in the West the meaning of truth was solidly on the belief side of the ledger. It was something that we strived, fought, and died for, and not, as expressed here, something that was inextricably bound up with our being and every action. To Buddhists, one's path in life is a recurring cycle of life, death, and rebirth that is circumscribed by one's actions, speech, and thoughts. What you do and what happens to you are fundamentally the same. Dharma provides the guidance and path to freedom from cyclic existence.

The booklet was hard to put down, in part because the familiar typeface insinuated that I had written it. Acknowledging that put me in a pensive mood. Here were my answers, or so it seemed to say with the disquietude of a *déjà vu*. I thought again of Plato's notion that we all have universal knowledge but must coax it out through experience. I recalled the crazy days in the Faroes when I shouted to the heavens for answers. I stiffened as I recalled the unfolding of the laundromat dream. I looked again at the familiar typeface, spellbound. *The Living Buddha.* Instead of relief, I felt anxious. I felt suddenly reconnected with the inexplicable events that had driven me to the brink. A queasiness stirred in my stomach.

Michelle entered quietly and beamed when she saw me examining the booklet. She carried a handful of the booklets with her, but probably had come for the vacuum. "Do you like?" she asked, nodding towards the booklet.

"I'm impressed. He did a very good job."

"He vorked wery hard. Until two or three at night sometimes." As she spoke she took a seat on the opposite side of the table and studied the inside of the vacuum with a grim expression. She looked up with a worried expression.

"It'll be ready in five minutes," I told her.

Minutes later, as we headed for the basement to vacuum the sauna, she related her interpretation of the mystery of the exploding light bulb. "The Karmapa broke the light bulb, don't you tink?" she asked. Her comment stunned me. "He did it to force us to clean the basement. To finish our work." My discomfort must have showed.

"He is in Sweden," I reminded her gently.

That didn't matter. She sought me out later to relate that she had talked on the phone with the Buddhists at Karma Ling. Shortly after I had vacuumed up the broken glass in the sauna and finished vacuuming the small area that had been left undone, His Holiness, as she now referred to the Karmapa, had changed his mind. He no longer wanted to use the sauna. To her this was definitive proof that the Karmapa had engineered the incident from a distance. He was renowned for such behavior, she informed me.

"Now vee learn that the Tibetans must have a kitchen for themselves. So meals at Activ Universite must end until after they leave," she told me carefully. Knowing that I had no money for food or lodging, she read the expression on my face as dismay. In truth, my thoughts swelled slowly with pleasure: this was the perfect opportunity to start up a coffeehouse across the street. It could serve as a kitchen for the hostel guests.

She loved the idea. Besides one more clean-up job, the only obstacle was turning on gas for the stove and boiler. That, and convincing the professor it was a good idea.

With Eric's help we set up enough tables and chairs to give the place the right look, prepared a sales pitch for the professor, then allowed Michelle to soften him up on the way over. As they entered the front door the professor wore that proud parent smile that had once led me to believe he was Eric's father. I could tell he was already sold on the idea. Michelle had convinced him on the way over. It should have been easy. The professor took pride in Activ Universite's mission and successes, and by hosting visiting spiritual leaders like the Dalai Lama, Kalu Rinpoche, and Karmapa, the Universite provided important services to the religious and intellectual community of northern Europe. It also served the city and region by offering inexpensive lodging for thousands of tourists each year. For travelers, part of that appeal lay in the fact that they also could get a nutritious meal at a fair price. So it was no surprise when the professor agreed to the idea. However, it caught us off guard when he asked that we serve supper that evening.

The deadline left no time to enjoy the good fortune. The whole place needed scrubbing and re-organizing. I attacked the kitchen. Eric and Michelle fetched pots, utensils, dishes, and other necessities from the Universite kitchen. With additional help from Amy, Beth, and a few volunteers, the inaugural meal of beans and rice was a triumph, although an hour later than planned.

The tables filled immediately after the doors opened. Rock music played over a radio that had been borrowed from the professor's belongings in the basement. The ambience did not rise above the level of student way station, due mostly to the number of backpacks scattered around and maps spread over tables, but the potential remained. Beth and Amy served as waitresses and recruited Laura, a friend. Together they cooked, served food, and collected money while I filled in where needed, which quickly evolved into scullery hand. Once, when I caught up, I indulged myself with a stroll among the patrons, chatting and fraternizing like Rick in *Casablanca*. The conversations were all about the Karmapa. I had been so busy that I had failed to mark his arrival.

Officially, supper ended at 7:30, but hungry people, mostly Buddhists who had spent the evening across the street hoping to see the Karmapa, trickled through the front door asking for a meal. A few had helped us organize earlier, so we continued cooking and serving small groups past ten o'clock. This hadn't been part of the rosy scenario I had painted for Amy and Beth.

With her long braid of black hair pasty from steam exposure, Beth plopped at the table nearest the kitchen doorway and declared, "I'm not feeding one more hungry Buddhist." Her comment seemed calculated to carry to the dozen or so tables occupied by Buddhists.

I tried to console her. "Sorry. I didn't realize it would be like this. I can find someone else to help from now on."

"It's not your fault that all these Buddhists think they're such hot shit."

"Be-eth?" implored Amy with a hand extended across the table. "Don't let it bum you out."

Amy and I stayed up late talking and kept the teapot going for others of a like mind. She apologized for Beth, who she admitted was "a spoiled brat." Beth had wanted to leave for home several days earlier, she confided, but had stayed on as a favor to Amy, who wanted to at least see the Karmapa once. That aside, she really wanted to hear about the trip to Sweden and my encounter with the Karmapa.

I recounted the journey and my impressions without voicing my disappointment. However, I quickly turned the conversation to my real passion, the coffeehouse. I desperately wanted it to flourish, for it to be a gathering place for artists and thinkers. After midnight Amy announced that she needed sleep and asked if my sleeping bag was big enough for two. Tellingly, I had not detected the soft angle of repose in her eyes until that moment. I felt like a fool and told her so. She gave me a quiet sign with an index finger to her lips and led me by the hand to the light switch.

I finally met Phil and Eva Humphrey the following morning at breakfast. Beth and Amy had raved about them. The Humphreys were engineers. Phil specialized in bridges. Eva was a civic planner. They had chosen a life of purposeful travel that they financed by designing a small bridge here, a drainage system there, and always by living close to the land and maintaining a cash reserve. They had been to dozens of countries and enjoyed sharing their vast store of travel tales, which gave them instant credibility among the Activ Universite crowd. They were Brits, thirtyish, educated, had good presentation skills, and were doing what many students promised themselves to do but never quite did: to travel after graduation. Phil, who was prematurely bald, wryly called his bare head a "solar panel." Eva seemed to have a smile on the ready at all times and so made a perfect foil for her poker-faced husband. I had come to tell them that breakfast hours were over after Amy had refused to do it.

I left the vacuum sweeper beside Amy at the top of the ramp, advanced to their table, and exchanged cordialities before getting to the point. "Hate to run you guys off after just meeting you, but we've got to clean up."

"Gracious man, can't you see we're in the middle of an earth-jarring discussion here," said Phil in crisp British diction. Eva was seated beside him, and a young American with a guitar across his lap was also seated at the table. "Roger here said that engineers are dorks."

"My name is Dennis," he clarified. "When I said 'I'll Roger that' I was agreeing with you."

"Yes, yes, I know," conceded Phil. "I was just playing the arse, as they say in the islands."

"You'll have to excuse my vapid spouse," said Eva to Dennis, "that was one of his humorless jokes."

"Vapid," he told Dennis behind his hand, "is German for fast." He turned to me and cocked his chin upward. "So what was your question?"

"He's asking that we leave, dearie," said Eva, who scooted her chair from the table.

There was a pause as Beth entered looking rested and renewed. Everybody watched as she approached. Sensing she was somehow in the spotlight, she sparkled and said with a matchmaker's smile, "You finally got to meet them." She stopped beside Eva. "I've been telling him about ya'll," she told them. "Between the three of you, you could probably talk around the clock without running out of ideas."

"That a compliment or an indictment?" asked Phil.

"I don't know," countered Beth, after a pause. "It's just that he likes to talk about philosophy and religion and you guys like to talk about philosophy and religion. I figured between the three of you, you could talk all night."

"Is that a compliment or an indictment?" repeated Phil in an effort to be funny again.

"Don't be so flip," said Eva, "Of course it's a compliment. And need I remind you that we've been evicted?"

Beth turned to me with a tell-me-it-ain't-so look, then looked at the vacuum sweeper, then Amy at the top of the ramp. When I didn't respond she asked, "It's not gonna hurt anything if they stay, is it?" She turned her head from me to Phil and Eva so fast that her braid swung onto her shoulder.

"We need to clean up. It's not just them, I asked everybody to leave."

Somehow this offended Beth. I could see the fires of injustice building behind that fresh application of eyeliner. "You let the Buddhists stay. Why can't they stay?" she asked.

"It's not a matter of Buddhists and others. Yesterday was an exception."

"Well, today can be an exception."

"You'll pardon us," interjected Eva softly, "but we really must go, irrespective of your good intentions."

I thanked them and politely retreated for the kitchen.

"It's just not right that you let the Buddhists come and go 'til midnight but then run Christians off," shouted Beth at my back.

"Just looking at things as right and wrong makes for a pretty small world view," I snapped.

Amy scowled in my direction.

"Oh, I see," said Beth mockingly. "If I don't see things your way then I'm small-minded, is that it?" The remark stung, and rightfully so. "Well, thanks but no thanks, Mr. Know-It-All." Phil, Eva, and Dennis were waiting for a moment to bid farewell. Beth, with a hand on Eva's shoulder, was pressing for them to sit down.

Amy pinned Beth and me with a firm expression. "You're acting like children. I'm gonna put you both over my knee if you don't stop squabbling."

"In that case, I'm staying," said Phil.

"We're leaving right now," declared Eva.

"Not before they apologize," said Amy. She trotted to the door to block their way. Beth and I apologized and Amy held the door open as the three departed.

In the afternoon I went looking for the professor to discuss the logistics of running the coffeehouse. Although I had been to the Universite dining hall the day before, so much had changed so quickly that it seemed like a week had passed. The door was closed. I had never seen it closed before. I couldn't decide whether to knock first or not. From down the hall the sound of bathers in the showers drifted my way, and to my back I heard the sound of feet treading up the stairwell. There was no sound from the dining hall. A young couple came strolling down the hallway arm in arm. My hand was poised to knock. "That's off limits, man," said the guy in a grave tone. I started to knock anyway but gave it a second thought. Suppose it interrupted a meditation session or something. I began to feel a bit like Beth must have felt. The dining room had always been a part of the public domain at Activ Universite and now suddenly it was taken over by others with unfamiliar routines. It made me feel like an outsider.

As I considered where to look next for the professor, the front door downstairs opened and closed and the familiar sound of Kristofer ascending the stairs two steps at a time arrived. A moment later he had an arm around my shoulder and was steering me down the hallway. "Vee cannot miss *pujah*," he declared.

We took the back stairs up to the third floor and entered the room directly over the dining hall. Thirty or so people filled the room that had been painted to resemble the interior of a monastery, complete with *trompe l'oeil* columns and ornamentation. We doffed our shoes, bowed three times with our hands pressed together, then joined the group of Buddhists on the floor. At the far end of the room, the Karmapa sat on a waist-high platform, looking vaguely different today, though seated in a lotus position again. He smiled casually at Kristopher, then me, his right hand rested on his knee, his left hand buried in the folds of his garments, and a four-foot-square screen covered with a richly colored brocade fabric behind him. To his right stood one of the prayer tables I had made. It looked great. This seemed the ideal time to ask to speak with him.

Along the long wall to the Karmapa's left sat ten or so lamas in maroon robes with a prayer table positioned beside or in front of each. One lama, I noticed, was an older woman with closely cropped white hair and glasses. Her pearl-white face stood in stark contrast to the dark and weathered faces of the Tibetans. I studied the woman for a short time but could not discern anything remarkable. Like the Tibetans, she was the picture of humility. I turned my focus to the horn players two stations away. As before, their backs were to the wall and the long brass horns extended to the center of the room where they rested on cushions. Shorter horns stood at arm's length beside them. I looked to the Karmapa. His eyes were closed and his lips moved rhythmically. Slowly and gently a liturgical murmur arose in the room, which slowly expanded into an enchanting swell of synchronized voices. After a while the horns joined in, their distinct sound rising slowly from a distant hiss until, catching some air, the sound swelled into the deep entreating strain. The Karmapa, I noticed, was chanting aloud and everybody, except me, had joined in.

My thoughts moved swiftly to Amy. If only I had known a few minutes earlier I could have fetched her. She had re-arranged her travel plans and risked alienating her best friend in order to see the Karmapa. She also had worked very hard to facilitate things for his arrival. She deserved it. But it was too late. I closed my eyes and listened to the soothing melody of the chant. I tried to comprehend the words so I could join in, but they were in Tibetan. Instead, I hummed along.

After a short while, I succumbed to the ineffable pull of the sounds and ritual and felt something welling in me. My chest expanded and flattened, my spine straightened as if being coaxed into good posture by a tailor. I could feel . . . something. I could feel . . . my body . . . the whole of it at once. I relaxed and just let it happen. Something was happening.

When the ceremony ended an hour later I didn't want to get up. I didn't want it to be over. I felt stilled. Becalmed though alert. As I moved, I became more aware of my body. The air passing through my nostrils rushed noisily in and out. I didn't know how it had happened, I just felt different. My eyes caught Eric and Michelle whispering near the front of the room. Michelle had that swoony look again. Perhaps I did too. I felt strangely taller as I walked to the pile of shoes at the door. Not taller really, just more aware than before of how far it was to the floor. I put on my boots with long arms and strode fluidly for the out-of-doors.

The day was cold but sunny. I paused at the corner for a moment, torn between a desire to share the experience with Amy and a desire to contemplate the *pujah* experience. The latter beckoned more eloquently so I walked to the Oster Anlaeg gardens nearby and sat cross-legged in a sunny spot among evergreens. As my eyes closed I let my body soak up the warmth of the winter sun. The sounds of midmorning traffic receded and the squawk of ducks and the sounds of splashing water and laughing children encircled me. I felt at peace. The songs of unfamiliar birds invited me to stay and listen as they conveyed something of their world in chirps and warbles and chatter. I stretched out onto my back, cushioned my head on my hands, and let my thoughts recline as well.

The meditation had put me into orbit around myself. I was aware of everything at once—my body, its functions, the cold earth beneath me, the timbre of city sounds impinging from beyond—while not focusing on anything in particular. Was this what the *The Living Buddha* booklet had characterized as "occupying your mind?" It was a seductive feeling. The meaningless chatter that ordinarily filled my head was no longer there. I felt clear-headed, unperturbed, truly relaxed. The only interruption to the serenity was my curiosity. How had I reached this state of mind?

I hadn't really chanted or meditated. Rather, I had hummed along and relaxed and listened. That's all. Could it have been the work of the Karmapa? Did he have that kind of power? The power to put people in orbit around themselves? Hadn't Michelle said as much on our way back from Sweden? She had described him as "the most powerful man in the world." And I had scoffed at the remark. I suddenly felt an urge to get up, to move around. I stood, then headed for the sidewalk. Had I been wrong about the Karmapa? Did he have extraordinary powers? It seemed just as unlikely now as it had before, but I had to admit that the meditation, the Karmapa, or something had put me in orbit.

Halfway across the park I stopped beside the manicured bank of a small duck pond and watched swans glide across the water. I no longer felt so serene and composed. Thinking about the experience seemed to have made the resulting emotions disappear. Whatever it was I had had, was gone.

A vision of Amy sprang into my thoughts as I returned to the coffeehouse. A vision of her walking away, hips and shiny blonde hair swaying in counterpoint. She turned slowly in my mind and displayed a big southwestern smile. She was a lovely woman with an alluring body. Sadly, she would be heading back to those wide open spaces in just a few days.

Amy and Beth sat at a table having tea when I returned. Amy pointed with a nod to a pair of Boston ferns hanging on chains in the front windows. "Look what Beth did," said Amy.

Beth smiled proudly. "What do you think?" she asked, her eyes wide open.

"They look great," I said, joining them at the table. "They really add a lot."

"That's exactly what I said," exclaimed Amy, her hands emphasizing the point. "Beth's an interior design major."

"So what's the occasion?" I asked Beth. They had cost her $20 at least.

"Oh, I don't know. I guess I wanted to make up for last night and this morning. I'm a real pain, I know." She poured tea into a cup and graciously handed it to me.

"It was my fault too," I apologized.

"See. I told you he wasn't mad," said Amy. She turned her soft blue eyes to me. "Beth and I had a brainstorming session to come up with a name for this place." She showed me the list, which included The Great Dane, Le Club Amerique, and The Danish Delight. To me, the doodles adorning the edges around the list were more interesting than the names. I borrowed the pencil and wrote Kierkegaard at the bottom of the list.

"Kierkegaard?" said Beth with a furrow of doubt. "You're beginning to sound like a Buddhist." She looked from me to Amy then back to me. She and Amy would discuss it back at the sorority house was the message.

"Here's a good name," I volunteered. "What do you think about Kierkegaard's Cafe?" I wrote it on the scrap of paper. "Or better yet, Kierkegaard's Pantry." In my imagination I could already see it painted on the front window, bracketed by the hanging ferns.

"Cafe with a K," said Amy. "That works better. But why are you so hung up on Kierkegaard?"

"He was a Dane, lived much of his life in Copenhagen, plus he wrote a lot about religion and philosophy."

I found the professor and Brigitte across the street in the hallway upstairs, where we settled on a system for resupplying the coffeehouse and other management issues. As usual, the professor was focused on something else, but he agreed. According to the plan, each morning I would submit a list of needed provisions and he would have it delivered that afternoon. The only conditions that he placed on the meals were that the price not exceed ten kroner, approximately $1.75, that they be vegetarian and nutritious, and that food costs not exceed the earned income. The conditions fit my expectations perfectly. By noon the next day Amy, Beth, and I had planned meals for the next three days.

Things went smoothly for a few days. I missed the early morning meditation sessions held in the third-floor meditation hall, but the afternoon sessions were at a convenient time. The coffeehouse meals and service improved as the three of us worked out the kinks. Amy and Beth were like housemothers. They enjoyed pleasing our "customers" and treated most of them like honored guests. The exception was between Beth and the Buddhists. For some reason she didn't like or trust them, even though the majority were exemplars of Christian virtue.

Eric and Michelle dropped by one night for tea. Gauging from their expressions, they had been watching me for a few minutes before I noticed them. I was singing along with the radio as I cleaned the prep area near the kitchen door. My singing was always good for a laugh. The three of us sat at a table near the back. Their faces radiated love and goodwill. They liked the name I had chosen for the coffeehouse. We talked for a long time. I learned that the woman in the Karmapa's entourage was Freda Bedi and that she was well known in India and had helped organize the Karmapa's visit to the West.

Eric and Michelle were totally entranced by the Karmapa. They reaffirmed my observations about the *pujahs*. "They are wery, wery powerful," said Michelle with a clenched fist. Eric said his legs wobbled afterwards. I was entranced by the Karmapa, but my fascination embodied a sort of ambient zeal that included Amy, Kierkegaard's Pantry, and feeling comfortable in Copenhagen.

I learned as we talked that meals for the Karmapa and his retinue had to be prepared according to very specific guidelines, which explained why the Tibetans had needed a kitchen of their own. Although eating meat generally was discouraged among Buddhists, the Karmapa ate meat, they explained carefully, because by consuming freshly slaughtered livestock "His Holiness" could hasten the progress of these creatures on the path to enlightenment. Animals were, after all, sentient beings that, like all other sentient beings, were on a spiritual sojourn.

The meat-eating rationale smacked of self-indulgence to me. I wasn't convinced that the Karmapa could influence other creatures after death, even though preparing for death was critically important to Tibetan Buddhists. But I recognized the appeal of believing that another person could solve one's problems. To me, it was an unacknowledged but central motivating factor in the development of organized religion. But the blind submission that always accompanied such relationships was, in my mind, the first step toward spiritual degeneration, the step that devolved spirituality into religion, religion into moral dogma, and morality into self-righteousness. Over the centuries this devolution had repeatedly served as the seedbed for otherwise unthinkable cruelty.

The unqualified good news was that the Karmapa was scheduled to do the Vajra Crown ceremony at a nearby auditorium. Amy had attended a *pujah* but had only heard about the Vajra Crown ceremony. She bear-hugged me when I informed her, then resumed trimming my hair.

Beth agreed to stay behind to receive a grocery delivery, which freed Amy and me to join a contingent of Buddhists in the twenty-minute walk to the auditorium near Kongens Nytorv, the King's New Market district.

The auditorium was nondescript—no marquis, neon inducements, not even the usual rows and rows of seats inside—but it was large, carpeted, and filled with hundreds of people. I was pleased to see that Kristofer was the master of ceremonies. From behind a podium onstage he spoke briefly on the history of Tibetan Buddhism, the Karmapa, and the Vajra Crown ceremony to a crowd that appeared to be non-Buddhist Danes, though the entire Activ Universite contingent seemed to be there. I translated what I could for Amy, including the request for donations that concluded the introduction. Kristofer signaled and rolled away the podium. The lights dimmed and the curtains opened slowly upon the Karmapa, with a row of lamas to his left. As before, the horn players sat midway along the row of lamas with their horns extending to center stage. We sat cross-legged on the carpet.

I decided on a different approach this time. Instead of trying to make sense of the ceremony, my plan was to just open my senses as wide as possible. There was utter silence in the auditorium as the lamas began with a slow, resonant chant in monosyllables. Amy and I added our voices to the chanting, although neither of us knew the words or meaning. The sound grew as a body. The chanting continued for perhaps fifteen

minutes when unexpectedly the long horns entered perpendi-
cularly with a long bass interlude and then fluttering asides. A
single, deep chanting voice carried through the exotic mix of
sounds. I opened my eyes briefly. The Karmapa lifted the Vajra
Crown to his head. I closed my eyes, my body snapped into the
lotus position as if programmed for it. I gently swept aside all
thoughts and opened my senses.

Moments later, I noticed that I could see the Karmapa
perfectly, although my eyes were closed. The image of the
Karmapa—the impassive expression and gaze, the Vajra Crown
held slightly askew on his head by his right hand—seemed
imprinted on my retina. Without hesitation, I swept away my
thoughts and opened up again. The sounds of the horns and the
single chanting voice enveloped me like a warm sea. Soon the
horns ceased in unison and the lamas and crowd took up the
chanting until, with a flourish of handbells and handdrums, the
lamas responded with a song-like liturgy over the
accompanying sound of handbell and drum. This stopped after a
long while and the lights returned slowly. The crowd rose, and,
with only a rustling sound amid a respectful silence, formed a
line at the right side of the stage.

The ceremony had only lasted an hour or so but the
individual blessings took much longer. Once again the
experience had left me feeling calm, centered, and introverted.
Not so for Amy. She felt confused and wanted to talk about it.
We took the long way back. "Do you think he's some kind of
god?" she asked. I gave it a lot of thought. I really didn't know
enough about Tibetan Buddhism to form an educated opinion.
Very few Westerners did. In one of my long chats with
Michelle and Eric and the Buddhist group I had asked for
recommended reading on the subject. None of them could name

a single English language book on Tibetan Buddhism. Rather, I was encouraged to read *An Autobiography of a Yogi* by Paramahansa Yogananda, a Hindu master.

She was not wanting an educated, impartial answer to her question or the Buddhist point of view. That was my impression. She wanted me to help her fit this into her belief system. She felt vulnerable and did not like it. Her feelings were not so different from my own. I wrapped an arm around her as we meandered slowly with our heads close together. There was nothing to do but tell her my take on things.

"No," I answered. "I don't think the Karmapa is a god. In fact, I don't subscribe to the notions of holiness, sin, or god. I agree with Blake when he said 'there is no natural religion.' To me the concept of god is a convenience, a human creation to explain the inexplicable and relieve human insecurity."

"The Buddhists think the Karmapa is a god. Did you know that?"

I nodded, but was aware from various sources that Buddhism was a nontheistic religion and from Kristopher's booklet that the Karmapa was regarded as a living Buddha, a *boddhisattva*. Still, there was pain in the way she had said it, as if the possibility that he was a god had violated something deeply held. God had always been something farther away, I suppose.

"I don't have any real answers, Amy. It's just too close to figure out right now. I do know that life can be frightening. And fear makes some people grasp for definitive answers to bolster their lives, while others are able to live with a greater tolerance for the unknown. For the insecure among us, a simple system of answers-from-on-high makes more sense than seeking answers within. And answers are important. Without them our everyday activities would lack structure and a meaningful foundation. But if you look at it honestly, embracing answers for the comfort they provide not only creates an unsustainable belief system, it results in a life of faithlessness. Faith, as I see it, is something more like openness to the unknown. All else is belief."

As we walked along the busy promenade, I admired in a peripheral way this beautiful and concerned woman who had entered my life like a sunny climate. Through her I saw a rerun of my confused state on the return trip from the Karma Ling retreat. It had all been too big to sort out in the immediate aftermath. It still was. I pulled her closer, remembering that a hug was what I had needed at the time. "We don't have to figure all of this out today," I soothed, a little amazed at my own manner. "We've got a lifetime of days like this still ahead."

288

Chapter 16 – K's Pantry

In many ways the evening meal that night marked the grand opening of Kierkegaard's Pantry. A two-day supply of rations had been delivered and that signaled good-bye to the bland rice-and-cabbage days and hello to more appealing fare.

"I've got another surprise," said Beth excitedly. She had us close our eyes for a long minute until the hiss of a struck match and the smell of sulphur hinted at what was to come, and she sang out, "Da-dum-m-m. You can look."

She had hung a green army blanket over the entrance ramp between the two dining areas to darken the smaller area, then lit several candles placed on tables. They were beautiful candles in small, tulip-shaped vases. They really added an elegant note to the table settings.

"Wow!" I called out. "I can't believe you, Beth!" I lifted her off the ground and spun her with a big hug then gently put her down with a kiss on the cheek. "They look great!"

She accepted the comments with a petite curtsy, daintily pulled out a chair and sat elegantly before a candle. "Do you really like them?" she asked, smiling with her head tilted coquettishly to one side.

Her tone conveyed doubt. I soon found out why. She had purchased the candles from the meal money collected the previous day. I was miffed but held fire. For better or worse, Beth had been instrumental in getting Kierkegaard's Pantry off the ground, and the purchase, though misguided and she knew it, had been made with the improvement of the coffeehouse in mind. Her behavior was not entirely a surprise. The real problem was how to pay for them. "That money is not ours to spend. It's our food allotment," I reminded her.

"I know," she cooed, "and I can pay it back if you get in trouble. It's just that . . . well, look how much they improve the place."

There was no disputing it, but I wanted to present an unambiguous response, so I turned my back on her, took down the blanket, and folded it with karate-chop motions. The unauthorized expenditure was partially my fault. I shouldn't have left the money in her hands. I had delegated my responsibility so I could spend more time with the Karmapa and Amy.

The professor dropped in that evening for the first time. Everything was perfect. The evening was dark and cold, so the candles and steamed windows beckoned to passersby. Once through the door, the professor was greeted by Amy and a room teeming with energy. The background music was compliments of a Copenhagen radio station. The professor expressed his approval with a gentle nod and a smile as he surveyed the room. He had not visited since the cold and dusty day when he had turned on the heat. I thought he had come by for a progress report, but instead he stopped to talk with Brigitte and the Aussie as they enjoyed creamed broccoli and cheese on pasta. He later made his way to the kitchen where I was struggling to keep the dishes in circulation. He expressed his satisfaction with the way things were going. He said that Brigitte had volunteered to pick up the money for him and collect the supply lists.

When the crowd thinned and I had some free time, I wrote "Kierkegaard's Pantry" on the outside of the front window with a bar of soap turned on edge. And though the skinny lettering was thoroughly amateurish and just barely visible, I felt like a miner who had found a vein of gold. As I returned to the kitchen, Phil Humphrey, who sat with his feet propped on a chair, a cup of tea in his hand, said, "If you meant to wash the windows, you forgot the water." At midnight I had to evict the Humphreys and a dozen others.

On one frosty morning, the Karmapa and a large group of followers were treated to a visit to the Copenhagen Zoo. Eric and Michelle dropped by afterwards to "wisit" with Amy and me. She recounted that while strolling at the zoo, the Karmapa warned those walking at the front of the group to watch out for broken glass ahead. His warning had come half a minute before they turned a corner and found a broken bottle underfoot. Michelle had related it in passing, sandwiched between the polar bears and cotton candy, apparently assuming that we knew the Karmapa could see around corners. Later, in what felt amusingly like a Buddhist double-date, the four of us walked to the auditorium for a Vajra Crown ceremony. This time a wealthy benefactor was allowed to sit on stage and face the Karmapa, but neither the man nor closed eyelids obstructed my view.

On the way back to the Universite I asked Michelle about seeing the Karmapa through closed eyes. She proclaimed the indelible image of the Karmapa as "wery auspicious" and clasped my hands excitedly. "You have strong karmic connections to His Holiness," she told me.

In the afternoon, Beth showed up at the coffeehouse carrying all of her gear. "I'm hopping mad," she blurted, after dropping her stuff on the floor in front of us. "I went to get some stuff out of my bag and some flimflam Buddhist had taken my bunk. Same with Bobby. It's the second time in three days" Her nostrils flared and went from bright pink to white as she spoke. "What really burns me up is the sonofabitch just tossed my stuff by the door and put his stuff on my bed. To be so full of peace-love, holy-cow, and all-is-bliss, the Buddhists are getting to be a pain in the ass."

"Report it to the professor," I suggested. "Most of them live right here in town. And the ones who don't are staying with the ones who do."

"Bullshit," said Beth. "Where have you been, baby. They've taken over. You gotta have a red string around your neck to get in the door over there. And I ain't got one . . . and I don't want one either."

"So what are you going to do?" asked Amy.

"I'm moving in here with y'all," she said with a smile as unyielding as a bench vise.

By supper time she was all sweetness and light. Brigitte had asked to be a volunteer. Beth was at her best when telling others what to do. And it was even better when the heartthrob of every male currently in residence at Activ Universite was asking her what to do.

I cornered Eric and Michelle after supper and asked them to intervene in the matter of the bunk thefts. "Everybody wants to be close to His Holiness," she explained, pressing her palms together as she used the Karmapa's name. As we talked it became apparent that she felt the bunk hijackings were acceptable behavior. Let the Buddhists be close to "His Holiness," had been her attitude. "His Holiness" will only be here for a few more days.

This shocked me. "What about the other people who are here to see the Karmapa? Where can they stay? And what happened to those vows of compassion?" It also annoyed me that both she and Eric were bowing in an abbreviated manner whenever they said "His Holiness." This, coupled with the abandonment of the obsolete term, Karmapa, looked to be step one of the deification process. I found it ironic that the Buddha, who found no need for a god, should be made into one by his devotees.

I recounted the conversation to Amy. "And then they come over here and expect to be treated like V-I-Ps or something," she said, sounding like Beth.

On Sunday I was seeing it differently, though. And the thing that changed my outlook was seeing many of the Buddhists in Sunday finery. Why the dressier clothes on Sunday, I asked myself, when several of the Buddhists showed up with polished shoes and dressy attire? The answer was simple: it was Sunday, a holy day to them for most of their lives. And though they were now Buddhists by affiliation, they had not fully discarded the habits and the Christian mindset. That mindset included an inclination to worship an exalted person, the inclination to deify.

The observation gathered strength the farther I took it. The "Zen Christians," as I now thought of them, equated concepts such as nirvana with heaven, samsara with hell, and dharma with truth, as if they were synonymous. They weren't even close. Nirvana means freedom from rebirth. Samsara refers to the suffering in the world of cyclic existence, and dharma, as I had learned from the booklet, was both the Buddha's teachings and the Buddhist path.

Useful though they were, my Zen Christian observations were no help in resolving the tension that grew between the Buddhists and non-Buddhists. Another factor that indirectly contributed to the friction between the groups was the Buddhists' informal schedule. Things just kind of happened while the Karmapa was there. Not wanting to miss a *pujah* or ceremony of any kind, the Buddhists were apt to linger in the corridors in case some unannounced something came up. This tended to exclude non-Buddhists from some activities.

I was drawn into one of these unscheduled events earlier in the week. I sat at a table by the front window in the coffeehouse when I saw a flash of maroon at the front door to Activ Universite across the intersection. A lama had poked his head out the door, looked up and down the empty sidewalk, and then withdrawn inside. It was the first time I had seen one of the Tibetans in a non-ceremonial setting, and that piqued my curiosity. I set aside the supply list, locked the door behind me, and gave chase. The same flash of maroon appeared at the end of the hallway when I reached the top of the stairs. I followed but pulled up short at the back staircase to the third floor. I felt like Alice chasing the White Rabbit when Anselm and Sara showed up. I hadn't seen them face-to-face since the trip to Sweden. They smiled approvingly, opened the door to the staircase confidently, and waited for me to go first. I returned the courtesy on the third floor, and followed them into the meditation hall.

Approximately fifteen individuals sat cross-legged on the wood floor with the Karmapa and three bare-headed lamas in maroon robes at the front. I bowed respectfully and sat. With palms pressed together, a lama chanted a memorized passage in Tibetan for several minutes, That was followed by a brief consultation among the lamas. Two of the lamas humbly stationed themselves among the crowd while the third, still sitting in front of the Karmapa, read from small slips of paper. The Karmapa watched over the proceedings but did not participate. As the lama at the front read the small notes he passed them to the lama in the center of the crowd who, casually casting an eye over our faces, handed the slips one by one to individuals. The hand-to-hand distribution system reminded me of "mail call" in the military. The second lama in the crowd followed the slips of paper to the recipient from whom he scissored a snippet of hair. After the lama snipped a locket from the top of my head, I looked at my fortune cookie-sized note, which featured a smudged red insignia stamped on one margin followed by two inches of handwritten Tibetan script. Like Arabic, I couldn't tell if I was looking at it right-side up, sideways, or what. I found out later from Sara that I had "taken refuge," the formal enrollment vow into Buddhism, and been given a Tibetan name.

Needless to say, I was anxious to find out more about my name. I caught Eric and Michelle in the hallway a short wait later and had them look at it. They recognized the Tibetan characters and pronounced my name as Karma Sonum Norbu. And while I was fascinated by having been given the name, I was much more fascinated with the casual manner in which it had happened.

Christmas Eve took me by surprise. I had heard there would be an afternoon *pujah* and shared the news with Amy. She couldn't attend, however, because she planned to shop with Beth. When I looked back quizzically, she responded with her you-must-be-crazy look and said, "Tomorrow's Christmas." Both the date and her response surprised me. Our paths were diverging, I realized. Amy and I had gone together to two *pujahs* but her experiences had been similar to my distracted first encounter with the Karmapa. Instead of emerging with a becalming feeling, she had experienced a Tibetan sing-along. There were other sides to the situation as well. Her stay in

Copenhagen would end in a mere forty-eight hours, and she was anxious about leaving and our impending separation. Plus, she was keen on mending fences with Beth, who had stayed because guru encounters were very trendy in the West.

After the *pujah,* I made tracks for the park. Sunny, warm weather had invaded, so I rolled up my sweater for a pillow and napped. I woke up some time later to goose bumps on my bare arms and darkness. It was after five o'clock, I recognized, as I set my course for Kierkegaard's Pantry. Car headlights were switched on. I was late again.

The place was open and booming. Amy had come through! She had even recruited male waiters. What a coup! And Beth, who usually handled the cashbox at the counter, was sketching decorative snowdrifts onto the window corners with a bar of soap. On the window sills she had spread a selection of fold-out paper bells, stars, and tinsel bunting.

Brigitte was at the counter collecting money. I waved appreciatively and strode into the kitchen to find Amy. She was ladling lentils onto plates held by a young kid trying to look like John Lennon. Her hair kept falling in her face as she blew at it angrily. I stopped, took a single step backwards and applauded. "Bravo! Bravo!" Then I gave her a hug. But she wasn't receptive. "Good job," I continued with an explanation of how I had fallen asleep in the park.

"It's not my doing," she said tersely. "You can thank Brigitte. She did it all." Her bottom lip trembled, and an incorrigible lock of hair fell over her face.

One of the other male helpers entered with a plate. "How about seconds?" he asked gamely. Amy looked at him then me and began to cry. I gathered her up and escorted her to our room in the back and gave her a big consoling hug and kiss. "I would have," she bawled, "but I didn't have the key."

She recounted the sequence of events. Basically Brigitte had stepped in with the keys, authority, and volunteers, while Amy had been left with the most unglamorous job because, or so Amy believed, she had sided with me and the Buddhists one time too many. I fetched her a damp cloth for freshening up and went back to the dining area where Beth, Phil, and Eva were squabbling with a Buddhist couple about the Christmas decorations.

The Buddhists asked politely that the explicit Christmas decorations be removed. Beth was not so polite. It took a while, but a compromise was forged. The Christmas decorations would be relocated to the smaller dining area since the Christians were a smaller contingent than the Buddhists, but the snow drifts would remain in the windows and anybody could eat where ever they wanted. I hated the senseless squabbling, the tribal attitudes, the partition.

As Beth marched off to relocate the decorations I joined Brigitte at the hot water urn and thanked her for covering. I then asked her about the professor's response. "Is he angry at me for being late?"

She pursed her lips seductively and shook her head. "He doesn't know. I had a key already. It was easy."

"Have trouble finding volunteers?" I asked facetiously.

She answered with a wag of her butt and an overtly flirtatious expression. I liked that. The honesty was a departure from her usual smug behavior. She seemed more relaxed and comfortable.

There was another *pujah* on Christmas day. I was pleasantly surprised to see Gellner in monk's garb, his shorn head shining white among the lamas flanking the hornplayers. I sought out those steady blue eyes but never connected. He had taken the vows. And his observation, which had merely seemed thoughtful at the time, suddenly seemed gilt-edged and eternal: "Only those who are capable of loving the world are capable of understanding it." Understanding is achieved through compassion.

I left the *pujah* giddy with my self-important insight, but distressed that the Tibetans were scheduled to leave in two days. Perhaps there would be one last Vajra Crown ceremony and another *pujah*. I asked around. Nobody knew.

Predictably there was a flare up between the Christians and the Buddhists during the Christmas meal that evening. This time it was more emotional and included more bodies on each side. And there was little doubt about how it got started. With encouragement and contributions from others, Beth had purchased a precooked ham for the Christmas meal. Naturally the vegetarian Buddhists were offended and repulsed by the meat in their midst. To them it seemed a provocation.

Until recently, I reminded them, many of the Buddhists had eaten fish and meat and the Christians did not wear red blessing cords around their necks. The Christians interpreted my position as siding with the Buddhists rather than advocating tolerance as I intended.

In another attempt at coming out on top, Beth instructed the Aussie to rehang the green army blanket like a partition from the ceiling between the two dining areas while she gathered the tabletop candles for use by the Christians only. I removed the candles and blanket. An informal truce was reached, but I had lost all respect from both groups. Their behavior had sullied what should have been a memorable day for all. It also reminded me of the crazy day prior to the Karmapa's arrival. Would his departure result in a similar scene?

I entered the last *pujah* disheartened by the imminent departure of two significant people in my life and the ugly squabble between the Christians and Buddhists. An hour later I departed feeling weightless, relieved of thoughts, unburdened, and acutely awake. Other such beings floated by and glided down the hall. I had been blessed by a meditation master who had dared to empty his mind of worldly thoughts and concepts. As the stream of everyday concerns began to trickle back into my thoughts, I wondered if I would one day regret not spending all my waking hours lingering in the hallways of Activ Universite, hoping to catch the Karmapa's eye, joining in one more *pujah,* or fetching at "His Holiness's" whim.

Feeling keenly aware of my surroundings, I crossed the street to the coffeehouse and passed through the empty dining area and kitchen to my room in back. With a couple of leisure hours before I needed to start prepping the evening meal, I felt it was time to wrestle with the Colossal Unknown that had dropped in my lap in the last several days. That is, the connection between my dreams and the 16th Karmapa.

Given the timing, location, and bizarre unfolding of the Laundromat Dream, there was little doubt in my mind that the dreams and coincidences I had experienced over the past year were connected to this encounter with the 16th Karmapa. But how? And for what reason?

I sat cross-legged on the carpet roll and focused on the logistics of the Karmapa's reincarnation, as it obviously defied the arrow-of-time concept on a much grander scale than my dreams. And the more I studied it, the more impenetrable it seemed. As explained to me, the 16th Karmapa had been a fully accomplished living Buddha for 800-plus years. And, over the span of those centuries and sixteen lifetimes, he had known when and where he would be reborn and in each case had shared the information well in advance in writing with the spiritual leaders at his monastery. At the appropriate time, several years after the death of each Karmapa, monks from the monastery would travel to the identified location to search for children whose age and circumstances matched the written description. When the child was located, they confirmed the identity as the Karmapa's reincarnation through the child's remembrance of key monastery figures and correctly identifying the Karmapa's personal items—favorite prayer beads, ceremonial implements, letters, and so on—when displayed alongside similar items belonging to others at the monastery.

Establishing a Karmapa connection to my portentous dreams obviously would require a thorough understanding of reincarnation. I laughed at myself for thinking I could make sense of the mysteries of death, rebirth, and time in an afternoon when serious scholars and spiritual seekers since the dawn of humankind had spent their lives attempting to do so. Still, my mental health demanded that I reach some reasonable explanation. I needed to live in a world that made sense. It was encoded in my DNA. So I asked myself how can a person be in charge of the death process since it requires knowledge that could only be ascertained by remaining conscious through the process? And, beyond that: How could a person accomplish anything at that point, supposing you knew what to do, since you would lack the wherewithal and the environment to actually do anything?

I searched my memory banks and quickly recognized I had no valuable information whatsoever about death. No doubt there was abundant information about life leading up to death and the experience itself, as witnessed by the living. But death, we are told, creates a wall between what we know and cannot know; between an empirical world in which we can act and a netherworld that we cannot with certainty even describe.

I recalled a pithy line from a Wallace Stevens poem, "Death is the mother of beauty." I had never read the poem and didn't know the title, but instantly recognized the soul-stirring irony contained in the poet's observation. Death is the one certainty in life, and that makes it the mother of all meaning—black, white, and every shade in-between.

Feeling the need to walk and ponder, I took a few brief turns around the windowless room. When I failed to retrieve anything from beyond the "wall," I sat again on the carpet roll and refocused, this time on rebirth, another piece of the reincarnation phenomenon.

The obvious questions arose: How can a person be in charge of the rebirth process? What is the rebirth process? Does such a process exist? My response was a shrug. I knew even less about this topic than I knew about death. Both subjects were well beyond my experience and scope of comprehension. I had read a number of articles about near-death and after-life experiences, but found them more speculative and provocative than informative.

My thoughts traveled back to the newborn baby in the acupuncture documentary. The roomful of spectators had gasped in disbelief when the doctor removed the bright red, fluid-streaked baby from the surgical opening and lifted it, the blue umbilical cord still attached, so the mother could see the child over the towel "fence." I wondered what was going through the baby's mind at that moment. Had the baby participated in any way in its own conception and birth? What conditions, knowledge, skills, and controls were needed for a living person to successfully orchestrate one's death, rebirth, and survival to adulthood? And what about the parents? How do they fit into the process?

In the documentary, the mother pleasantly nibbled on orange slices while separated by the fence from the pain and complexity of a Caesarian section and the birth of her child. I imagined for a moment that the baby was a Karmapa reincarnation and imagined everything needed for the baby to draw its first breath of air. The immediate question that came to mind was how would a deceased being select the parents for a rebirth? And, while considering that piece of the process, I quickly recognized that in some cases the Karmapa's note to the elders at the monastery would likely predate the marriage of his future parents. The thought jolted me. It introduced a whole new level of complexity.

I did the math in my head. If the Karmapa submitted the note seven years before his death, eighty-four months in advance, then the selection of parents could easily predate the marriage of his prospective parents and the conception of a child. That's because the monks were said to wait no longer than six years, or seventy-two months, after the Karmapa's death to begin searching for the newly incarnated Karmapa. At that point a five-year-old child would have lived sixty plus nine months, counting gestation, and that could easily fit within an eighty-four-month advance notice period. It was a staggering addition to a highly complex situation. It meant the Karmapa must have a mind that encompasses all human beings, all thoughts, all interconnections. The Karmapa must be omniscient, as the Buddhists claimed. In some ways omniscience would simplify the process, since such a being would have no need to travel to the future and back for information about the suitability of prospective parents living in a yurt or stone dwelling in premodern Tibet. But that too seemed a flagrant violation of the arrow of time concept.

As every new line of inquiry added new layers and new pathways to the labyrinth, I once again acknowledged the futility of my quest. I had no direct knowledge, evidence, or proof that the Karmapa had been reborn sixteen times, or that he was a master of time travel. Still, I was certain that the dreams were his work and the sum of circumstances, including sixteen reincarnations, obviously would require a master of time travel.

I had spent a lot of time thinking about the nature of time since the *Marite* adventure and had arrived at a couple of interesting observations. First, I realized that time only exists as *now*. The future and the past exist in our imagination and memory only. What we call the future is actually an educated guess of what *now* will look like in seventy-two hours or twelve months or on New Year's Eve. And the past is simply the memory of *nows* that we have already experienced. And the real clincher is that by the time we have thought about it, or acknowledged a momentary *now*, it is already in the past. Simply put, the past and future seem real because people around the world have implicitly agreed to organize their lives around an internationally accepted notion of time, which in most of the Westernized nations is based on the Gregorian calendar.

The annual New Year celebration in Times Square offered an illustration of the complexities involved. Using the Gregorian calendar, thousands of people make plans each year to meet in the future on December 31st in Times Square just before midnight to celebrate the end of one calendar year and the beginning of another. This event, with its official countdown to the New Year and the glittering ball that descends to street level in sync with the countdown, has been so successful for so long that similar events are now celebrated in a similar manner in most big cities around the world, and some of them are celebrated twelve hours earlier than the New York City event. These events, celebrating the exact same moment in time, are staged with great precision, yet half a day apart, and can be done so without confusing most people due to the widely accepted concept of time.

Another widely accepted convention is that day and night are a universal phenomenon, that all days are divided roughly into halves consisting of the same number of hours in the day as at night. However, this is true only on rotating heavenly bodies that do not emit light—such as planets, moons, and asteroids—and those bodies comprise an infinitesimally tiny proportion of the objects in the universe. And yet the notion persists in our imaginations that the entire universe is conveniently divided into days and nights.

The many hours I had spent obsessing over the nature of time had produced a second interesting observation, this one about the arrow of time. It was prompted by Kierkegaard's comment that we have to live life moving forward, but can only understand it by looking backward. This self-evident observation, although a simple rendering of a complicated phenomenon, underscores again the notion that time is a series of *nows* that can only be experienced in the past, after they have occurred. It also presents two directions for the arrow of time: one directed to the future, which consists of experience-based activities, and one directed to the past, which consists of previously experienced activities that have acquired content and can be analyzed and organized into a comprehensible narrative. This duality raises an interesting question about the arrow of time. Should it be pointed toward the future, where we are exposed to a constant stream of raw experience, or toward the past, where our experiences can have meaning? The obvious answer seems to be both, since the arrow would have to have meaning before you could even identify the direction it points. At the same time, that constant stream of raw experience that we call life and experience as a changing set of conditions internally and externally requires that we focus on the future, that we maintain a posture of readiness, that we be informed and ready to deflect and absorb and process our experiences or risk being waylaid by them.

Humans seem predisposed to a simple description of the world, especially when it involves a complicated matrix of constantly changing conditions that need to be viewed through the prism of lives, deaths, suffering, happiness, and survival. Given the way we experience the world, it makes sense that we would presume that the arrow of time points toward change, toward our challenges, and yet must originate out of our understanding of the world and how we fit into it.

I returned to Kierkegaard's Pantry, pausing in front to gaze through the window. Half of the tables were occupied. As before, Brigitte had everything under control. I entered, looked around for Amy, then made for the kitchen. "Sorry mate," said an English youth. "Staff only." He held out an arm to bar my entrance.

"I am staff," I told him.

"'ard to tell 'round this place," he muttered as I walked by.

Brigitte was in the kitchen unpacking more tulip vases at the counter by the sink. I stopped in the doorway. She paused to push a stick of chewing gum in her mouth then looked my way. She smiled a nervous but resolute smile. A prologue to some tempered words, I guessed.

"Not a big crowd," I opened. "Guess I got lucky."

She stopped chewing and looked up with steely eyes. "Some stuff came for you." She pointed toward the back room. "Hedda brought them over. A typewriter and a box."

"Thanks. I guess I owe you another thanks for opening up. It was the final *pujah*. It won't happen again."

She took the last candle from the box, dropped the box to the floor, and pushed it under the over-sized stainless steel sink with her foot.

She hadn't responded. "Where did the candles come from?" I asked.

She stopped chewing gradually and then swallowed. "I bought them. Now there's one for each table. They're beautiful, don't you think?" She looked over her shoulder for my reaction with her head tilted as if looking over bifocal lens. "The professor has given me two thousand kroner to fix up the place. I'm going to get some artwork, more plants, and bigger speakers. What do you think?"

She had slowly turned to face me. Behind the good looks and tall winning figure was sterner stuff, the stuff of a warrior.

"Sounds like I need to talk to the professor," I said unsteadily.

"It won't do any good." She paused to let it sink in, then added, "It's mine now." A gritty smile surfaced, then disappeared. She was chewing the gum again. Her brown eyes didn't flinch. I knew what she was saying was true. "I like the name. But I think I'll change it to Kierkegaard's Cafe with a K. It's Beth's idea, really."

Oddly, the words didn't sting as they should have. Rather, her words felt familiar, as if marking my return to reality from the seductively real illusions of a dream or a willing suspension of disbelief. "You can stay here as long as you want," she told me. "The professor likes you." She picked up three tulip vases in each hand and headed for the dining areas.

I headed through the kitchen to the room that had been my home for more than a week, moved the box and typewriter from the bed to the floor, and sat on the corner of the mattress. The box had "Don" marked on a flap. I opened it. It was full of clothes. I immediately recognized them as Gellner's. I held up a pair of blue-green underwear in a lively paisley design. They looked like a playboy's underwear rather than a man who would disown them to wear a monk's robe. I tried on the jeans. They fit perfectly. Definitely a step up from the rags I had been wearing.

I found Amy's note on the pillow. Somebody had delivered it for her. She had not wanted to make me choose between escorting her to the train station and attending the last *pujah,* so she and Beth had left early. She left her love, her Texas address, and promised to write. In a postscript she added that the Aussie was traveling with Beth to London.

Amy had gone. My little utopia was unraveling.

The Karmapa left the following morning in a chartered bus with maroon curtains hung over the windows. Their next stop was Scotland. I joined a large swarm of devotees who gathered on the sidewalk in front of the Universite to bid a farewell to the Tibetans and to those who were going to follow in a caravan. The anxious mood of the crowd flickered from joy over being so near the Karmapa to the sadness of impending departure. I looked through the windshield for a last glimpse, but saw nothing.

During the Tibetans' ten-day visit I had only seen the Karmapa in ritual settings. Performances, some might say. The only departures from the routine of these ceremonies had been one brief smile prior to the first *pujah* and the informal ceremony when I took refuge and received a Tibetan name. Those two encounters had been the closest thing to a direct relationship with the 16th Karmapa. And yet I had been substantially touched. Changed, really. I knew I would never be the same. The dreams, riddles, and coincidences that had marked my journey from San Francisco to this moment had not been mere coincidences. Something much more profound was at work. The things I had done and the things that had happened to me had been connected, and sometimes at the surface level. Those two aspects had merged as one enough times over the last nine months that I had felt guided by the coincidence.

A loud cheer went up behind me. I turned and followed the eyes of the crowd to the front door of Activ Universite as Kristofer emerged, crossed the street, and began to make his way through the ecstatic Buddhists. His smile told it all. He would travel in the bus with the Tibetans. Tears of joy and sorrow came streaming uncontrollably down my cheeks. Everybody wanted and got their moment with Kristofer. We connected at curbside near the back of the bus. With the light of love and joy in his eyes he placed a boxer's hand behind my neck and pressed his forehead to mine as if wanting to transfer a spark of infinite wisdom before departing. I asked him to translate my name before he left.

"Karma Sonum Norbu," he repeated slowly and caressingly. "The Karma of Married Jewels." He smiled robustly. "And it is true, my friend. You are a man of many blessings." He pressed his forehead to mine again and with passion as the tears poured from my eyes.

"Your scribe machine?" he asked.

I nodded affirmatively. "I got it last night."

He looked into my eyes for a long moment then said, "Journey safe, my friend."

I watched from among the crowd as Kristofer made his way to the bus, mounted the steps, and, after a final wave, climbed onboard and disappeared into the folds of maroon in back. A crescendo of emotions collided inside me. My body vibrated. The tears flowed. My lungs heaved. Twenty-plus years of pent-up emotion streamed uncontrollably from my body in an undifferentiated expression of love.

310

Chapter 17 – The King's New Market

The engine on the huge stainless steel bus grumbled to life and sent the crowd at curbside scrambling from the exhaust fumes as I said good-bye to Eric and Michelle. They had joined up with Anselm and Sara, and the four of them planned to follow His Holiness in the Volkswagen bus for as long as the gas, money, and good fortune held out. When the vehicles in the convoy started their engines, Michelle hurriedly wrote something on a piece of paper, folded and refolded until it was a small wad, then pressed it in my palm as if passing directions for a top secret mission. It was an odd thing to do, I realized, when I unfolded the note later and found she had written: *Autobiography of a Yogi* by ParamahansaYogananda. It was the book the Buddhists had recommended a week earlier. I guess she felt as if she were leaving a wounded soldier by the roadside.

I did not embrace the religious side of Buddhism with the same zeal and immediacy as others who had participated in the Karmapa's activities, because I had internalized a working atheism over the years, and, unlike the others, had been seduced by the coffeehouse opportunity. There was a trace of sorrow in Michelle's smile as we said goodbye. Following Kristofer's example, she and Eric individually pressed their foreheads to mine and then, with moist eyes and palms pressed together, they backed away, climbed into the Volkswagen bus, and closed the doors. Within minutes they were all gone, the 16th Karmapa, the monks, and the caravan of devotees.

Again I felt alone in a crowd. I brushed the feeling aside and weaved through the lingering spectators on the sidewalk and returned to Kierkegaard's Pantry, now Kierkegaard's Kafe.

For the first time in weeks I felt like a visitor in Copenhagen. I listened wistfully as bells all over town marked the hour. I would miss the bells of Copenhagen, but it was time to move on, to find a place where I could make sense of my encounter with the 16th Karmapa and put it in writing. An awesome task, I realized. Still, in the same way that the mythical Gordius was motivated by gratitude to attach his wagon to the temple with an elaborate knot, increasingly I felt an obligation to share my experiences.

I walked through the empty dining area and recalled a conversation I overhead earlier in the week about a Confucian philosopher who maintained that our minds work exactly the way we think they work. I had given this observation considerable thought in the days since and concluded that it was a convincing explanation for how the world's billions of individual people can all view themselves as right-minded even while experiencing vastly different versions of the world and behaving in very different ways. It was an elegant explanation of how we as Buddhists and Christians, Hitlers and Pollyannas, men and women, givers and takers, and people of every conceivable complexity acquire and maintain purpose and structure, which give us a measure of comfort and deliberation in a world of bewildering complexity. Without purpose and structure in our intellectual lives, there is no sanity, no basis for a meaningful life.

Eventually I came to envision the mind as a porous vessel, like a colander, that is constantly being filled and emptied by the world of stimulation around us, and the flow of stimuli through this vessel is largely controlled by the purpose we give ourselves. However, some people want a bowl instead of a colander and accomplish this by stopping the flow with mind-made answers and beliefs. Others thrive on overflow and never learn of the structure or the orderly pattern of pores or the stimuli that escape through them. A majority probably sees the external stimulation only and regards life as something that happens to them despite their best efforts to control it. Still others recognize that even thoughts are subject to the laws of cause and effect, a distinction that separates Buddhist thought from modern science.

I took a seat at the back of the dining area near the kitchen entrance and gazed over the tables and through the windows to the sidewalks and intersection outside. I was penniless, homeless, and threadbare. I had just watched my only local friends leave town, friends that I had hoped could help me find work and establish a foothold in Copenhagen. Given my situation, I should have been a total wreck. Instead, I felt that same calmness of spirit I first noticed when Brigitte stated she would be managing the coffeehouse going forward.

Confidence. That's what I felt. Not the ego-based confidence one gets from winning a sporting event, amassing a large bank account, or marrying your dream lover. Rather, in a world that seems to have no purpose, no direction, and no explanation, I was confident from the certainty of knowing one thing only: that I was supposed to meet the 16th Karmapa in that small barn in Sweden, that I was supposed to be at that place at that hour in December 1974.

For me—and I suspect for many others—it is tempting to attribute meaning to single snapshot moments such as my encounter with the 16th Karmapa in Sweden. However, the dozens of small coincidences and symbolisms that tested my sanity almost daily were equally important, since they provided a set of small steps in a spiritual journey that cannot be made in a single step or a single day.

Around nightfall, one of Brigitte's helpers brought an envelope that had been delivered by a tall sailor with long red hair and a beard. The envelope from Dalton contained the $50 that Ike owed me and a request that I meet Dalton at a local pub at eight o'clock. I had spent the afternoon making up for a week of neglect in my journal and thinking about where I would go next and what I would do. Like the changing of Kierkegaard's Pantry from my hands to Brigitte's, the note from Dalton did not surprise me. Only a month ago the timing of the note would have irritated me, but on this day it felt more like the final scene in a Greek drama. I studied it briefly, like a player appreciating the final piece of a puzzle that, when set in place, would dissolve the lines between pieces and allow the picture to be viewed unmediated for the first time. And the puzzle picture I saw was that of an exceedingly intricate knot, with no loose ends, that connected the spiritual and material worlds.

At seven thirty that night I stood in front of Kierkegaard's Kafe in the cold night air with my belongings on the sidewalk beside me. The sound of an unseen hound baying at an unheard siren caught my ear as I considered which route to take to rendezvous with Dalton. I didn't like any of my options with Dalton. The journey from the spiritual summits of Tibet to a tall ship under construction at sea level would involve a significant descent, I knew. Faced with the material facts of life, I lifted the typewriter to my side, enjoying its heft for a moment, like a warrior reassured by his sword, and headed for Kongens Nytorv, the King's New Market. I'd had a shower and a hot meal, and I felt like a king.

Epilogue

In the closing days of my two-week experience with the 16th Karmapa in Copenhagen in December 1974, I realized my life would be different going forward, although I could not say at the time what would change or how. I did know without hesitation that my aspiration to be a tall ship sailor had been extinguished. Although I stood in awe of the ships themselves and found the work to be gratifying, the opportunities were scarce, unlawful labor practices were common, and—with no heat, indoor plumbing, running water, or personal space—the living conditions were coarse even while in port.

The one aspect of my new life that I could identify was the recognition that I needed to share with others the incredible journey I had made from those mornings in the rigging on the *Balclutha* in San Francisco to the feet of the 16th Karmapa in a small barn in Sweden. I had begun that journey as a curious, small-town artist-wannabe; now I found myself the denizen of a cosmic world well beyond my scope of comprehension. I also knew that the transition from the spiritual heights with the Karmapa to my former lifestyle would involve a dramatic change in altitude.

I returned to the Korsør shipyard late in the day on January 1, 1975, to discover an empty dock space where the ferry I called home had been moored. I found Benny sitting on a duffel bag, head in hands, on the dock where the gangway to the ferry had been located. The green duffel bag of belongings I had left behind in the shipyard was plopped on the dock alongside Benny's stuff. He informed me that the ferry had been sold the day before and had motored away to a new location just hours before I arrived. Benny had been evicted with only an hour's advance notice. This left the two of us homeless, with very little money and no prospects, as evening fell on the small Danish town of Korsør. As twilight arrived, Bruce came by to celebrate New Year's Day with us. Thinking it would cheer us up he lit up a joint that had been sent to him for a New Year's celebration by a friend in San Francisco. The three of us smoked it and watched spellbound as the streetlights came on. That was my last-ever puff of marijuana.

Defying Dalton's instructions, Benny and I moved onboard the *Apollodora,* because we had no other place to go. I worked a few additional months with Dalton in an unsuccessful effort to save $600 for return airfare to the U.S. Fed up with a hand-to-mouth existence and Dalton's unpardonable behavior, I moved to the little trailer on the farm in Skaelskor, where I helped harvest and package Brussels sprouts, roughed out the first few chapters of this book, and managed to save a small amount of money.

Eventually I borrowed the money for airfare from the president of the wholesale art company I cofounded, agreeing to work there until I paid off the loan. That turned into an after-school job when I returned to the University of Oklahoma, where I subsequently graduated with a bachelor's degree. When I returned for graduate studies in the professional writing program in 1981, a professor described the *Footloose* chapters I had written up to that time as "rough as a corncob." Within a year I married an architecture student with a two-year-old daughter, and two years later we welcomed a new baby daughter. I became a trailing spouse several years later when my wife took a tenure track teaching position at a large university.

Since my return to the U.S. from Denmark in 1975, Tibetan Buddhism has become an important part of my life. I traveled to Colorado in the winter of 1976 to see the 16th Karmapa during his second visit to the U.S. Upon arrival I learned at the Shambala Meditation Center in Boulder, the organization hosting the Karmapa, that his schedule had been revised and that he was slated to arrive later in the week. Lacking the money for an extended stay, I drove back to Norman nonstop through an ice storm, disappointed to have missed the opportunity.

Shortly after I moved to Chicago in 2003, I joined a Karma Kagyu dharma group that had just purchased a building to establish a dharma center for Karmapa devotees in the Chicago metropolitan area. While looking for a job for half of that first year, I spent nearly every weekend and many weekdays rehabbing and transforming the building with other center members and with guidance by fax and telephone from Bardor Tulku Rinpoche, one of the resident Tibetan teachers at the Karma Triyana Dharmachakra monastery in New York, the Karmapa's North American headquarters. Months later, when I spoke with Bardor Tulku Rinpoche in person at the Chicago center, I learned he was one of the lamas who had participated in the ceremony at Activ Universite when I took refuge with the 16th Karmapa.

In the summer of 2009 I traveled to Tibet with Bardor Tulku Rinpoche, acupuncturist Kirk Moulton, solar energy specialist Walt Ratterman, registered nurse Sharon Osel, and others to carry out a Raktrul Foundation project to establish a medical clinic and install solar lighting systems in a monastery, a nunnery, a community center, and three schools.

His Holiness the 16th Karmapa died in Zion, Illinois, just
north of Chicago, in November, 1980. His Holiness the 17th
Karmapa, Ogyen Drodul Trinley Dorje, was born in Tibet in
1985, as predicted by the 16th Karmapa in a letter, and returned
to Tsurphu Monastery, the traditional seat of the Karmapas, in
1992. In late December, 1999, at age fourteen, and after years
of *de facto* house arrest in his monastery in Chinese-controlled
Tibet, the 17th Karmapa escaped over the Himalayas—while
much of the world was celebrating the beginning of the new
millennium—and arrived on January 5, 2000 in Dharamsala,
India, where he was enthusiastically embraced by the Dalai
Lama.

Today there are thousands of Tibetan Buddhist centers and
study groups in the West, thanks to the pioneering work of
Chogyam Trungpa, who established the Boulder Shambala
Meditation Center, the 16th Karmapa, the Dalai Lama, Kalu
Rinpoche, and many others. There also are hundreds of books,
CDs, DVDs, and opportunities to learn about Buddhism and its
many manifestations. When you meet a Western Buddhist
practitioner, let me recommend that you ask them how they got
involved in Buddhism. Many of their stories will astound you.

One of the issues I struggled with in writing this book is
how to explain that my prophetic dreams stood out in part
because they were the *only* dreams I've remembered from my
adult life. Since nearly everybody dreams nearly every night
and they often recall their dreams in the morning, it's quite a
stretch to expect normal dreamers to appreciate the significance
of, say, having only one dream in an entire year, as I had in
1973, or of having only four dreams in 1974, or of having no
dreams whatsoever for years on end. Having the images from

those dreams unfold before my eyes several months later in the real world was thus an especially powerful experience. Our nervous systems are not equipped to process such things. When confronted with cognitive disconnects of that magnitude, the natural response is to deny it happened. That was my immediate response as well.

Since the prophetic dreams in 1974 that nearly made me crazy I have had two additional dreams. The first was in the summer of 1999, while I participated in a two-week Kalachakra empowerment presented by the Dalai Lama in Bloomington, Indiana. Following the actual empowerment session in the afternoon, he told the participants to expect to have a dream about it that night, that it would be the last dream of the night. It was both the first and last dream of the night for me and featured the single image of a spiritual figure in robes in the sky encircled by radiating streams of colored light.

The last dream, the seventh, occurred in the fall of 2000 when I lived in St. Louis. In the dream, I was playing basketball in a gymnasium and was called away into a dimly lit hallway where a small man in a crumpled blue uniform had a package for me from Tibet. It was covered in change-of-address labels, all with my name on them, and all the labels, except my current address label, were crossed out with a large X. I signed for the package and the man departed. End of dream.

The basketball setting was not unusual, since I played on a handful of park district teams over the years, until I dropped out with a pair of broken ribs in the summer of 2000. In the spring of 2003, after I had moved to Chicago, a U.S. Postal Service mail carrier in a crumpled blue uniform delivered a package in the dimly lit hallway of my northside apartment building. Three sides of the package featured previous mailing addresses and

"Return to Sender" stickers that reflected my history of divorcing in 1996, followed by two moves, then remarrying in 2001 with another move, then moving a fourth time, to Chicago. The package was from Lama Lodo Rinpoche, the spiritual director of the Kagyu Droden Kunchen (KDK) dharma center in San Francisco, whom I had met years earlier through a St. Louis branch of the KDK group. I became one of Lama Lodo's students and learned in one of our first conversations that he also had been one of the lamas in the Karmapa's entourage in Copenhagen and that he was one of the two lamas who had conveyed to me the small card with my Tibetan name on it. The package from Lama Lodo contained an elegant bronze statue of Chenrezig, a Tibetan Buddhist deity revered as the embodiment of compassion. The gift has special meaning, since the Karmapa is considered to be an incarnation of Chenrezig. The statue resides on a shrine table in my home, a daily reminder of the importance of Buddhism and compassion in my life.

Made in the USA
Lexington, KY
12 July 2013